Mike Peters
Birgit Pikkemaat
Editors

Innovation in Hospitality and Tourism

Innovation in Hospitality and Tourism has been co-published simultaneously as *Journal of Quality Assurance in Hospitality & Tourism,* Volume 6, Numbers 3/4 2005.

Pre-publication
REVIEWS,
COMMENTARIES,
EVALUATIONS . . .

"RESEARCHERS ESPECIALLY, BUT ALSO PRACTITIONERS AND STUDENTS WILL PROFIT from reading these well-rounded contributions by internationally renowned authors. This book answers the questions of how new services can be developed, what innovation means in various tourism sub-branches, and how innovations can be measured."

Dr. Bibiana Walder
Project Manager and Senior Lecturer
Institute for Tourism
and Leisure Research
Chur University of Applied Sciences

More pre-publication
REVIEWS, COMMENTARIES, EVALUATIONS . . .

"**P**rovides tourism professionals with theory-based TOOLS, CONCEPTS, AND MODELS GROUNDED IN EFFECTIVE PRACTICE. . . . A perfect mix of contributions dealing with innovation and product development. . . . Links theoretical concepts and models with practical industry needs. The authors have done a superb job."

Dr. Hans H. Hinterhuber
Univ-Prof, Dipl-Ing
Professor and Head
Department of Strategic Management
Marketing & Tourism
University of Innsbruck, Austria

"**I** RECOMMEND THIS BOOK TO TOURISM RESEARCHERS, PRACTITIONERS, TEACHERS, AND TOURISM BUSINESS STUDENTS. It gives a versatile and high-level review of the latest academic research on innovation in hospitality and tourism."

Raija Komppula, DSS
University of Joensuu
Department of Business and Economics

THHP

The Haworth Hospitality Press®
An Imprint of The Haworth Press, Inc.

Innovation in Hospitality and Tourism

Innovation in Hospitality and Tourism has been co-published simultaneously as *Journal of Quality Assurance in Hospitality & Tourism,* Volume 6, Numbers 3/4 2005.

Innovation in Hospitality and Tourism, edited by Mike Peters and Birgit Pikkemaat (Vol. 6, No. 3/4, 2005). *Vital information on how to measure innovation in the control and sustainable management of new service development in hospitality and tourism.*

Hospitality, Tourism, and Lifestyle Concepts: Implications for Quality Management and Customer Satisfaction, edited by Maree Thyne and Eric Laws (Vol. 5, No, 2/3/4, 2004). *A comprehensive review of current theory and case studies of the application of lifestyle marketing to the hospitality and tourism industry.*

Current Issues and Development in Hospitality and Tourism Satisfaction, edited by John A. Williams and Muzaffer Uysal (Vol. 4, No. 3/4, 2003). *Focuses on emerging approaches that measure customer satisfaction and how to apply them to improve hospitality and tourism businesses.*

Knowledge Management in Hospitality and Tourism, edited by Ricarda B. Bouncken and Sungsoo Pyo (Vol. 3, No. 3/4, 2002). *"Of great value. . . Introduces the concepts associated with knowledge management and provides examples of these concepts through case studies and unique real-world applications. . . . A lot of great information on a fascinating topic. . . ." (Cary C. Countryman, PhD, CHE, CHTP, Director, Technology Research and Education Center, Conrad N. Hilton College of Hotel and Restaurant Management)*

Benchmarks in Hospitality and Tourism, edited by Sungsoo Pyo (Vol. 2, No. 3/4, 2001). *"A handy single volume that clearly explains the principles and current thinking about benchmarking, plus useful insights on how the techniques can be converted into profitable business operations. Includes conceptual, practical, and operational (or 'how-it-is-done') chapters." (Chris Ryan, PhD, MEd, MPhil, BSc (Econ) Hons, Professor of Tourism, The University of Waikato, Hamilton, New Zealand)*

Innovation in Hospitality and Tourism

Mike Peters
Birgit Pikkemaat
Editors

Innovation in Hospitality and Tourism has been co-published simultaneously as *Journal of Quality Assurance in Hospitality & Tourism,* Volume 6, Numbers 3/4 2005.

The Haworth Hospitality Press®
An Imprint of The Haworth Press, Inc.

New York • London • Victoria (AU)
www.HaworthPress.com

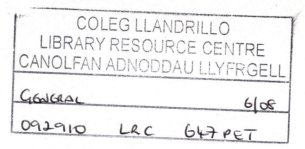
Published by

The Haworth Hospitality Press®, 10 Alice Street, Binghamton, NY 13904-1580 USA

The Haworth Hospitality Press® is an imprint of The Haworth Press, Inc., 10 Alice Street, Binghamton, NY 13904-1580 USA.

Innovation in Hospitality and Tourism has been co-published simultaneously as *Journal of Quality Assurance in Hospitality & Tourism,* Volume 6, Numbers 3/4 2005.

The development, preparation, and publication of this work has been undertaken with great care. However, the publisher, employees, editors, and agents of The Haworth Press and all imprints of The Haworth Press, Inc., including The Haworth Medical Press® and Pharmaceutical Products Press®, are not responsible for any errors contained herein or for consequences that may ensue from use of materials or information contained in this work. With regard to case studies, identities and circumstances of individuals discussed herein have been changed to protect confidentiality. Any resemblance to actual persons, living or dead, is entirely coincidental.

The Haworth Press is committed to the dissemination of ideas and information according to the highest standards of intellectual freedom and the free exchange of ideas. Statements made and opinions expressed in this publication do not necessarily reflect the views of the Publisher, Directors, management, or staff of The Haworth Press, Inc., or an endorsement by them.

Cover design by Lora Wiggins

Library of Congress Cataloging-in-Publication Data

Innovation in hospitality and tourism / Mike Peters, Birgit Pikkemaat, Editors.
     p. cm.
     "Co-published simultaneously as Journal of Quality Assurance in Hospitality & Tourism, Volume 6, Numbers 3/4 2005."
     Includes bibliographical references and index.
     ISBN-13: 978-0-7890-3270-6 (hard cover : alk. paper)
     ISBN-10: 0-7890-3270-8 (hard cover : alk. paper)
     ISBN-13: 978-0-7890-3271-3 (soft cover : alk. paper)
     ISBN-10: 0-7890-3271-6 (soft cover : alk. paper)
     1. Hospitality industry. 2. Tourism. I. Peters, Mike, 1966- II. Pikkemaat, Birgit, 1967-

TX911.3.M27I52 2006
647.94–dc22

                                                 2005036307

Indexing, Abstracting & Website/Internet Coverage

This section provides you with a list of major indexing & abstracting services and other tools for bibliographic access. That is to say, each service began covering this periodical during the year noted in the right column. Most Websites which are listed below have indicated that they will either post, disseminate, compile, archive, cite or alert their own Website users with research-based content from this work. (This list is as current as the copyright date of this publication.)

Abstracting, Website/Indexing Coverage . . . . Year When Coverage Began

- **CIRET (Centre International de Recherches et d'Etudes Touristiques). Computerized Tourism & General Bibliography** <http://www.ciret-tourism.com> 2000

- **EBSCOhost Electronic Journals Service (EJS)** <http://www.ejournals.ebsco.com> 2001

- **Elsevier Scopus** <http://www.info.scopus.com> 2005

- **Google** <http://www.google.com> 2004

- **Google Scholar** <http://www.scholar.google.com> 2004

- **Haworth Document Delivery Center** <http://www.HaworthPress.com/journals/dds.asp> 2000

- **HTI Database (Hospitality, Tourism Index); EBSCO Publishing** 2003

- **IBZ International Bibliography of Periodical Literature** <http://www.saur.de>. 2000

(continued)

- *INSPEC is the leading English-language bibliographic
  information service providing access to the world's
  scientific & technical literature in physics, electrical eng.,
  electronics, communications, control eng., computers
  & computing, and information tech
  <http://www.iee.org.uk/publish/>* 2000

- *Internationale Bibliographie der geistes- und sozialwissenschaft
  Zeitschriftenliteratur . . . See IBZ <http://www.saur.de>* 2000

- *Leisure, Recreation & Tourism Abstracts
  (c/o CABI Publishing) <http://www.cabi.org>* 2000

- *Links@Ovid (via CrossRef targeted DOI links)
  <http://www.ovid.com>* 2005

- *Management & Marketing Abstracts <http://www.pira.co.uk>* . . . . . *

- *New Zealand Bibliographic Database
  <http://www.mngt.waikato.ac.nz> (U of Waikato–
  not Database)* 2003

- *Ovid Linksolver (OpenURL link resolver via CrossRef targeted
  DOI links) <http://www.linksolver.com>* 2005

- *Referativnyi Zhurnal (Abstracts Journal of the All-Russian
  Institute of Scientific and Technical Information–
  in Russian) <http://www.viniti.ru>* 2006

- *Scopus (See instead Elsevier Scopus)
  <http://www.info.scopus.com>* 2005

- *Soils & Fertilizers Abstracts (c/o CABI Publishing)
  <http://www.cabi.org/AtoZ/asp>* . . . . *

- *Tourism Insight <http://www.tourisminsight.com>* 2003

- *TOURISM: an international interdisciplinary journal* 2000

- *"Travel Research Bookshelf" a current awareness service
  of the Journal of Travel Research "Abstracts
  from other Journals Section" published by the Travel &
  Tourism Association* . . . . *

- *World Publishing Monitor* . . . . *

  *Exact start date to come.

(continued)

Special Bibliographic Notes related to special journal issues (separates) and indexing/abstracting:

- indexing/abstracting services in this list will also cover material in any "separate" that is co-published simultaneously with Haworth's special thematic journal issue or DocuSerial. Indexing/abstracting usually covers material at the article/chapter level.
- monographic co-editions are intended for either non-subscribers or libraries which intend to purchase a second copy for their circulating collections.
- monographic co-editions are reported to all jobbers/wholesalers/approval plans. The source journal is listed as the "series" to assist the prevention of duplicate purchasing in the same manner utilized for books-in-series.
- to facilitate user/access services all indexing/abstracting services are encouraged to utilize the co-indexing entry note indicated at the bottom of the first page of each article/chapter/contribution.
- this is intended to assist a library user of any reference tool (whether print, electronic, online, or CD-ROM) to locate the monographic version if the library has purchased this version but not a subscription to the source journal.
- individual articles/chapters in any Haworth publication are also available through The Haworth Document Delivery Service (HDDS).

Innovation in Hospitality and Tourism

CONTENTS

ABOUT THE EDITORS

Mike Peters is Assistant Professor in the Department of General and Tourism Management at the University of Innsbruck, Austria. He is the author and editor of five books in the field of tourism research. He has written more than 50 professional articles in well-known journals, on international tourism conferences and in edited books. He started his career with an apprenticeship in the restaurant industry and has worked about seven years in the hospitality industry. In 1995 he finalised his studies in the field of social sciences and was Visiting Scholar and Project Assistant at the Innsbruck University School of Management, Innsbruck, where he conducted and coordinated several research projects in the field of tourism and hospitality. He received his doctoral degree in the year 2001 for his study on the internationalisation behaviour of small and medium sized tourism businesses. Since then his research interests focus on the processes of entrepreneurship and associated problems, such as succession planning, product development and innovation. He is a member of international tourism experts' networks, such as AIEST (International Association of Scientific Experts in Tourism).

Birgit Pikkemaat is Associate Professor in the Department of General and Tourism Management at the University of Innsbruck, Austria. She is an expert in the fields of tourist decision behaviour and has published books on consumer behaviour in tourism and quality perceptions of tourists. She received her doctoral degree in the year 2000 for her insights into the information search behaviour of tourists. She has also conducted several research projects in the fields of innovation and innovative behaviour in tourism and revealed severe product and service development problems in small and medium sized businesses. She has analysed the perception of quality attributes on the tourism demand side. She has published more than 30 papers and articles in well known tourism journals and books, and was involved in more than 20 international tourism conferences.

Innovation in Tourism

Mike Peters
Birgit Pikkemaat

SUMMARY. An overview of the importance and the concept of innovation is given prior to an illustration about important areas of innovation research in tourism. The ten papers of this special issue are briefly introduced and a final statement about the status of innovation research in tourism is presented. *[Article copies available for a fee from The Haworth Document Delivery Service: 1-800-HAWORTH. E-mail address: <docdelivery@ haworthpress.com> Website: <http://www.HaworthPress.com> © 2005 by The Haworth Press, Inc. All rights reserved.]*

KEYWORDS. Innovation, new service development, tourism

Innovation and new service development are important strategic features to assure growth and sustainable wealth for every industry, but in particular for those industries where markets are saturated and clients choose products and services from all over the world, such as is the case in tourism. There are various definitions of the term "innovation,"

Mike Peters, Assistant Professor, and Birgit Pikkemaat, Associate Professor, are both affiliated with the Center for Tourism and Service Economics, Innsbruck University School of Economics, Austria, Universitätsstrasse 15, A-6020 Innsbruck (E-mail: mike.peters@uibk.ac.at) or (E-mail: birgit.pikkemaat@uibk.ac.at).

[Haworth co-indexing entry note]: "Innovation in Tourism." Peters, Mike, and Birgit Pikkemaat. Co-published simultaneously in *Journal of Quality Assurance in Hospitality & Tourism* (The Haworth Hospitality Press, an imprint of The Haworth Press, Inc.) Vol. 6, No. 3/4, 2005, pp. 1-6; and: *Innovation in Hospitality and Tourism* (ed: Mike Peters, and Birgit Pikkemaat) The Haworth Hospitality Press, an imprint of The Haworth Press, Inc., 2005, pp. 1-6. Single or multiple copies of this article are available for a fee from The Haworth Document Delivery Service [1-800-HAWORTH, 9:00 a.m. - 5:00 p.m. (EST). E-mail address: docdelivery@haworthpress.com].

doi:10.1300/J162v06n03_01

1

which derives from the Latin "innovatio" which means to create something new. The diversity of definitions lies in the different purposes of examining this phenomenon. Probably the most useable definition is that provided by the late Schumpeter (1934) who distinguished five areas in which companies can introduce innovation: (1) generation of new or improved products, (2) introduction of new production processes, (3) development of new sales markets, (4) development of new supply markets, and (5) reorganisation and/or restructuring of the company. This categorization clearly distinguishes innovation from minor changes in the make up and/or delivery of products in forms of extension of product lines, adding service components or product differentiation.

As Hjalager pointed out, innovation in tourism industry is characterized by limited research and political considerations (1997, p. 35). As a point of departure innovation (in contrast to invention) can be defined as the market-based application of new processes, products or forms of organisation. Thus, the mere idea for a new process or product does not suffice; the idea has to have the potential to be commercialized and has to be developed to the point of being market-tested. Using an example from tourism as a product "alpine wellness tourism" is still an idea (invention) whilst Ayurveda treatment-based tourism constitutes already a novel or innovative new product in the family of spa (health) tourism. What are the main drivers of innovation in the market place or in the tourism enterprises, and what distinguishes innovative firms from those which merely follow market trends? Analyzing existing research in tourism it becomes obvious that there is a lack of radical innovations in comparison to incremental innovations. As a consequence innovation rates are low.

Without doubt new product development and innovation have the capacity to create additional value for customers and sustainable growth for entrepreneurs. However, management processes leading to new products or innovations are highly complex, in particular in a service dominated industry like tourism. Figure 1 presents the main research areas in the fields of innovations in tourism covered in this special issue.

The ten papers included in this special issue discuss at least one research area, such as, e.g., the measurement of innovations or new service development processes in tourism enterprises. Another stream of papers gives examples (and explanations) of innovation and related management processes in special areas of the tourism value chain.

Anne-Mette Hjalager discusses the marriage between welfare services and tourism focussing thereby on its driving force for innovation. Prior to a discussion about the welfare state and welfare trajectories in-

FIGURE 1. Selected Research Areas

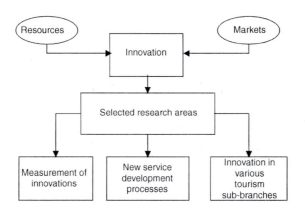

novation in tourism is briefly stated. In the main part of the paper six welfare trajectories in the Danish welfare concept are explored: the human capital trajectory, the environmental protection trajectory, the discouragement-of-noxious-behaviour trajectory, the work-for-all trajectory, the Beaux Art trajectory, and the health trajectory. The paper outlines that internal and external driving forces are continuously challenging welfare models and that the pressures and the opportunities are transmitted to tourism and innovation as well.

The second study, conducted by Harald Pechlaner, Elisabeth Fischer and Eva-Maria Hammann, is about leadership and innovation processes focussing thereby on the development of product and services based on core competences in tourism destinations. The innovation process is interpreted as an inter-organizational network process. As cooperation and networks play a minor role in the small and medium sized Alpine tourism at the present, the question is raised "how to overcome the obstacles of cooperation and to initiate network activities to foster innovation networks within tourism destinations?" The results of their empirical study show that specific forms of cooperation are able to strengthen and reinforce innovation in a destination.

Klaus Weiermair analyzes the innovation potential throughout the tourism value chain from the supply side focus. Assuming that innovations will only be undertaken when there is a sufficiently high innovation dividend which pays for the added cost and risks of innovation the paper investigate the innovation potential in terms of the innovation dividend to be expected in different parts and places of the tourism value chain. The discussion includes various dependent variables, such as firm size, economics of scale, proximity to relevant science and technology or forms of organisation.

The fourth paper is written by Serena Volo and deals with consumer-based measurement of tourist innovation. After a literature review of current innovation research and its measurement in tourism a model which categorizes innovation along two dimensions ("invention-adop-tion" continuum and an "impact-on-the-tourism-experience" dimension) is presented. The aim of this model is the aggregation of tourism inno-vation statistics across products, providers, markets and geopolitical re-gions. The economic impact of the innovation as a third dimension is added to the model as well as the research needed to empirically test the model is described.

Birgit Pikkemaat and Mike Peters discuss innovation as competitive advantage in the Alpine tourism and in particular, in the small and me-dium sized hotel industry. Prior to the presentation of the empirical study the results of other current empirical innovation studies in tourism are analyzed and hypotheses are derived. The findings of the study in the small and medium sized Alpine hotel industry point out that process innovations are the dominant type of innovation activities and product innovations are hardly found. Moreover, only a minority of innovation activities in the Alpine hotel industry can be interpreted as others than incremental innovations.

"An Investigation of the Factors Affecting Innovation Performances in Chain and Independent Hotels," authored by Michael Ottenbacher, Vivienne Shaw and Andrew Lockwood, emphasizes on the process of new service development as well as on its success factors. The aim of the study was to compare success factors of service development in ho-tel chains and independent hotels. The study's results suggest that mar-ket attractiveness, process management, market responsiveness and empowerment predict new service development success within chain affiliated hotels. While empowerment and market attractiveness are also related to new service development success in independent hotels, this is also linked to effective marketing communication, employee commitment, behaviour based evaluation, training of employees and marketing synergy.

In the paper of Joerg Frehse the process of product and brand devel-opment in hotel operations is discussed using AltiraSPA as a case study. The resources based view of innovation is emphasized and after a dis-cussion about the process of new product development the case of

AltiraSPA, a wellness concept of the ArabellaSheraton group under-lines the principles of that innovative product development processes.

"Challenges in Mobile Business Solutions for Tourist Destinations–The Trial Case of St. Moritz," authored by Pietro Beritelli and Matthias Schuppisser in its introduction discusses mobile business solutions and travel recommender systems for tourist destinations. After the descrip-tion of the technical background a trial case is presented which involves visitors as well as tourism enterprises. With the help of a newly devel-oped system called Destination-Pilot mobile business solutions have been tested regarding acceptability, usability, and market potential for mobile information services in a real environment situation.

Claudia Klausegger evaluated internet portals and conducted "an em-pirical study of acceptance measurement based on the Austrian Na-tional Tourist Office's service portal" which focuses on the evaluation of Internet portals by tourism professionals. Analyzing the relevant lit-erature about the measurement of the acceptance of Internet portals a working model is described and used for the empirical part of the paper. Significant differences are identified between four user groups exam-ined in the B2B field (provincial tourism organizations, hotels, travel agencies/operators and associations) as well as between age groups and genders in the various dimensions of Internet portal evaluation.

Robert A. Home, author of "A New Tune from an Old Instrument: The Application of SERVQUAL to a Tourism Service Business," uses the SERVQUAL questionnaire for his empirical study in Australia. After an overview about the conceptual development of service quality and its measurement the study which uses the case of a small brewery tour oper-ator is presented. The results show that unlike in other studies empathy seems to be the most relevant factor influencing perceived service qual-ity. In addition, the author points out how important service quality mea-surement instruments are to secure a proactive product development in tourism service businesses.

Although all authors agree on the importance of new service devel-opment and innovation in tourism various difficulties have to be over-come to strengthen innovation in tourism. Innovation research and its implementation to tourism have been very limited and are still in its in-fancy. Until today, research dealing with innovation in tourism or new tourism product and service development has been dominated by con-ceptual papers rather than empirical studies. The limited number of in-novation studies in tourism reveals gaps in the process of new service development as well as in its control and sustainable management. This special issue attempts to fill some of these gaps. Given the fact that on a

European level still no sufficient (data) basis for the measurement of new services development processes and innovation management processes in tourism exists, the paper of Serena Volo presents a conceptual measurement model which is able to reduce this deficit. However, further research and collaborative innovation studies are needed to strengthen and increase the knowledge about innovation and new service development in tourism research as well as in related tourism industries.

REFERENCES

Hjalager, A. M. (1997). Innovation patterns in sustainable tourism–an analytical typology. *Tourism Management 16* (3), 35-41.
Schumpeter, J. A. ([1934] 1961). *The Theory of Economic Development*. New York: Oxford Univ. Press.

The Marriage Between Welfare Services and Tourism– A Driving Force for Innovation?

Anne-Mette Hjalager

SUMMARY. This paper discusses the linkages between the welfare state and tourism, and attempts a definition of the phenomenon. It suggests that the specific features of welfare ideologies and practices influence the scale and scope of tourism in many ways. Six welfare trajectories, containing examples of similar modes of thinking, are explored: the human capital trajectory, the environmental protection trajectory, the discouragement-of-noxious-behaviour trajectory, the work-for-all trajectory, the Beaux Art trajectory, and the health trajectory. Innovativeness in tourism is more likely if welfare-based sectors are well connected with other sectors, including the voluntary sector. Both internal and external driving forces are continuously challenging the Danish welfare model. The pressures and the opportunities are transmitted to tourism, albeit not uniformly. There are good reasons for commercial and non-commercial tourism and leisure facilities to keep up to date with the various welfare ideologies. *[Article copies available for a fee from The Haworth Document Delivery Service: 1-800-HAWORTH. E-mail address: <docdelivery@haworthpress.com> Website: <http://www.HaworthPress.com> © 2005 by The Haworth Press, Inc. All rights reserved.]*

Anne-Mette Hjalager is Senior Consultant and Researcher with Advance/1, Science Park, Gustav Wiedsvej 10, 8000 Aarhus C., Denmark (E-mail: anne-mette. hjalager@advance1.dk).

[Haworth co-indexing entry note]: "The Marriage Between Welfare Services and Tourism–A Driving Force for Innovation." Hjalager, Anne-Mette. Co-published simultaneously in *Journal of Quality Assurance in Hospitality & Tourism* (The Haworth Hospitality Press, an imprint of The Haworth Press, Inc.) Vol. 6, No. 3/4, 2005, pp. 7-29; and: *Innovation in Hospitality and Tourism* (ed: Mike Peters, and Birgit Pikkemaat) The Haworth Hospitality Press, an imprint of The Haworth Press, Inc., 2005, pp. 7-29. Single or multiple copies of this article are available for a fee from The Haworth Document Delivery Service [1-800-HAWORTH, 9:00 a.m. - 5:00 p.m. (EST). E-mail address: docdelivery@haworthpress.com].

doi:10.1300/J162v06n03_02

KEYWORDS. Discontinuity, globalisation, innovations, tourism products, trajectories, quality, welfare state, Denmark

INNOVATION AND TOURISM

Talk of industrial innovation rarely brings the tourism industry to mind. Social and economic research focuses most of its attention on such innovative industries as the pharmaceuticals, IT, biotechnology, instruments, and materials industries. The occurrence of innovation with wide economic impacts is also often closely linked to university R&D departments and prestigious military and space projects (Dosi, 1982; OECD, 2000).

In recent years, however, the concept of innovation has been increasingly linked to the service sectors (Metcalfe et al., 1999), with research projects investigating how radically new concepts of services are developed and implemented, and how knowledge and creativeness are transgressing previous boundaries. In banking, for example, the interaction between customers and providers of financial services is being remodelled, with automation for some services and new personalized counselling for others. As in many other categories of services, the new combinations of services in banking have been made possible by massive IT investments. During this process, face-to-face contact is often replaced altogether. As noted by Barras (1986), IT is often the starting point of the "reverse innovation cycle" in services. Initially, the provision of services is rationalised and made more efficient, but soon after IT opens up new opportunities for providing services, e.g., speedier or more precise delivery. The service sector is thus setting the new agendas for the development of technology through a gradual, but quite significant, reengineering of the whole portfolio of services.

One of the key difficulties of studying innovation in the service sector is that it has many facets, which tend not to be uniformly connected to a specific and tangible product. Innovation in services may consist of:

- Product innovations–new products or services, which are regarded as such either by customers or providers, or both.
- Process innovations–new ways of providing the services, including new roles for customers in the service delivery process.
- Market innovations–new modes of communicating with customers.

- Logistics innovations–new constellations of services and the organisation of flows.
- Institutional innovations–the emergence of new organisations and new ways of providing financing, marketing, production, collaboration, etc. (Hjalager, 2002).

From employing rather static approaches, research is increasingly addressing the determinants and outcomes of dynamic change in the tourism sector. For the most part, the starting point of such research is in the fluctuating market conditions and features connected to demand (Baumol, 2000). Innovation studies are gradually becoming more common in tourism research, although most agree that present conditions for innovation processes in tourism are not particularly propitious (Gallouj and Sundbo, 1999; Hjalager, 2002; Jensen et al., 2001). In general, tourism businesses have been found to be mainly imitators and adaptors rather than innovators. There has been much research and policy focus on, for example, managerial improvements, and considerably less so on how public subsidies and other measures can enhance knowledge transfers and thereby competitiveness.

The disproportionately low occurrence of innovation in the tourism sector is often connected with knowledge (transfer) deficiencies. Structural conditions obviously play a large part in this, e.g., the fairly small average size of firms in the sector, and the high firm mortality and start-up rates compared with other sectors. The collection of information, and the analysis and transformation of this information into knowledge, together with subsequent creative innovations, can be seriously hampered by high structural change rates (Laffary and Fossen, 2001). "Adherence" of knowledge is lost when people and capital move, unless other structures and institutions cover this loss. More than in other industries, the efficient codification of knowledge in the single enterprise, or in the industry as a whole, is crucial. For instance, this sometimes occurs through franchise set-ups (Darr et al., 1995). However, the study of such compensatory mechanisms and alternative routes to innovative development is all but absent in tourism research.

The seasonality-based low profitability of tourism enterprises can also be an obstacle to the "optimal" rate of innovation (Syrjämaa, 2001). However, much innovative effort is concentrated on finding ways to raise business activity in off-peak periods and reduce costs. Problems such as the lack of managerial and human resources are also important, inasmuch as they impede the appropriate acquisition of knowledge and its transformation into business strategies and practices.

Research into innovation in tourism is still sparse and fragmented, in spite of the fact that innovation is considered a prerequisite of economic development. There are thus many reasons for studies of innovation in tourism, not least to try to determine why and how tourism manages to develop in spite of discouraging odds. That is exactly where the notion of the welfare state and its ideological, financial and structural impacts comes in. The purpose of this article is to investigate the linkages between the welfare state and innovation in tourism and to offer a conceptualisation of this phenomenon.

THE WELFARE STATE AND TOURISM

Traditionally and ideally, one of the important roles of the welfare system was to ensure both internal coherence in society and the redistribution of resources, balanced against the need to curb a free market-based accumulation. Social and egalitarian objectives are crucial, but measures should be kept at a level where the private economic dynamics are not compromised (O'Brien and Penna, 1998). The literature on the Nordic model suggests that the welfare state operates not only in the social fields for the benefit of the disadvantaged, but comprises ideologies that are embedded in almost all corners of policymaking and administration (Eriksen and Loftager, 1996). Eriksen and Loftager (1996) characterise the nature of the Scandinavian welfare economies as "impressive and robust inventions," noting that:

> . . . the public sector is designed to counterweight the market, to compensate for its dysfunctions and negative by-products and to substitute for its failures. However, viewed functionally the public sector may also be conceived of as an organizing principle of industrialism parallel to the market as it is marked by systemic mechanisms of integration. While the market is legitimate purely on grounds of efficiency and is integrated via the medium of money, the public sector is correspondingly an arrangement for producing public benefits via the medium of legal sanctions–power–and professional skills. (p. 3)

Welfare state logic thus pervades politics, no matter whether it involves education, labour markets, infrastructure, social service, housing, environment, or the arts. It is naturally manifested in welfare programmes, such as the distribution of resources and opportunities, and it transcends the agendas of social patterns of access, participation, security, inclusion and exclusion. The influence and involvement of the public sector comes as somewhat of a surprise to some writers from other cultures, particularly those from the Anglo-Saxon world, where personal and economic liberalisation is taken for granted, and where welfare services are mainly in the hands of private (non-profit) organisations. As recalled by Taylor (2003), the Celtic tiger has been liberated through the dismantling of "the labyrinthine bureaucratic structures that has crowded out investment, created a culture of dependency, and undermined the emergence of an entrepreneurial spirit" (p. 212). Taylor's point is that, in the case of Ireland, the welfare concept has not so much been undermined as replaced by corporatist, collaborative structures where incentives are critically and continuously reconsidered.

Hardly anyone doubts that the Nordic welfare organisations–e.g., government bodies at all levels–are powerful agents. But they are far from being isolated from the private sector. Boundaries are crossed all the time. Even in the Nordic countries there is an extensive contract culture, which goes hand in hand with the welfare concepts. New Public Management or Management By Objectives are just two of the methods that are being developed and refined (Eikås and Selle, 2002). An underlying rationale of the contract culture is its aim of enhancing the development of welfare services in ways that would be impossible if it were solely in the hands of public or private actors.

The welfare state has come under increasing fiscal pressure over the past two decades. A lot of effort has been made to ensure a higher degree of private (commercial) involvement though outsourcing and collaboration. In addition, there has been more emphasis on alleviating activities by integrating "civil society" and social entrepreneurship (Barr, 2004; Ascoli and Ranci, 2002). There is a also a need to view the development of the welfare state in a global context, where welfare arrangements increasingly lose power as capital, labour and other economic resources are no longer confined within the borders of a purely self-contained national environment (Södersten, 2004). The migration of retired people to the coastal areas of Southern Europe is a good example of the spill over between the welfare state and tourism (Williams, 1999). There is an increasing focus on the disincentives of the welfare state, e.g., the inclination to enjoy and not to contribute, which are a result of both fiscal constraints and foreign access to the generous Scandinavian benefit systems (Lindbeck, 2004). In spite of attempts to "fix" the welfare state, a consensus on its desirability remains elusive, yet for most voters in the Nordic welfare states, dismantling it is out of question.

The most straightforward connection between the welfare state and tourism is the phenomenon of social tourism, which is (or was) quite widespread in many countries (Haulot, 1981; Zamelska, 1986). Traditionally, social tourism included the provision of facilities to enable disadvantaged groups, such as single mothers or children from city slum areas, to take a holiday away from home. However, although in this sense social tourism is also an ingredient in the Nordic welfare concepts, the implication of welfare governance on tourism is substantially wider-and perhaps also subtler. The general view is that the activities of a welfare state may have direct as well as indirect impacts on the private sector. Opportunities for starting new businesses and implementing innovations by hanging on the coattails of the welfare system are particularly decisive.

WELFARE TRAJECTORIES

In innovation and economic development research, the term 'trajectory' is used to describe the essence of technological development and its embeddedness in institutional and mental frameworks. Dosi (1982) notes: "Let us define technology as a set of pieces of knowledge, both directly" practical (related to concrete problems and devices) and "theoretical" (but practically applicable, although not necessarily already applied), know-how, methods procedures, experience of successes and failures, and also, of course, physical devices and equipment (p. 151-152). Dosi draws a parallel to the conception of Kuhnian "normal science": "A "scientific paradigm" could be roughly defined as an "outlook" which defines the relevant problems, a "model" and a "pattern" of inquiry" (p. 152). In this sense, being on a trajectory, the actors are "blind" to opportunities that challenge or threaten the basics of the original model.

A development trajectory, which represents an accumulation of targeted knowledge, is very powerful. It also indicates a certain direction of determined action and progress. In addition, the operational methods and problem-solving involve specific formats, which have been demonstrated to be efficient and feasible through an intensive use and continual, albeit incremental, adjustment. The methods used help to focus, but they also rule out deviating and competing paths of operation. A trajectory is supported by a range of other institutional set-ups, e.g., learning curricula in the educational system, legislative features and frameworks, the general image in media and public opinion, etc.

In this paper, we suggest a parallel between technological and economic trajectories and the development of the welfare state. Thus, *categories of tourism developments that rely on welfare state trajectories* are defined in the following way:

- Tourism trajectories that relate to comprehensive welfare state concepts are characterised by the *embracement and adaptation of principal and sustained ideologies* of justice, social and economic redistribution, fulfillment of human needs, participation, equal access to social resources, and the protection of the weakest.
- Within the prescriptions of the welfare logic and legislation, the tourism trajectory continually *enforces creative mutations of existing products and services*, and it operates towards new frontiers of innovation.
- Because of clustering around the dominant and pervasive welfare concept, the tourism trajectories *share a knowledge base with governing structures and institutions,* and there is a call for an ongoing, long-term, consensus and *joint accumulation of knowledge.*
- There is a *multiplicity of risk-taking,* as tourism trajectories are embedded in collaborative institutional structures with a lack of or *modest commercial pecuniary compulsion.*
- At best, the outcome of the trajectory is a *path-dependent, progressive movement* that adds strategically to quantities and qualities of the tourism product.
- The threats to the welfare-related tourism trajectories are *consistent with the challenges the welfare state faces,* albeit transposed, due to goal ambiguity and harsher consequences for coat-tailing tourism than for mainstream welfare activities.
- The welfare-related tourism trajectories meet only *limited opposition* due to the comprehensive *general legitimacy* of the welfare state, but there is some *jealousy* from commercial and market-based tourism enterprises.

In practice, the welfare state has many faces, and it is this pervasiveness, which makes it difficult to determine its nature with any great precision. We can, however, define six distinct trajectories that have had implications for innovativeness in tourism:

- The human capital trajectory
- The environmental protection trajectory

- The discouragement-of-noxious-behaviour trajectory
- The work-for-all trajectory
- The Beaux Art trajectory
- The health trajectory.

In the following, examples will be given of the tourism implications of each of these trajectories.

THE HUMAN CAPITAL TRAJECTORY

The importance of education, which is one of the oldest concerns of the Danish welfare state, has steadily increased throughout successive welfare regimes. Children's education has been compulsory since the first comprehensive school legislation was passed in 1814. From the beginning of the 20th century, the educational agenda gained importance as a major factor in attempts to deny privileged access to certain positions and opportunities in society. However, the educational systems were also agents in the general enlightening and transfer of cultural knowledge and consistent worldviews.

Over the past 30-50 years, education has moved radically beyond the confines of traditional educational institutions. An understanding has emerged that children and young people will also benefit from other learning environments. Increasingly, whole areas or countries have being regarded as "learning fields." Tours and camps are organised in order to enhance social and other skills, but wider learning elements depend on the setting, e.g., history, science, literature, etc. Basically, the choice of learning environment (for example, a visit to a farm, a waste water treatment plant, a natural site, a museum) was at the discretion of the individual teacher, who, in organising such trips, had to rely solely on their own (limited) networks.

A side effect of the increased focus on excursions is that children start their careers as curious and critical tourism consumers quite early in life, and what they will be learning is that tourism is not an exclusively hedonistic exercise.

Gradually, a commercial and non-commercial sector has emerged to accommodate the ideologies embedded in the (dominantly primary school) system, which at the same time makes life easier for teachers. Museums and other attractions have principal-pragmatic-developers in this field. Innovation takes place at the meeting point between the ideological and practical demand from schools and teachers. At the same time, this is likely to result in a greater attraction, both vis-à-vis school-children and for other visitors.

The Distribution Center for Teaching Materials ("Amtscentralen for Undervisningsmidler") and professional media for teachers are very important "umbrellas" for the dissemination of knowledge of ex-tramural learning objects. Thus, the clustering of the teaching profession in dense networks and the intermingling of these networks with the attractions sector has been of enormous value for the quantity and quality of the global tourism product.

The propensity to develop edutainment facilities in connection with museums and visitor attractions has grown dramatically, and these days there are few of the larger places that do not employ a whole range of in-terpretative facilities, which allow children to be investigative alone and in groups. The amendment of the Labour Market Holiday Foundation's statutes in 1990, which resulted in a substantial increase in funds to at-tractions, gave a further boost to these facilities. The funds were given only to projects with distinct learning objectives (Hjalager, 2005). The foundation is a part of the Danish social and labour market and social

FIGURE 1. The Viking Ship Museum in Roskilde provides a whole range of edu-cational facilities for school children. The museum has its own teachers, who guide tours around the fjord in full-scale models of Viking ships. During the tour, they provide living narratives of the lives and deeds of the Vikings. In controlled environments the children can experiment with materials and crafts methods of the Viking age. According to the museum, seen in isolation the schools are not economically viable, but many children later revisit with their parents. In addition, the Viking Ship Museum is located next to a youth hostel, whose profits depend to a large extent on visits to the museum by schools and sports groups.

Photo: Werner Karrasch. Copyright: The Viking Ship Museum, Denmark.

security system; the human capital issue is thus crucially embedded in mainstream welfare state logics.

THE ENVIRONMENTAL PROTECTION TRAJECTORY

The protection-of-the-weakest ethos is a prominent part of the welfare state concept. But while this was originally conceived to include only the particularly disadvantaged, i.e., those suffering from illness, poverty or lack of abilities, in recent decades it has become much more broadly applied to also include, for example, the environment. The

FIGURE 2. "Tracks in the landscape" is a joint project developed by the small rural municipality of Norhald, a number of local citizens' associations, local environmentalist organizations, and farmers. The idea is for groups of tourists to systematically walk through the landscape and on the way listen to the narratives of those who live and work there. The narratives are collected and edited to track-maps that can guide tourists through the landscape and give them more personal and vivid interpretation of modern rural life, buildings, landscapes, flora and fauna, etc. An added bonus of the project is that farmers have become considerably less hostile to interventionism from the local government, and they are starting to cooperate in developing dedicated tracks for riding and mountain biking.

Used with permission.

FIGURE 3. Symbiosis' is a term used to characterize the co-location and cooperation between enterprises that can recycle each others' by- and waste products. The same thinking has fueled new tourism concepts. In Odense, a large
power plant/district heating plant has long provided citizens with reliable energy at the cheapest possibly price. Comprehensive energy planning has been
a key concern of the public sector since the energy crises of the 1970s, and is
fully in line with welfare thinking. The power plant produces excess hot water,
particularly during the summer, autumn and spring, when the demand for dis-
trict heating is low. A project has been launched to build heated outdoor swimming basins and a long basin for all-year rowing in the old inner-harbor area.
The basins are supervised, so that they can also be used for training purposes
and fun rides. The location in the harbor area coincides with attempts by the
city council to revitalize and recycle the area for new housing and other urban
purposes. The area will become much more attractive to tourists in general.

Used with permission.

Brundtland Committee phrase "to interact with the natural resources today so that the opportunities of future generation are not compromised,"
has caught on as a framework for action that fits well with an expansive
welfare ideology.

   There are numerous interlinkages between the tourism case and the
protection case. As in most other countries, there has been a distinct
effort to protect areas of particular natural beauty and value, many of

which are publicly owned, and to guarantee free access for (non-disturbing) leisure purposes. The "State Forest Agency" ("Statsskovvaesenet"), which is a major actor in the protection of and access to nature, has for many years been an active partner in this area vis-à-vis tourists, and this role has increased as the timber market has more or less collapsed. Thus, in recent years, the Forest Agency has increasingly cooperated with commercial actors to replace activities that are no longer viable with tourist products. The wider objectives ensure that, for example, catering facilities operated privately are made available at appropriate locations, which do not compromise the protection agenda.

The protection of natural resources has always been a battlefield, with landowners ideologically opposed to the welfare state, at least when the ideology affects their own operations. The EU's Common Agricultural Policy presents a serious challenge to modern, industrialised agriculture, however. Danish farmers are likely to see an increased need for links with actors in tourism and leisure, which will open up new possibilities for income (Hjalager, 1996).

THE DISCOURAGEMENT-OF-NOXIOUS-BEHAVIOUR TRAJECTORY

Gambling has been subject to moralising for centuries, but the welfare state has chosen not to moralise, but rather to use its right to tax the passion for gambling which, taken to excess, may lead to poverty and misery. The revenue from these taxes is placed in the "Lottery Foundation," which supports a wide range of sound leisure activities, particularly (but not exclusively) for youth. It goes without saying that this should create attractive alternatives for tempted souls.

The "Lottery Foundation" subsidises open-air and sports facilities, and also supports the work of voluntary organisations such as sports clubs, scouts organisations and neighbourhood committees. In particular, the Foundation ensures the financing of equipment and infrastructures, while manpower for building the facilities is supposed to be mainly voluntary. Thus, there is a strong inclination to promote the concept of the "civil society" in the fields of leisure and culture, and the involvement of the welfare state is only secondary, at arm's length.

Increasingly, there is an overlap between leisure and tourism. Many facilities are freely accessible, e.g., nature guides, who operate from nature centres and nature museums throughout the country. Facilities include bird watching towers, game watching sheds and angling facilities, which are very popular among (German) tourists along the Danish west coast.

Cultural grass-roots organisations, leisure clubs and sports organisations help improve international relations, and cross-border project cooperation with similar interests groups abroad is increasing. This institutionalised "special interest tourism" is often overseen in tourism research, but is of considerable (though unquantified) importance for turnover in tourism-related trades. For example, a youth sports event is a source of revenue for the hosting club, but also for the local area. Parents and relatives who come as spectators push up occupancy rates in hotels and camping sites. For example, Frederikshavn football club organises "Danacup,", an event greatly appreciated by the local tourist industry, in spite of the fact that all visiting young people are put up by private families or in school facilities.

FIGURE 4. DGI-Byen in Copenhagen is a complex of sport facilities owned and managed by the largest voluntary sports organization in the country. The complex contains a range of facilities, but with an emphasis on swimming. The "Water Culture House" is a spectacular facility, which focuses on wellness rather than competition. The complex also contains a modern hotel, which is increasing used by others than participants in the sports events. Increasingly, DGI-Byen is used for international conferences of all kinds.

Used with permission.

THE WORK-FOR-ALL TRAJECTORY

Employment is one of the most crucial issues in the welfare state. Both the Scandinavian models and others emphasise the fact that full employment is a condition for general affluence. There should always be incentives to work (Gallie and Esping-Andersen, 2002; Jessop, 2002). Most people regard employment as a "human right," and there is an implicit obligation for the welfare state to combat disincentives to work.

The recession, which lasted from the mid-seventies to the mid-nineties, resulted in massive unemployment. Measures such as job-training and other compulsory schemes were meant to keep spirits/morale and qualifications intact, and to top up (public) services where this was considered particularly necessary. This period was in many ways a golden era for welfare institutions, e.g., services for children and the elderly. But the availability of funds and human resources also motivated many public and voluntary organisations to develop new tourism and leisure products.

Large numbers of the unemployed were assigned to positions in museums and attractions, in part to help build new facilities, and the abundance of extra manpower meant that many other organisations were also given an opportunity to expand. As considerable numbers of the unemployed had some kind of further education, administrative routines, marketing, documentation and other tasks became thoroughly professionalized.

In relation to tourism, the cleaning of beaches, trail making in forests and natural areas, upgrading of marinas and camping sites, organisation of playgrounds, trimming of golf-areas, etc., was both visible and qualitatively appropriate. However, an unintended side effect was that many of the projects became "institutionalised," and launched facilities that demanded continuous maintenance. The unemployment rate declined again from 1993, and quite a few of the projects and their spectacular facilities had to close down. It became clearer that employment-related activities in a welfare context should be reversible and robust, even under changed circumstances. It also illustrates the vulnerability of connecting the provision of tourism facilities too closely to the operations of the welfare state, whose main objectives are not congruent with those of tourism.

THE BEAUX ART TRAJECTORY

The public sector is the most important patron of arts in modern welfare economies. Although it claims to operate on an "arm's-length" principle, there is little doubt that the funding of are from public

FIGURE 5. The Citybike project in Copenhagen is a combined employment, environmental and promotional scheme. Bicycles are provided in the inner city, and can be borrowed by placing a refundable DKK 20 deposit (3 EURO) in a box. The idea is to give visitors and locals a costless means of transportation and thereby prevent traffic congestion and pollution. The bicycles are specially designed to prevent theft and vandalism. The organisation in charge of managment and maintenance is mainly staffed with unemployed persons on job training. All bicycles are sponsored by private enterprises, and carry advertisements on the wheels. This project seems to be quite viable, and has built a considerable reputation for innovativeness. However, without the indirect subsidy of unemployment benefit it would be unlikely to be feasible.

Used with permission.

sources is of major importance for the artists and arts institutions concerned. While art is intended for the enjoyment and enlightenment of the native population, foreigners are usually allowed access on equal terms. Increasingly, the public sector sees itself as a provider of frameworks and favourable economic conditions for arts, while the content and performance is entirely in the hands of the artist.

Initial public and private investments in arts are recognised to lead to significant spin-offs (Erhvervsministeriet and Kulturministeriet, 2001; Pine and Gilmore, 1999). The Danish welfare state is becoming increasingly aware of the potentials (Dansk Industri, 2003), and designs its policies in such a way that the opportunities for a secondary commodification can be grasped and further developed by private actors. The welfare state is not creative in an artistic sense, although there is an ongoing discussion about the indirect influence of politicians and officials.

FIGURE 6. Roskilde Rock Festival, which each summer attracts thousands of young people and performing artists from all over the world, has existed for many years. More than 70,000 paying guests attend the rock festival every year, which relies heavily on voluntary help (20,000 volunteers), but there is also a considerable degree of commercialism. Over the years, merchandising has expanded dramatically. The Festival Organization, which has become increasingly professional, also has a tendency to experiment and innovate. For example, it has developed an environmental sustainability concept, and after a fatal accident several years ago, safety issues have been given higher priority and much managerial and creative attention. Recently, new institutional constellations have been created for the purpose of launching the Roskilde area as a 'Musicon Valley,' including the establishment of educational facilities in music and arts management. Collaborative agreements have been made with research centres in order to explore innovative potentials in sound technologies. Links to the educational sector are regarded as crucial. The Roskilde area wants to expand the notion of a music-related "economic cluster," with far-ranging economic implications. Tourism is obviously a part of the committed network, although the roles of the commercial tourism actors are not yet well defined.

Used with permission.

Filmmaking is one of the sectors that has been quite successful over the past decade. The so-called "dogme-films" have won an international reputation. These films make a virtue of necessity by, for example, using hand-held cameras, no artificial lights, no special effects, shooting on location, using natural sounding, etc., (www.dogme95.dk; Hjort, 2001). Yet, without public financial guarantees, the films would probably never have been made. The production of dogme-films has since become more and more of an international affair, involving famous actors and foreign locations. However, the courage and reputation of the Danish directors have made it easier for others to arrange successful film festivals and film events on a more commercial basis. For example, the Copenhagen Film Festival attracts many visitors. The dogme-films attracted curiosity about the country and its population, which in some cases makes better tourism marketing than glossy pictures in brochures.

THE HEALTH TRAJECTORY

Health services are the most important element of the Danish welfare system. Nearly all health services, most of which are provided within the publicly owned and operated health system, are free of charge. The public sector has (quite restrictive) contracts with general practitioners, dentists and other private suppliers of health services, whose activities are partly or fully paid via taxes. In recent years, private hospitals and health services have been established on market conditions. These are mainly aimed at those who want to bypass waiting lists or who have private medical insurance. The appearance of private hospitals was a controversial issue, on account of the break with the idea of egalitarianism. Some of the private health services have experienced substantial difficulties, since Danes are not used to paying for health care. However, alliances with insurance companies and with employers who pay for heath services for key employees has a created a market–albeit limited–for private health services.

It should be noted that the organisation and financing of health services is still a closed world, where medics are accused of wanting to stay in quite narrow institutional and professional settings without much thought about the future. Tourism-related innovations are not easily embedded in this system.

The generous and free health system has made it necessary to try to limit demand. New treatments are costly, and patients tend to want them

FIGURE 7. Sundhedshøjskolen Diget has found a way to avoid being trapped in the health hegemony. Diget is a folk high school, financed over the education budget rather than the health budget. This means that the health and prophylaxis challenges are replaced by knowledge or educational challenges. The school has boarding facilities, and its situated at an attractive coastal location near Skagen. To some extent, the facilities resemble a commercial health farm. Courses in healthy lifestyle are offered to those who want a more "holisitic" approach to their health. The school can help persons with eating disturbances or other health-related problems, which the official health system is less geared to. Foreigners are welcome, but only Danes qualify for reduced fees.

Used with permission.

as soon as they are available. This means that prophylactic treatments, whose impacts are uncertain, are seldom included in the portfolio of the public health service. For example, prescriptions for spas and health resorts are rare, as in other countries (Hall, 2003). It has often been argued that prophylactic treatment of the body and soul will have positive impacts on hospital costs. However, the causal relationships are not convincing enough to shift political priorities.

Private actors have attempted to establish comprehensive spa facilities and health resorts in Denmark on several occasions, so far without success. The financing constraints, where health expenditure is so strictly incorporated in the public sector, is the main reason for this (Tetzschner and Herlau, 2003).

DISCUSSION

The above sections have outlined some important trajectories in the Danish welfare concept and related these to the provision of tourism facilities and services. It has been shown that, in many cases, concepts and ideologies are transposed and reinterpreted to make room for innovations in a tourism context.

The examples demonstrate that the modern welfare state goes considerably beyond what is considered as basic human rights and needs. What makes a cross-fertilisation between tourism and welfare services possible is that the welfare concept increasingly includes enjoyment and entertainment as essential qualities of life. Thus, the Danish welfare state is not particularly concerned with providing access to (cheap or free) holiday facilities for the poor and disadvantaged in isolated social tourism reserves, as is the case in some countries. Rather, individual choice of holiday and leisure activity is retained by means of income transfers that can be used at the receivers' own discretion; this means that even disadvantaged citizens should feel they are on equal terms with the rest of the local community. Subsidised, high-quality leisure facilities are offered to all citizens with no social distinction made. Precisely by being open, accessible and reasonably priced, welfare-based facilities end up being genuine parts of the tourism product.

There are many examples of the ongoing innovative mutation of existing products and services. Perhaps unsurprisingly, the new frontiers of innovation are most prevalent in the cultural sectors/beaux art. Possibly, the arm's length principle can ensure that actors are not locked into traditions and institutions. If arts people want to remain in the arena, they have to continually apply for funds for creative new projects. However, public funding is not enough to ensure continuation, renewal and efficient brokerage. The clustering of public, voluntary and private agents is taking place around global concepts, as we saw in the "Musicon Valley" and film industry examples. Clustering also occurs in other parts of the sector, e.g., the "Design" cluster, where attempts are being made to enhance innovation through a collaborative environment consisting of design schools, exhibition centres, arts and crafts producers, artists, the media, and tourism marketers. The "Play" cluster is a meeting place for producers of toys, playground equipment, teacher's associations, pedagogical research, and leisure organisations. It is likely that public funds can be a mediator and a factor in the sourcing, not only of money but also in terms of knowledge (Erhvervsministeriet and Kulturministeriet, 2001).

It was suggested in the definition that, because of clustering alongside the dominant and pervasive welfare concept, the tourism trajectories share a knowledge base with governing structures and institutions. This is particularly the case in the environment-related projects. The mode of regulation in the environmental sector is characterised by a considerable consensus and joint accumulation of knowledge. There is a certain flow of manpower between various categories of jobs and positions, and the interlinkages with the leisure grassroots have existed for many years. A new angle to innovation is the more forceful inclusion of agriculture. In large part, this is because the CAP (Community Agricultural Policy) reforms encourage farmers to find alternative long-term uses for their land and buildings.

There is a multiplicity of risk-taking, as tourism trajectories are embedded in collaborative institutional structures with a lack of or modest commercial compulsion. This is especially the case in the sports and leisure sector, where public funds are given "in exchange" for voluntary commitment and work. Voluntary work is in a (perhaps delayed) internationalisation process, alongside the globalisation that has occurred in many other sectors. To some (unexplored) extent, therefore, in- and outbound tourism is the result of a push through the welfare economy.

At best, the outcome of the trajectory is a path-dependent, progressive movement that adds strategically to quantities and qualities of the tourism product. Many tourism facilities would never have had the extent and quality they have today without public interference, including most museums, performing arts establishments, and leisure facilities such as marinas, golf courses, trails and tracks, etc. It can be argued that taxpayers' money is used to raise standards beyond the level that the average Dane (and foreign tourists) is willing to pay for. Many facilities of the kind mentioned here would not be able to survive on purely commercial terms. There is a tacit understanding that facilities should be kept up to standard and further developed along the same paths. There are many advantages of path-dependency, e.g., edutainment has benefited from a strong pedagogic tradition, and from the consistent, long-term interaction between teachers, attractions and the voluntary sector. There has been a strong and mutually beneficial "tandem" development that has also acquired a solid international reputation.

However, things change, and even successful and progressive development paths are challenged occasionally. The threats to the welfare-related tourism trajectories are consistent with the challenges that the welfare state faces, albeit transposed, due to goal ambiguity, to harsher consequences for coat-tailing tourism than for mainstream welfare activities. For example, changes in employment conditions and policies to combat unemployment have already had severe negative effects on many tourism-related activities. However, there may be beneficial effects elsewhere. If the government decided to privatise or cut expenditure on, for example, education, leisure provision, environmental management, etc., to a higher extent than at present, it could lead to a variety of impacts, although it is not possible to determine whether it would be uniformly catastrophic in relation to tourism. However, many facilities would probably suffer from this discontinuity for shorter or longer periods, since there are few areas that would attract private investors.

At present, the welfare-related tourism trajectories meet only limited opposition due to the general legitimacy of the welfare state (Rohtstein, 1998; Svallfors and Taylor-Gooby, 1999). Danes appreciate the provision of welfare to an extent that they generally accept high taxes, as long as they feel that they receive a decent share of the benefits.

When the present liberal government took office, it found it had to retract its intentions to privatise and reduce state involvement. In terms of welfare, its policy is hardly distinguishable from social democratic policy.

Membership of the EU means that Denmark faces pressure to harmonise the levels and formats of welfare provision, including making welfare available for all EU citizens and being less restrictive with regard to the flow of resources across borders.

Right from the start of the welfare era in the late 1960s commercial and market-based tourism enterprises have complained about unfair competition from organisations, which receive state support, e.g., the sports, and youth movements, which have established their own facilities instead of using commercial ones. And criticism increased when publicly co-funded facilities started offering their services and facilities to non-members as well. Notwithstanding, many private enterprises benefit quite substantially from welfare-related tourism and leisure provision. Those who can join clusters are likely to be exposed not only internally, but also in larger markets abroad.

Tourism research can with some right be criticised for being *either* over-occupied with the commercial side *or* focusing exclusively on the public governance. Too little emphasis has been placed on the creative clustering of public and private driving forces. Emerging institutional and knowledge structures transcend boundaries. If tourism research has the intention of understanding the dynamics of modern integrated and globalised format of tourism, there is much to be investigated in greater depth.

REFERENCES

Ascoli, U., and Ranci, C. (2002). The context of new social policies in Europe. Ascoli, U. and Ranci, C. (Eds): *Dilemmas of the welfare mix*. New York, Kluwer, pp. 1-24.

Barr, N. (2004). *The economics of the welfare state*. Oxford, Oxford University Press.

Barras, R. (1986). Towards a Theory of Innovation in Services. *Research Policy 15*, pp. 161-173.

Baumol, W. J. (2002). *The free-market innovation machine. Analyzing the growth miracle of capitalism*. Princeton: Princeton University Press.

Dansk Industri (2003). *From beauty to business*. Copenhagen.

Darr, E. D., Argote, L., and Epple, D. (1995). The acquisition, transfer, and depreciation of knowledge in service organizations: Productivity in franchises. *Management Science 41*, pp. 1750-1762.

Dosi, G. (1982). Technological paradigms and technological trajectories. *Research Policy 11*, pp. 147-162.

Eikås, M., and Selle, P. (2002). A contract culture even in Scandinavia. Ascoli, U. and Ranci, C. (Eds): *Dilemmas of the welfare mix*. New York, Kluwer, pp. 47-76.

Erhvervsministeriet & Kulturministeriet (2001). *Denmark's creative potential*, Copenhagen.

Eriksen, E.O., and Loftager, J. (1996). Introduction: Challenging the normative foundation of the welfare state. Eriksen, E. & Loftager, J (Eds): *The rationality of the welfare state*. Oslo, Scandinavian Universities Press, pp. 1-11.

Gallie, D., and Esping-Andersen, G. (Eds) (2002). *Why we need a new welfare state*. New York, Oxford University Press.

Gallouj, F., and Sundbo, J. (1998). *Innovation in services in seven European countries*.: Roskilde, Roskilde University.

Hall, M. (2003). Spa and health tourism. In: Hudson, S. J. (ed), *Sport and adventure tourism*, Birmingham, Haworth Hospitality Press, pp. 273-292.

Haulot, A. (1981). Social tourism. Current dimensions and future developments. *Tourism Management 2*(4), pp. 207-212.

Hjalager, A. M. (1996). Diversification in agricultural tourism. Evidence from a European Community programme. *Tourism Management 17*(2) pp. 103-111.

Hjalager, A. M. (1997). Innovation patterns in sustainable tourism-an analytical typology. *Tourism Management 16*(3), pp. 35-41.

Hjalager, A. M. (2002). Repairing innovation defectiveness in tourism. *Tourism Management 23*(5), pp. 465-474.

Hjalager, A. M. (2005). Innovation in tourism in a welfare state perspective. *Scandinavian Journal of Hospitality and Tourism 5*(1), forthcoming.

Hjort, M. (2001). Dogme 95: A small nation's response to globalization. *Film, Politik & Samfund*, 4, p. 3.

Jensen, C.F., Mattsson, J., and Sundbo, J. (2001). *Innovationstendenser i dansk turisme*. Roskilde University, Center for Servicestudier.

Jessop, B. (2002). *The capitalist state*, Cambridge, Polity.

Lafferty, G., and van Fossen, A. (2001). Integrating the tourism industry. Problems and strategies. *Tourism Management 22*(1), pp. 11-19.

Lindbeck, A. (2004). An essay on the welfare state dynamics. Södersten, B. (ed): *Globalization and the welfare state*, Houndsmill, Palgrave Macmillan, pp. 149-171.

Metcalfe, J. S., and Miles, I. (Eds) (1999). *Innovation systems in the service economy. Measurement and case study analysis*, Boston, Kluwer Academic Publishers.

O'Brien, M. & Penna, S. (1998). *Theorising welfare. Enlightenment and modern society*, London, Sage.

OECD (2000). *Knowledge management in the learning society*. Paris.

Pine, J., and Gilmore, J. (1999). *The experience economy*. Boston Mass, Harvard Business School Press.

Rothstein, B. (1998). *Just institutions matter: The moral and political logic of the universal welfare state*. Cambridge, Cambridge University Press.

Syrjämaa, T. (2001). Challenging seasons. Pros and cons of changing seasonality. Toivonen, T. & Honkanen, A. (Eds): *Proceedings for 7th ATLAS International Conference*, Savonlinna 2001, pp. 69-79.

Svallfors, S., and Taylor-Gooby, P. (Eds) (1999). *The end of the welfare state?: Responses to state retrenchment*. London, Routledge.

Södersten, B. (2004). The welfare state as a general equilibrium system. In: Södersten, B. (ed), *Globalization and the welfare state*, Houndsmill, Palgrave Macmillan, pp. 96-127.

Taylor, G. (2003). Bargaining Celtic style: The global economy and negotiated governance in Ireland. van Waarden, F. and Lehmbruch, G. (Eds), *Renegotiating the welfare state. Flexible adjustment through corporatist concertation*, London, Routledge, pp. 191-224.

Tetzschner, H., and Herlau, H. (2003). Innovation and social entrepreneurship in tourism–a potential for local business development? Working paper 49/03, Syddansk Universitet.

Williams, A. M. (1999). International retirement migration and rural transformation in Southern Europe. Paper presented to the Sustaining Rural Environments Conference, 20-23 October, Flagstaff, Arizona.

Zamelska, M. (1986). Recreational migration within social tourism. In Vetter, F. (ed): *Grossstadttourismus. Tourisme de grandes villes. Big city tourism*, Berlin: Dietrich Reimer Verlag, pp. 466-481.

Internet sources: *www.dogme95.dk,* retrieved June 2005.

Leadership and Innovation Processes– Development of Products and Services Based on Core Competencies

Harald Pechlaner
Elisabeth Fischer
Eva-Maria Hammann

SUMMARY. The new challenge for destinations is to professionalize the continuous development process of innovative products and services. In this context, innovation is regarded as a bipolar process between market and resources. From the resource-oriented perspective, the concentration on regional core competencies will therefore become a source of innovation for destinations while the customer is the source of innovation from the market-oriented perspective. Resulting from the nature of the destination product, the innovation process is interpreted as an inter-organizational network process. The aim has to be the imple-

Harald Pechlaner (Foundation Professor of Tourism), Elisabeth Fischer (Assistant Professor), and Eva-Maria Hammann (Assistant Professor), are all affiliated with the Foundation Professorship of Tourism, Catholic University of Eichstätt-Ingolstadt, P.-Phil.-Jeningen-Platz 2, 85071 Eichstätt, Germany (E-mail: harald.pechlaner@ku-eichstaett.de) (E-mail: elisabeth.fischer@ku-eichstaett.de) or (E-mail: eva.hammann@ku-eichstaett.de).

[Haworth co-indexing entry note]: "Leadership and Innovation Processes–Development of Products and Services Based on Core Competencies." Pechlaner, Harald, Elisabeth Fischer, and Eva-Maria Hammann. Co-published simultaneously in *Journal of Quality Assurance in Hospitality & Tourism* (The Haworth Hospitality Press, an imprint of The Haworth Press, Inc.) Vol. 6, No. 3/4, 2005, pp. 31-57; and: *Innovation in Hospitality and Tourism* (ed: Mike Peters, and Birgit Pikkemaat) The Haworth Hospitality Press, an imprint of The Haworth Press, Inc., 2005, pp. 31-57. Single or multiple copies of this article are available for a fee from The Haworth Document Delivery Service [1-800-HAWORTH, 9:00 a.m. - 5:00 p.m. (EST). E-mail address: docdelivery@ haworthpress.com].

Available online at http://www.haworthpress.com/web/JQAHT
doi:10.1300/J162v06n03_03

31

mentation of continuous innovation processes in the form of networks within a system of a learning destination. Given the fact that, especially for innovative activities, networks play a minor role in tourism at present, the question is raised of how to overcome the obstacles of cooperation and to initiate network activities to foster innovation networks within a destination. A study was conducted that focused on the identification of forms of cooperation that strengthen and reinforce innovative behavior in a destination. The article aims at discussing the enhancement of the attractiveness and the quality of innovative network activities by increasing the value of cooperation for the providers of the destination. *[Article copies available for a fee from The Haworth Document Delivery Service: 1-800-HAWORTH. E-mail address: <docdelivery@haworthpress.com> Website: <http://www.HaworthPress.com> © 2005 by The Haworth Press, Inc. All rights reserved.]*

KEYWORDS. Innovation process, tourism product development, leadership, networks

INTRODUCTION

The development of innovative marketable products and services is one of the most discussed topics in tourism science and practice at the moment. The increasing national and international competition and the saturation of markets in particular do not only force regular business players to intensify their endeavor for innovativeness but the tourism industry is also asked to successfully develop innovative services and products (Weiermair, 2003; Keller, 2002). The creative use of local resources and a more consequent customer orientation are essential in order to create an innovative offer of a destination. The constant development of new innovative offers, products and services will be the challenge for the future of a destination. Thus, practitioners and scientists are needed to create and implement an efficient innovation process within the destinations.

The first section of this paper deals with the destination product and innovation in tourism and gives an overview of the recent literature of the processes of innovation in tourism and a typology of the innovation of tourism products. Considering the innovation as a market or resource-driven output, innovation is regarded as either a push or a pull innovation process. The article discusses two important sources of innovation for the destination product: the region and its core competencies as well as the market with the innovative impulses of customers and the entrepreneurial behavior of the service providers of a destination.

The innovation process for a destination itself will be discussed in the second section of the paper. Given the nature of the destination product, cooperation and competition are two important determinates of innovation. The innovation process is therefore regarded as an inter-organizational network process–a hybrid process between regional core competencies and the market. The aim must be the implementation of a continuous innovation process through networks within a system of a learning destination. Therefore, five important forms of cooperation are identified along the innovation process: exchange of knowledge, exchange of specific experiences, co-determination and impact on regional competence development, common utilization of specific resources and acquisition of techniques/technologies of other regional players. Furthermore, these networks need to be managed and coordinated. As such, the topic of inter-organizational innovative networks and leadership is dealt with in the third section.

Despite their importance for destination development, networks play a minor role in the tourism industry at present because of the high costs and a certain unwillingness of the small and medium sized enterprise (SME) to cooperate. With respect to their essential role for the innovative output of a destination, these obstacles have to be overcome and the initiation of innovative networks within the destination has to be enforced. This leads to the central questions of research: What forms of network activities foster innovation within a destination and how can they be initiated in order to overcome the obstacles of cooperation? In summer and autumn 2004, a study was conducted among forty service providers in a Bavarian region to identify the forms of cooperation that strengthen and reinforce innovative behavior in a regional network.

The focus in the discussion of the results is made on how to increase the attractiveness and the value of innovative cooperation for service providers of a destination by raising the quality and reducing the costs of innovative network activities according to the concept of customer value management in order to boost the innovation process within the destination. Therefore, the tool of the customer value map is used. Supporting cooperation of high value and therefore the innovation process within the destination could be the task of the "*decentred leader*" as an intermediate position between two sources of innovation-regional leadership and entrepreneurial management of the destination–by creating and offering favorable conditions that reduce costs and raise the quality of network activities.

The results should allow important implications for tourism policy and practice to fight the unfavorable positioning of cooperation and thereby improve the innovative behavior resulting from network activities in a destination. Finally, indices for further research are given.

INNOVATION AND THE DESTINATION PRODUCT

At the moment, the traditional tourism countries face problems of productivity and growth. Consequently, innovation as a motor of growth is intended to be the answer (Sancho, 2005; Bieger, 2005; Flagestad, 2005; Hjalager, 2002; Keller, 2005). Nevertheless, most innovations in tourism come from outside, initiated by people from other industries and sectors. Innovations in terms of creating experiences often emerge between sectors (e.g., Cinema and Tourism, Industry and Tourism). In other industries the innovation process is standardized as a matter of routine but not so in tourism where this culture is still missing. It is a fact that the tourism industry differs considerably from other industries in its structure, developmental dynamics, heterogeneity and human resource capacities. The reason why innovators often come from outside are the difficult structural and behavioral preconditions for innovations in the tourism industry (Hjalager, 2002):

- The tourism sector is dominated by small and medium-sized enterprises and most of them are owned and managed by a single person or family. Innovation capacity is closely and positively correlated with the size of firms (Rogers, 1983; Dosi, 1988). In these firms daily operations tend to have first priority. It is impossible for SMEs to screen and process the huge amount of information to an operational form. SMEs simply lack time, money and knowledge for innovative activities. Moreover, industry insiders are often too technical and too less experience-oriented.
- Large tourism enterprises are more quickly implementing new ideas, processing information and thus creating competitive advantages. Small enterprises tend to follow and imitate.
- Moreover, there is a culture of little trust among firms in tourism. Because of the problem of free riding, collaboration is mostly the result of intermediation by other organizations, e.g., tourist offices/boards, where activities are undertaken at "arms-length" from

the individual proprietors balancing some of the potentials of knowledge transfers.
- The destination product compromises services form several segments of suppliers.
- There is a high volatility of ownership of tourism businesses. In general, new owners make considerable investments; they are more change-oriented and innovative but when the changes are too fast, the establishment of trust-based collaborative relations in destinations will be difficult.

Innovation holds huge potential for the destination to create customer value and to attract people with high purchase power. In order to exploit this potential, the development of a process of innovation facing the problems mentioned above is the future challenge for tourism destinations.

After the following typology of innovations adapted from Hjalager (1994) to the service sector, innovation can take place in one or a combination of the following five categories: product innovations, process innovations, management innovations, logistic innovations and institutional innovations. Other researchers stress the involvement of customers by the production of services and add the dimensions of service innovation and involvement innovation (Bieger, 2005).

With the focus on innovation management in tourism, three different product levels can be distinguished: The first is the service product itself; the second element is the attraction as nuclei producing the experience; and finally, the destination product as network of bundles of products and services. The third element mentioned is the center of the discussion of this article. In consideration of the characteristics of the destination product, the following typology of innovation (Hjalager, 2002) distinguishing the types of innovations by their constellation of consequences in terms of knowledge and collaborative structure fits best:

- Architectural innovations tend to change general structures, establish new rules and therefore may change not only the industry but also the society.
- Regular innovations are at least radical, conserve existing collaborative structures and competences but the impact over time can be radical.
- Revolutionary innovations keep external structures unchanged but they have a radical effect on competences.

- Niche innovations challenge collaborative structures but not basic competences and knowledge.

In order to develop innovations on the level of the destination, an institutionalized innovation management in destinations is needed. Therefore, the destination has to become an innovative system (Flagestad, 2005) guaranteeing dynamics by sharing a vision, a certain ownership structure of firms, demanding customers, a strong brand and finally a critical size. A future requirement for innovative organizations in tourism is to look after the innovation process (Bieger, 2005).

In the tourism industry the innovation process itself is widely under-researched, especially on the level of the destination and in comparison to other industries. Latest research see the innovation process as a process of knowledge management for innovative experiences (Stambouis and Skayannis, 2003). Hjalager (2002) also regards the innovation process as a transfer process between the core tourism businesses and the four determinates of innovation: the trade system (market surveys, best practice, certification standards, IT systems etc.), the technological system (equipment and technological semi-manufacturing, outsourcing) the infrastructural system (natural and cultural attractions, traffic, transport) and the regulation system (safety control, economic control, environmental systems, labor regulations etc.). Hjalager (2002) considers that the "bright brains of importance for innovation in tourism are just not employed in the tourism industry, but elsewhere" (p. 437). The innovation potential is seen outside the core tourism industry. She regards the four systems mentioned above and their organizations as responsible for research. The tourism industry is not involved at this early but important stage of the innovation process. With it, Hjalager (2002) suggests to "outsource" the research activities in order to overcome the obstacles of the difficult structural preconditions of the tourism industry. This would leave research and invention out of the destinations management influence. Despite the fact that fundamental innovations can not be planned, such a process might be adequate to an additional forecast system for screening environmental determinants. But innovation as an institutionalized management process should become a matter of routine and therefore lasting influence of independent innovators should be aimed. In this paper, a first attempt to develop such an innovative process is made.

Firms are basically conservative; if they are not challenged or threatened, they will tend to be attached to usual procedures. Innovation research regards two different motivators for speed up changes: Push factors (new technologies, appropriate methods that offer more effective solutions) and pull factors (reflected in the demand from individual customers). Both factors operate at the same time (Hjalager, 2002). Tourism is an industry very close to the customer; nevertheless, most innovations are pushed and are often too technology-driven and not customer-friendly in its outputs (Bieger, 2005). Paradoxically, most innovations in other industries are customer-driven. This is due to the reasons mentioned above as they feature high transaction costs, and they lack time and financial resources. The consequences are less market research and late decision time.

The involvement of customers in the innovation process is important for the development of ground-breaking services and products because very often customers make substantial contributions through the articulation of their ideas, wishes and needs (Bieger and Gräf, 2004). The accumulated knowledge due to interaction with tourists can be incorporated in intelligence (Stamboulis and Skayannis, 2003). This intelligence is destination-specific and user-oriented, thus, providing an intangible (and consequently less replicable) source of competitive advantage. Moreover, the customers or guests become a source of innovation.

In the tourism industry, the environmental view of strategy is still predominant (Bieger, 2002). It is a fact that tourism destinations and products include external factors as climate and topography what made the orientation on internal factors as core competencies unnecessary for a long time. Former experience shows that destination strategies oriented on market and environment add value for the customer by offering coordinated marketable products on a short-term perspective, but they do not lead to competitive advantages in the long run. The lack of differentiation makes it easy to be imitated and replaceable: The focus on specific recourses and cultural identities is also missing. A more "resource-based" view (Barney, 1986; Penrose, 1959) in contrary to a "market-based" view (Porter, 1990) should therefore be targeted. In competition, a destination has to find out what resources are available in the region and what competencies exist for the future. For the determination of competitiveness the focus has clearly to be made on the specific resources and processes of the region. The region is regarded as a source of innovation in tourism.

A significant differentiation of regions and tourism destinations arises from the comprehension of leadership. From the perspective of the destination, the managers of tourism organizations engage in regional management but from the potential guest's point of view they engage in destination management (Pechlaner, 1999).

The definition of a destination is characterized by a process-oriented but also a customer-and market-oriented view. Parts of the destination product offered are on the one hand services like information, accommodation, food, transport, activities etc. and on the other hand available resources and components as landscape and inhabitants of the region. The destination product mainly consists of services and experiences provided by different individual suppliers of a destination. In fact, it is the overall performance of the destination which is judged and valued by guests and which can therefore be regarded as the marketable product unity of a destination (Pechlaner and Tschurtschenthaler, 2003). Co-operation between the different service providers of a destination is highly demanded as it is central for the long-term competitiveness of a destination.

Contrary to knowledge or finance-oriented services, the destination product needs a stage in the form of mountains, beaches, artificial infrastructure, shopping-centers, etc. Thus, these services are closely tied to a location because the guest has to come to the location for consumption (Bieger and Gräf, 2004). This implies that the region itself has a big impact on the design and development of the destination product. The unique marketable product of a destination is a combination of recourses, knowledge, know-how, experiences, technologies, abilities and competencies of a region (Pechlaner et al., 2005). Consequently, it is essential to adjust the demand of the market and the real conditions of the location.

The competitive advantages of a region arise from the dynamic interaction of determinants such as supply and demand, quality and structure of organizations, markets and industries as well as specific strategies and goals (Porter, 1990). This emerges e.g., from the availability of a well educated staff, sufficient size of respective markets and when related also supplying industries exist in order to both develop and exchange competencies and management strategies. The combination of different competencies, resources and factors of a region direct their development. In the course of time, unique location-specific resources, capabilities, knowledge and technologies, the development of different industries, the creation of a special focus in the education-system, the get-together of different interest-groups are built up. Core competencies can be created by systematic development of the bundle of competencies. Core competencies offer access to various markets; they are the source for product development and successful innovation (Prahalad and Hamel, 1990). Consequently, a combination of outstanding competences of the region, which are highly valued by guests, can be the source for the development of innovative new destination products; they enable the development of a unique profile and allow the access to a number of new markets (Pechlaner et al., 2005).

The regional core competencies have to be continuously developed and managed by regional governance. In doing this, the regional governance becomes a co-producer not only by offering attractive public goods, optimizing size and surplus of positive externalities and setting an innovation-oriented tourism policy but also by regional development.

Providers of the tourism destinations must have the possibility to co-determine regional planning and development and accordingly adjust tourism planning. Regional and tourism planning need to be coherent.

This discussion shows that for the innovation process both the determination of customer needs concerning the destination's services and products and the identification of the region's unique competencies, namely the core competencies and their value for guests, are important.

This leads to the conclusion that the destination innovation process is a bipolar process between the two opposite poles of market and resource orientation.

INNOVATION PROCESS
AS INTER-ORGANIZATIONAL NETWORK PROCESS

Given the nature of the destination product, cooperation is one of the most important strategies in order to develop innovative products in tourism (Keller, 2002; Weiermair and Walder, 2004). Destination products can feature vertical cooperation on the different levels of production, lateral cooperation with other industries of other levels of production, or horizontal cooperation within the same industry on the same level of production (Bieger/Scherer, 2003). But tourism products are always in spatial regions what make the exchange in the destination important. The balance between competition and cooperation is the key for the development of innovations in tourism (Franke, 1999; Keller and Smeral, 2001). The form of cooperation of the network players is not intended to diminish competition. This would minimize the dynamic of innovation. Indeed, too much competition also reduces innovation (Sancho et al., 2004) because the product development costs are too high. Therefore, a healthy competitive situation is required to force the development of the product (Peters and Weiermair, 2002). The development of fostering balance has to be assured by the emergence of the network.

The innovation process itself can be seen as a five step process.

1. Positioning of the Destination

First of all, the innovation process starts with the analysis of the current positioning and performance of the destination. On this basis, a development plan with the strategic positioning should be formulated to assure the right and coherent direction of the development by all players. The development of a destination has to be planned as a whole. In order to receive a long-term profitable and competitive strategic positioning of the destination, it is necessary that all providers and suppliers are involved in the planning process of a destination. An overall tourism concept or a destination strategy can not stand alone; it has to be implemented in a superior plan of the region and in the downstream plans of the individual regional companies.

2. Identifying Themes Based on Regional Competencies

During the next step the destination can define the themes for their core products and services and also make concrete offers based on the value of a regional core competency. Themes can more easily be communicated to customers.

3. Building Networks Based on Themes

Furthermore, marketable tourism products and services, and subsequently, specific offers can be created on the basis of these core products and services. This happens by newly defined networks. Therefore, in a third step, networks with potential partners and providers of the new innovative destination product have to be built. It can be ascertained that there is a permanent challenge concerning the use of regional core competencies as a basis of product and service development in tourism and their continuing enhancement. As the destination product has previously been defined as a bundle of competencies, different players within the region are linked together. Depending on the defined themes, the network also includes players of other industries as well as providers of tourism core businesses.

4. Producing Innovative Products and Redefining Value Chains

Through cooperation and collaboration between various entrepreneurs and companies along a new defined destination product value chain, innovations that provide access to new markets and customers are made.

5. Managing and Monitoring of the Innovation Life Cycle Course by Learning Processes

Finally, in order to provide a continuous innovation management to fully tap the success potential of the innovation brought to the market by managing its course in the life cycle, the destination has to become a "learning destination." This task can only be accomplished when the players within the destination manage to create a general framework to trigger transindustry learning processes or networks that culminate in the transition of core competencies in core products and services. This continuous learning process for the further innovation management is essential since innovations of intangible products imply high customer involvement, as it is the case in tourism. The problem of the trial and error arises. There are no pilot markets and it is often an animated innovation what means the guest has to be convinced to use it. The customers have to learn and invest a lot of time and energy what reduces the customer value; they waste time and interest. As such the innovative service provider needs to reduce these costs for the customer (Bieger, 2005). For the innovation of the destination, product knowledge management is therefore closely linked with innovation management (Pikkemaat and Pfeil, 2005). From the consumer's perception and the communication in general, the destination product is a network. Innovation management is based on the identification of knowledge, the use and codification of knowledge and the competence creation within the network (von Krogh and Venzin, 1995, p. 425).

Generally, the tourism innovation process can be seen as an inter-organizational network. Along the production and product development process five possible forms of cooperation emerge: the common utilization of specific resources, the exchange of knowledge, the exchange of specific experiences, the co-determination and the impact on regional competence development and the acquisition of techniques/technologies of other regional players. They are identified as potential sources of transaction costs (Williamson, 1975) when it comes to cooperation.

This innovation network has to be a strategic network and differs from typical regional networks. The latter ones typically do have neither explicit aims nor role distribution nor an identity. They are rather characterized by informal processes without strategic leadership. Strategic inter-organizational networks are emerging from market-networks that follow organizational rules (e.g., franchising). They differ from organizational-networks where organizations are achieved by principles of the market (e.g., decentred directed groups). Such cooperation forms are hybrid arrangements on the continuum of possible economic cooperation between the one extreme-loose flexible arrangements of the market ruled by the mechanism of price-and the other extreme of technocratic, co-ordinate hierarchical organization-forms aiming for stability (Hinterhuber and Stahl, 2000). This compromise between both poles is an inter-organizational network that is characterized by emergence.

Innovations are finally developed through the networking of individual suppliers and companies in the destination. As discussed in the beginning, small and medium-sized enterprises (SMEs) do not have the resources to innovate products and services by themselves. Because of their small size investment in knowledge, concepts and innovation could not be multiplied and profitably managed. SMEs can be highly adaptive to external pressures and potentials but R&D results must usually be of a practical nature if they are applied in this type of firm. Researchers have observed the expectations of this behavior where SMEs are units in chains and franchisees (Hjalager, 2002). Constellations in collaborative structures can help SMEs to overcome some difficulties of innovation when a head office screens and precedes the vast amounts of information into useful units for the firms. The collaboration with suppliers, partners and customers concerning research work, the development of products or the innovation process itself is vital. The coordination and initiation of the networking process has to be done by the co-operative tourism organization (Keller, 2002). The individual providers and suppliers of a destination need a strong partner that brings them together. This coordinating instance–e.g., the tourism organization–has to provide the sustainability and stability of the network.

Today, the tourism business still more or less ignores the importance of cooperation and networks. High transaction costs and a certain unwillingness to cooperate are mainly the reason why networks do not emerge or fail in practice (Weiermair and Walder, 2004). To foster innovative activities and the innovation process, cooperation and network activities among providers of the destination product has to be more attractive.

In this context, cooperation is regarded as offering exchanges in the destination. The suppliers of a destination can be regarded as "internal customers" within the destination system demanding cooperation as a form of exchange. By offering cooperation of high value for the suppliers of a destination product, cooperation activities can be raised among the different organizations. Therefore, it must be the task of a destination to foster cooperation and innovative behavior by offering and creating favorable basic conditions for the cooperation of high "customer value." The aim must be to raise the value of the different forms of cooperation for the suppliers of a destination product. The customer value is the difference between perceived benefits and costs. For Gale (1994), "customer value is market perceived quality adjusted for the relative price of your product" (p. xiv). Here, value is understood and measured on the perceived costs and benefits of the different form of cooperation. Matzler et al. (2002) regard value of a product/service as a ratio between the perceived tangible and intangible costs of an exchange (perceived price) and its perceived tangible and intangible benefits (perceived quality). For the customer the value of perceived alternatives is also relevant. Thus, value for the customer is created when the perceived benefits of a product/service exceed the perceived costs. Superior customer value is achieved when an exchange is more attractive by offering greater value as a result of perceived relative quality and costs compared to other opportunities.

INNOVATION AND LEADERSHIP

Keller (2002) regards leadership as a key factor for the development of innovations in tourism. A retrospective analysis shows that leadership in tourism brought innovations to the market through the implementation of visions in new business models.

Corresponding to the idea of leadership as a process in which individuals emerge as leaders (Stogdill, 1974; for a general overview Wren, 1995; Northouse, 1997; Judge et al., 2002), all players of the destination, but in particular members of tourism organizations, have to become more entrepreneurial and must show the willingness to communicate and mediate in the sense of shared values and goals within the destination. As Heifetz and Laurie (1997) state, leaders must have the emotional capacity to tolerate uncertainty, frustration, and sometimes pain while they raise questions and at the same time communicate confidence that they can assume the tasks. Confidence is the major source of competitive advantages in the network context (Hinterhuber, 2001, p. 86).

Today, innovation is organized as a management process and can be planned systematically. The network for an innovation process concerning the destination product development has to be a strategic network and not just a regional network without leadership. Consequently, leadership is the challenge for creating an innovative competitive destination.

Given the actual situation that the destination is characterized by a multitude of different tourism entrepreneurs and service providers, only very few of these different players have a complete understanding of both the conditions within the region and consolidated knowledge about political, social, ecological and economic structures, resources, market conditions and customer needs (Porter and Stern, 2001). As such, it is impossible for individual service providers, suppliers or even governmental officials to keep up with the great amount and complexity of available information.

To be innovative and stay competitive in the future, the actors of a destination have to cooperate in order to be able to identify opportunities within the destination, share resources and capabilities or formulate strategies, which give guidance for the development of marketable products and services. The innovation process can therefore only be accomplished if the following levels and potential sources of innovation are involved (see Figure 1): *Leaders* within a destination are e.g., members of political authorities that have to define the overall concept for the regional development and regional core competencies as important source of innovation. *Managers* (tourism entrepreneurs such as hoteliers or people working in the leisure industry) on the other hand, are very often too occupied with the process of product and service optimization and therefore miss to abstract from their specific services in order to reach a higher level where they could identify the core competencies behind the particular services. But they have access to customers whose contributions, ideas and needs in particular promote the development of ground-breaking services (Bieger and Gräf, 2004). Both are necessary, as the innovation process is located between the two opposite poles of market and resource orientation.

Corresponding to the complexity of the innovation process and the multitude of different actors, the need for a mediator or connector becomes obvious. This mediator has to assure that both the knowledge flow between all those regional players' works, and costs and risks of cooperation are reduced. Managers of tourism organizations have to become *"decentred leaders"* (see Birkinshaw, 2000; Drumm, 1995 for an overview).

Decentred leaders have five specific competences namely the epistemic competence, the heuristic competence, the relational competence, the reputation-related competence and finally the integrative competence (Hinterhuber and Stahl, 2000). For the successful management of the innovation process as an inter-organizational network and

FIGURE 1. The Role of Decentred Leadership Concerning the Deduction of Core Services to Services

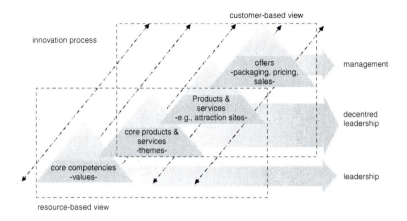

cooperation process within a destination, these five competencies are essential.

THE STUDY

Despite their high relevance for the destinations development, networks and cooperation play in fact a minor role in tourism practice at present. The main reasons are high costs and risks compared to the benefits resulting from these activities. Regarding the innovations process for the destination product as an inter-organizational network process, the question is raised which network activities can foster new product development and how it can overcome the major obstacles of cooperation. The study which was conducted gives an insight into the interaction of innovative behavior and network activities by answering the central question of research: What forms of network activities foster innovation within a destination and how can they be initiated in order to overcome the obstacles of cooperation?

The study was conducted in spring and autumn 2004 among service providers in the region around Eichstätt, a cultural tourism destination amidst the natural park Altmühltal in Central Bavaria (Germany). The survey focused on various network activities influencing the innovative performances. Furthermore, the current value of the different forms of cooperation for the service providers of a region was examined.

The Questionnaire

The marketable destination product is defined as a combination of recourses, knowledge, experiences, technologies, abilities and competencies of a region. Therefore, in the discussion mentioned above the following five forms of cooperation are key factors for the development of innovative destination products resulting from network activities: the common utilization of specific resources, the exchange of knowledge, the exchange of specific experiences, the acquisition of techniques of other regional players, and the co-determination and impact on regional competence development. In this context, the innovation process resulting from network activities is operationalized by these five items.

For the main survey, a questionnaire was developed to measure the impact of the five forms of cooperation on innovative behavior resulting from network activities. For each item the two following direct questions were asked: How much effort (monetary and non-monetary) do the providers invest for this activity at present? What benefit emerging from this activity do they perceive? The two components were directly measured by a rating scale from 1 (very high) to 5 (very low). As the depending variable, the overall innovative performances resulting from networking activities were questioned. In this context, the respondents were asked to evaluate their innovative performance resulting from network activities from 0 percent (non existent) to 100 percent (highly existent). Finally, the service providers were asked about their personal arguments for and against innovation networks with two open questions.

The Sample

In order to answer the question for the most fitting form of cooperation fostering innovative behavior, regional service providers as potential actors of an inter-organizational network aiming at the development of the innovative tourism destination Eichstätt should be asked by the quantitative survey. Thus, prior to the main survey a qualitative preliminary study was conducted to define the population of competent regional service providers bearing regional core competencies and therefore being a potential source of innovation. The purpose of the preliminary study was to get an idea of the regional core competencies. This permits to determine the geographical site and business sectors for service providers as potential actors of an innovative inter-organizational network.

The respondents were identified by analyzing the existing tourism offers of the destination and the economic structure of the region. For the preliminary study 34 semi-standardized qualitative interviews were conducted with important actors along the economic and tourism value chain of Eichstätt. Interviews were carried out with the local stone processing industry (12), tourism organizations (6), service providers in the cultural sector (arts, museums, etc.) (7), restaurants (3), and other service providers along the tourism value chain (6). The interviewees were asked about their economic performance, how they create value for whom, about their strengths and weaknesses on the micro-level of the firm and the macro-level of the region, and finally, about their perspectives of future development. The further findings of the core competency resulting from the preliminary study are not presented in this paper.

Derived from the findings of the regional core competencies, the population could be defined and the representative sample size for the quantitative study could be determined. Thus, most potential regional service providers, in terms of possessing the regional competences, could be identified and selected for the main survey. Bearing regional competences were the main criteria for defining the sample of the service providers. They were potential members of an inter-organizational network possessing regional resources and competences as a source of innovative behavior. The sample for the main study included service providers of the hotel and restaurant industry (14), service providers in the cultural sector (arts, museums, etc.) and nature (bike and boat rental, tour operators etc.) (11), the financial sector (7) and the public sector (8). The 40 service providers of the region were interviewed in the form of a standardized questionnaire. The survey was conducted by interviewers in face-to-face meetings. The results of the paper are presented and analyzed as follows.

The Results

To answer the central question of research, which forms of cooperation foster innovative behavior, a correlation analysis after Pearson with the SPSS 11.5 was conducted. The results are presented in Table 1.

The following three items show a significant correlation with the dependent item "*Innovative performance resulting from network activities,*" namely the "*costs of exchange of knowledge,*" and the "*cost exchange of specific experiences.*" The third item that also correlates with the innovative performance is the "*benefit of exchange of specific expe-*

TABLE 1. Results of the Survey

Innovative performances resulting from network activities:						
	Costs			Benefits		
Item	inexistent	Mean[1]	Correlation-coefficient	inexistent	Mean[2]	Correlation-coefficient
Common utilization of specific resources	52.5%	2.84	n.s.	52.5%	3.63	n.s.
Exchange of knowledge	10%	3.28	0.422	7.5%	3.92	n.s.
Exchange of specific experiences	25%	3.33	0.486	22.5%	4.13	0.389
Co-determination and impact on regional competence development	45%	3.00	n.s.	40%	3.75	n.s.
Acquisition of techniques/technologies of other regional players	55%	2.89	n.s.	52.5%	3.63	n.s.

[1] Mean, Ranking 5 very high costs to 1 very little costs
[2] Mean, Ranking 5 very high benefit to 1 no benefit
[3] Correlation-Coefficient (Pearson) −1= r = 1, with "Innovative Performance resulting from network activities"

riences." Subsequently, the investments for the exchange of knowledge and specific experiences and the quality of the specific experiences do have an impact on the innovative behavior resulting from network activities.

The percentage of "*inexistent*" gives information about the current use of the form of cooperation. According to the results, 90% of the service providers questioned invest in the exchange of knowledge and 75% in the exchange of specific experiences. Thus, these two forms of cooperation are common in practice.

As shown in Table 1, the other forms of cooperation as the "*common utilization of specific resources,*" the "*co-determination and impact on regional competence development,*" and the "*acquisition of techniques of other regional players*" do not have an impact on the innovative performances resulting from network activities. Moreover, about half of the service providers interviewed neither invest resources nor do they see any benefit deriving from these three forms of cooperation. The results show that existing innovative cooperation is dominated in the service sector by knowledge management-the exchange of knowledge and specific experiences.

By analyzing the current value of the different forms of cooperation for the providers, implications can be drawn for how further cooperation fostering innovative behavior can be initiated.

The perceived value is presented and analyzed by a two-dimensional matrix (see Figure 2) according to the customer value map with the di-

FIGURE 2. The Customer Value Map Applied to Measure the Value of Cooperation Forms

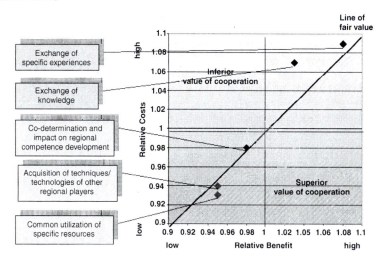

(Source: own illustration based on Gale 1994)

mension of relative perceived costs and relative perceived benefit/quality (Gale, 1994). The line of fair value presents the balanced relationship between costs and benefits as perceived by the providers and divides the matrix into areas of low and high value. The slope of the line represents the level of price/benefit sensitivity. The position of the individual forms of cooperation in the map arises from the deviation of the average perceived costs/benefits in percent and presents the different values.

As a result, the cooperation forms of "*exchange of specific experiences*" and "*exchange of knowledge*" on the right above the line are of relatively low value for the providers. The reason is that the benefit is too low in relation to the costs. The two forms of cooperation "*common utilization of specific resources*" and "*acquisition of techniques/technologies of other regional players*" on the left below the line offer high value. The rather high benefit is offered for relatively low costs. Actually, the network activity "*co-determination and impact on regional competence development*" shows a balance of costs and benefits.

When taking a closer look at the results, it becomes obvious that the two forms of cooperation "*exchange of specific experiences*" and "*ex-

change of knowledge" are of low value but the cooperation is of relatively high quality positioned in the upper field on the right. These two network activities also do have a correlation with the innovative behavior resulting from networks in comparison to the "*co-determination and impact on regional competence development,*" the "*acquisition of techniques/technologies of other regional players*" and "*common utilization of specific resources*" where the costs are relatively low but the benefit is also below the average. The low quality of this cooperation might be the reason why they do not have a significant correlation with the innovative activities resulting from networks.

In order to answer the question of how to increase network activities fostering innovation, the question of how to increase the value of cooperation has to be answered. Generally speaking, the aim of value increasing strategies must be taken at shifting the positioning of all cooperation forms in the right section of the value map. Basically, in order to do so the following possibilities exist: to improve the benefit at constant costs, to reduce costs at constant quality, or to attempt a combination of the two strategies.

The fair value line representing the balanced relationship between costs and benefits as perceived by the providers is from high relevance to conclude further implications. In this context, it is seen as a slope of 45° that indicates a linear progression of marginal costs of cooperation. The slope implies that quality and price have the importance attributed to them by the cooperation, for example a 10% increase of quality would justify a 10% increase in price. This does not correspond to the reality. Obviously the sensitivities regarding price and quality differ what has to be expressed by the slope of the fair value line. It is flat for cost-conscious providers and steeper for quality-conscious providers. Price and benefit sensitivity depends on various factors (Nagle, 1987) and may change over the time. A change of the fair value line also changes the position of the individual item together with their value.

Furthermore, it has to be considered that there may be a minimum limit of benefits or a maximum limit of price which has to be identified. This is not included in this study but relevant for deducing implications. The rising or declining marginal costs must also be taken into account.

DISCUSSION

Concluding from the results of the study that cooperation forms of low quality do not have an impact on innovative performance, it seems that a certain minimum quality has to be existent so that the cooperation serves the purpose of service providers and fosters the innovative output of the destination.

Consequently, the perceived value of the following three cooperation forms (1) "co-determination and impact on the regional competence development," (2) "acquisition of techniques/technologies of other regional players," and the (3) "utilization of specific resources" is too low for investing (see Figure 3).

As presented above, the innovation process needs all five forms of cooperation. Currently, only cooperation in the form of exchange of knowledge and experience (4)/(5) is relevant for innovative performance as mentioned above. The aim for boosting innovative behavior must be to achieve all five forms of cooperation actively performed by the providers of the destination product. Therefore, all five have to be shifted to the field of superior value (i.e., the section below the line of fair value). This challenging process of sophisticated networking demands competent network leadership. This has to be performed by the coordinator of the network, e.g., the managers of the tourism organization who have to become and act as decentred leaders. The following section deals with this network leadership challenge in the context of the innovation process:

FIGURE 3. The Minimum Quality of Cooperation

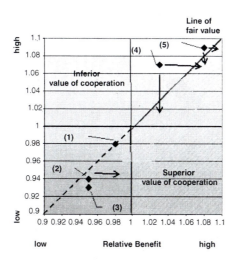

1. According to the innovation process, the "co-determination and impact on the regional competence development" is the important basis for the creation of unique products and services in the destination. Based on the shared and developed values of the regional core competency, themes for the creation of core products and services are delivered. Assuming that a minimum quality of cooperation is regarded as a precondition for the functioning of network activities resulting in innovative output, the quality of this form of cooperation is too low and as such not attractive for investment. Consequently, the quality has to be raised. It is the task of the decentred leaders to ensure the prerequisites for high value cooperation. His heuristic competence mentioned above allows him to handle a situation in an entrepreneurial manner, i.e., to manage different contexts and players. It allows him to be the mediator who can provide all relevant information about market and resource situations for the participants of the network and then give them sufficient space to participate in the determination and the definition of the destination's competence profile. His integrative competence, i.e., his capability to evaluate network relations from a more objective position, allows him to integrate different views of tourism entrepreneurs as well as regional governmental planners acting as co-producers in the process of innovation in order to develop and enhance a shared regional development.

2. The "acquisition of techniques/technologies of other regional players" is the second form of cooperation that is important for the development of a destination's innovative output. Due to the small size of small and medium-sized enterprises, their resources are quite limited and it is almost impossible for them to acquire techniques from other industries in order to develop innovative products and services on their own. Consequently, inter-industry learning by sharing knowledge and technology with other network members is a very resource-consuming task for small tourism entrepreneurs. Thus, the decentred leader should apply his epistemic competence. This competence allows him to successfully work in network structures where he acquires know-how about social, economic, technological and ecological structures and market conditions. Behind this knowhow he can then make the information visible, accessible and understandable for small entrepreneurs so that they are able to assimilate the new know-how and subsequently enhance their own knowledge. Moreover, through his relational competence he becomes the missing link between both geographical, social and contextual distances and different regional players. His engagement leads to "boundary spanning" which is set up on a wide range of social

capabilities such as understanding the partners' expectations, allowing him to develop his/her identity and also give him/her an insight into his own identity. This sets up a culture of trust among the members of the network and raises the confidence in the perceived value by establishing long-term relationships in order to develop unique destination products and services together.

3. The third form of cooperation, the "common utilization of specific resources," showed relatively low quality which definitively has to be increased. As certain resources are fixed to a certain location as a part of the destination product they are not transferable. Despite the fact that the access to certain resources is difficult, they provide great potential for synergy effects and cost reductions, particularly for small tourism entrepreneurs, when used among different actors. In general, interviewees stated that due to the chances they already highly assess innovation networks to exploit synergy effects, to have less coordination and marketing efforts or to be strained time and costs. The perceived uncertainty about the existence and access of resources as well as the integrity of the intentions of the network partners is still too high. The decentred leader has to set up all destination players at one table as well as to promote the dialog between them. The decentred leader's ability to transfer knowledge about markets and resource situations is subsumed under his reputation-related competence.

4. The "exchange of knowledge" and know-how of other network members is seen as one of the major advantages for innovation networks stated in the literature and also for the interviewees. At present, this form of cooperation features high rated benefits but also high costs. These costs have to be reduced as the exchange of knowledge keeps the innovation process alive and alters a "regular" destination into a learning destination. The concern of tourist SME entrepreneurs is that the ratio between sharing and receiving information and knowledge among the network partners will be unbalanced and stacked against them due to the fact that they are partly unaware and not sufficiently informed about each other's activities and capabilities. This calls for someone who sets up a platform for interaction and dialog. The existence of profound and valuable knowledge about each other is the basis for good cooperation and finally leads to the actors' perception and conviction of an adequate benefit of the cooperation compared to the time and resources invested. The decentred leader's relational competence is therefore highly relevant. Moreover, his integrative competence gives him an understanding of the "big picture" of the destination and also the ability to more easily

deal with uncertainty and the dynamics of knowledge. Thus, he is able to create an atmosphere of trust among the network participants.

5. The same applies for the "exchange of specific experience." The fifth form of cooperation is also highly assessed by SME entrepreneurs in the destination but the costs are very high. They also have to be reduced as the exchange of experience is also a very important part in the innovative process of the destination. Like knowledge exchange, the exchange of experience requires trust-based and long-term relationships among the players of the destination. Costs are high if SME entrepreneurs have to invest great amounts of time and money to find reliable partners. Therefore, the decentred leader has to apply his epistemic competence which allows him to successfully work in network structures by means of accumulated expert knowledge and experience. He knows the players and is able to bring them together and finally convince them that this form of cooperation will have major benefits when it comes to the development of unique products and services. In reducing uncertainty among network partners, he may lower their concern about cooperation and its perceived costs.

CONCLUSION AND IMPLICATIONS

The paper shows a first attempt to develop a framework for an institutionalized continuous innovation process on the level of a destination. The reason for the long absence of such a managerial infrastructure can be explained by the difficult structural and behavioral preconditions of the tourism industry and the fact that most innovations in tourism were initiated from outside.

To go further than recent research on the innovation process, the aim of the paper is to suggest a first conceptual framework for an active and continuous innovation process of a destination. In this context, not only an environmental but also a resource-based view is followed by the concentration on regional core competencies and the customer as a source of innovation.

The innovation process is presented as an inter-organizational network process where the exchanges of knowledge and experiences could be identified as the forms of cooperation correlated with innovative behavior in destinations. Other essential forms of cooperation, such as the co-determination of the development of regional competences, the exchange of technologies and the common use of resources for the innovation process do not have an impact on innovative behavior at the moment. In future, destinations have to place the emphasis on a more resource-oriented management.

The decentralization of leadership will play an essential role in the future. The conditions to enable cooperation of high value for the providers of innovative destination products are also provided. They finally reinforce innovative behavior.

Regarding this paper as a first approach towards the innovation process and its management in a destination, further research is needed. Concerning the determination of the value of cooperation, essential questions are for example if there is a minimum quality or a maximum of costs as well as if there is a sensitivity of price/quality of regional players. Furthermore, it should be questioned if the perceived costs and benefits are multi-attributive? Are the networks built in a limited or constant way? Furthermore, the question of the implementation of such an innovation process in an existing destination organization comes up. The impact of such an innovation process and its management to the destination system, the individual tourism entrepreneurs and the tourism organization has to be explored.

REFERENCES

Barney, J.B. (1986). Strategic factor markets–expectations, luck and business strategy. *Management Science (32)*10, pp. 1230-1241

Bieger, T. (2002). *Management von Destinationen*, 5. Auflage, Oldenbourg, München.

Bieger, T. (2005). On the Nature of the Innovative Organisation in Tourism: Structure, Process and Results. *Workshop on Innovation and Product Development in Tourism*, Innsbruck (January 25).

Bieger, T., and Gräf, H. (2004). Das Konzept Attraktionspunkte-Ein Innovationskonzept für standortgebundene Dienstleistungen. In Bruhn, M. and Stauss, B. [Eds.] *Dienstleistungsinnovationen*, Forum Dienstleistungsmanagement, Gabler, Wiesbaden, pp. 497-529.

Bieger, T., and Scherer, R. (2003). Clustering und integratives Standortmanagement-von einem theoretischen Konzept zu konkreten Handlungsstrategien. In Bieger, Th. and Scherer, R. [Eds.]. *Clustering-das Zauberwort der Wirtschaftsförderung*, Haupt, Bern, pp. 9-27.

Birkinshaw, J. (2000). *Entrepreneurship in the global firm*, Sage Publications, London.

Dosi, G. (1988). The nature of the innovation process. In Dosi, G., Freeman, C., Nelson, R., Silverberg, L. and Soete, L. (eds.) *Technical Change and Economic Theory*, London, pp. 221-238.

Drumm, H.J. (1995). The paradigm of a new decentralization-Its implications for organizations & HRM, *Employee Relations* 8(4), pp. 29-45.

Flagestad, A. (2005). Destination as an innovation system for non winter tourism: Development of a model. *Workshop on Innovation and Product Development in Tourism*, Innsbruck (January 25).

Franke, E.S. (1999). *Netzwerke, Innovationen und Wirtschaftssystem-Eine Untersuchung am Beispiel des Druckmaschinenbaus im geteilten Deutschland (1945-1990)*, Steiner, Stuttgart.

Gale, B.D. (1994). *Managing Customer Value*, Free Press, New York.

Gattermeyer, W., and Neubauer, R.M. (2000). Change Management zur Umsetzung von Strategien. In Hinterhuber, H.H., Friedrich, St.A., Al-Ani, A. and Handlbauer, G. (eds.) *Das Neue Strategische Management*, 2. Auflage, Gabler, Wiesbaden, pp. 241-260.

Heifetz, R.A., and Laurie, D.L. (1997). The Work of Leadership, *Harvard Business Review 75*(1), pp. 124-134.

Hinterhuber, H.H., and Krauthammer, E. (2001). *Leadership-mehr als Management*, 3. Auflage, Gabler, Wiesbaden.

Hinterhuber, H.H., and Stahl, H.K. (2000). Unternehmensnetzwerke und Kernkompetenzen. In Hinterhuber, H.H. and Stahl, H.K. (eds.). *Unternehmensführung im Wandel*, Band 1, Expert, Renningen-Malmsheim, pp. 239-263.

Hjalager, A. (1994). Dynamic innovation in the tourism industry. *Progress in Tourism Recreation and Hospitality Management* (6), pp. 197-224.

Hjalager, A. (2002). Repairing innovative defectiveness in tourism. *Tourism Management* 23(5), pp. 465-474.

Judge, T.A., Bono, J.E, Ilies, R., and Gerhardt, M.W. (2002). Personality & leadership. A qualitative & quantitative review, *Journal of Applied Psychology 87*(4), pp. 765-780.

Keller, P. (2002). Innovationen im Tourismus. In Bieger, Th. and Laesser, Ch. (eds.). *Jahrbuch 2001/2002-Schweizerische Tourismuswirtschaft*, IDT-HSG, St. Gallen, pp. 179-197.

Keller, P. (2005). Towards an innovation oriented tourism policy: A new agenda? *Workshop on Innovation and Product Development in Tourism*, Innsbruck (January 25).

Keller, P., and Smeral, E. (2001). Inno Tour-Erfolg eines tourismuspolitischen Programms. In Bieger, Th. and Laesser, Ch. (eds.). *Jahrbuch 2000/2001-Schweizerische Tourismuswirtschaft*, IDT-HSG, St. Gallen, pp. 141-159.

Matzler, K., Smeral, E., and Pechlaner, H. (2002). Customer Value Management as a Determinant of the competitive Position of Tourism Destinations. *Tourism Review 57*(4), pp. 15-22.

Nagle, T.T. (1987). *The Strategy and Tactics of Pricing*. Prentice Hall. Englewood Cliffs.

Nootboom, B. (1996). Trust, opportunism and governance. A process and control model, *Organisation Studies 17*(6), pp. 985-1010.

Northouse, P. G. (1997). *Leadership-Theory and Practice*, Sage Publications, Thousand Oaks.

Pechlaner, H. (1999). The Competitiveness of Alpine Destination between Market Pressure and Problems of Adaption, *Turizam/Tourism 47*(4), pp. 332-343.

Pechlaner, H., and Tschurtschenthaler, P. (2003). Tourism Policy, Tourism Organisations & Change Management in Alpine Regions & Destinations: A European Perspective, *Current Issues in Tourism* 6(6), pp. 508-539.

Pechlaner, H., Hammann, E., and Fischer, E. (2005). Leadership und Innovationsprozesse: Von der Kernkompetenz zur Dienstleistung. In Pechlaner, H., Tschurtschenthaler, P., Peters, M., Pikkemaat, B. and Fuchs, M. (eds.). *Erfolg durch Innovation-Perspektiven für Tourismus und Dienstleistungswirtschaft*, DUV, Wiesbaden, pp. 63-85.

Penrose, E.T. (1959). *The Theory of the Growth of the Firm*. Basil Blackwell, Oxford.

Peters, M., and Weiermair, K. (2002). Innovationen und Innovationsverhalten im Tourismus. In Bieger, T. and Laesser, Ch. (eds.). *Jahrbuch 2001/2002-Schweizerische Tourismuswirtschaft*, IDT-HSG, St. Gallen, pp. 157-179.

Pikkemaat, B., and Pfeil, S. (2005). Knowledge Management as Precursor for Innovation: The case of Family Homes in Tyrol. *Workshop on Innovation and Product Development in Tourism*, Innsbruck (January 25).

Porter, M. (1990). *The Competitive Advantage of Nations*, Free Press, New York.

Porter, M.E., and Stern, S. (2001). Innovation: Location matters, *MIT Sloan Management Review 42*(4), 28-37.

Prahalad, C. K. and Hamel, G. (1990). The core competence of the corporation, *Harvard Business Review 68*(3), pp. 79-91.

Rogers, E. (1983). *Diffusion of innovation* (3rd ed.), Free Press, New York.

Sancho, A. (2005). Innovation and Profitability in the Hotel Industry: Specialization and Concentration effects. *Workshop on Innovation and Product Development in Tourism*, Innsbruck (January 25).

Sancho, A., Cabrer, B., Gonzalo, M., and Rico, P. (2004). Innovation & profitability in the hotel industry: Specialization & concentration effects, Conference paper, *ENTER-conference*, Cairo.

Stambouis, Y., and Skayannis, P. (2003). Innovative strategies and technology for experience-based tourism, *Tourism Management 24*(1), pp. 35-43.

Stogdill, R.M. (1974). *Handbook of leadership: A survey of theory & research*, Free Press, New York.

von Krogh, G., and Venzin, M. (1995). Anhaltende Wettbewerbsvorteile durch Wissensmanagement, *Die Unternehmung 49*(6), pp. 417-436.

Weiermair, K. (2003). Product improvement or innovation: What is the key to success in tourism?, *OECD Conference on Innovation & Growth in Tourism*, Lugano (September 18-19).

Weiermair, K., and Walder, B. (2004). Produktentwicklung im Tourismus. In Bieger, T., Laesser, C. and Beritelli, P. (eds.). *Jahrbuch 2004/2005-Schweizerische Tourismuswirtschaft*, IDT-HSG, St. Gallen, pp. 93-113.

Williamson, O. E. (1975). *Market & Hierarchies: Analysis & Antitrust Implications*, Free Press, New York.

Wren, T.J. (1995). *Leader's Companion: Insights on Leadership through the Ages*, New York.

Prospects for Innovation in Tourism: Analyzing the Innovation Potential Throughout the Tourism Value Chain

Klaus Weiermair

SUMMARY. The tourism product is a composite one with its production, distribution and marketing being configured along a value chain involving many activities which are vertically, horizontally and diagonally related and integrated in varying degrees. Both orthodox and non-orthodox economists agree that innovations will only be undertaken when there is a sufficiently high innovation dividend which pays for the added cost and risk of innovation. Thus profitability appears to be the strongest explanatory variable both behind investment and innovation. Based on the notion that expected profitability from innovation can serve as the primary independent variable determining innovation behaviour across different economic sectors and/or sub branches of tourism, the paper sets out to establish the innovation potential for each of the tourism value creating economic activities from the provision of information to prospective customers (tourists) in the sending region to post-trip (after sale) services. In addition to the usual profit-generating forces of costs and revenues, such dimensions as firm size and economics of scale,

---

Klaus Weiermair is Professor and Head of the Center for Tourism and Service Economics, University of Innsbruck, Universitätsstrasse 15, A-6020 Innsbruck, (E-mail: Klaus. weiermair@uibk.ac.at).

[Haworth co-indexing entry note]: "Prospects for Innovation in Tourism: Analyzing the Innovation Potential Throughout the Tourism Value Chain." Weiermair, Klaus. Co-published simultaneously in *Journal of Quality Assurance in Hospitality & Tourism* (The Haworth Hospitality Press, an imprint of The Haworth Press, Inc.) Vol. 6, No. 3/4, 2005, pp. 59-72; and: *Innovation in Hospitality and Tourism* (ed: Mike Peters, and Birgit Pikkemaat) The Haworth Hospitality Press, an imprint of The Haworth Press, Inc., 2005, pp. 59-72. Single or multiple copies of this article are available for a fee from The Haworth Document Delivery Service [1-800- HAWORTH, 9:00 a.m. - 5:00 p.m. (EST). E-mail address: docdelivery@haworthpress.com].

proximity to relevant science and technology (know-how for innovation) through human capital and forms of organisation (e.g., network-organisation and/or clusters) will equally be taken into consideration. This analysis will therefore help in pinpointing those areas of the tourism value chain where innovations are most likely to occur. The paper concludes with the presentation of a model aimed at empirically testing innovation behaviour across the tourism value chain. *[Article copies available for a fee from The Haworth Document Delivery Service: 1-800-HAWORTH. E-mail address: <docdelivery@haworthpress.com> Website: <http://www.HaworthPress.com> © 2005 by The Haworth Press, Inc. All rights reserved.]*

KEYWORDS. Innovation in tourism, innovation potential, tourism value chain

INTRODUCTION

Following Schumpeter's analysis of innovation five different types of innovation can be distinguished, all of which can also be found in the tourism industry or industries broadly defined: (1) the creation of new products or services, (2) new production processes, (3) new markets, (4) new suppliers and (5) changed organisation or management systems (Schumpeter, 1934). From a micro (tourism enterprise) perspective innovation and innovative behaviour can be viewed as the result of appropriate entrepreneurship, leadership and a host of sound management practices dealing with human resource development, technology, quality and service process management to name only the more salient micro determinants (Schumpeter, 1934; Foster, 1986; Tidd et al., 2003; Fitzsimmons and Fitzsimmons, 2003).

Innovation can however also be analysed as a market phenomenon occurring as it were in the various interrelated tourism markets or sub-branches of tourism. The latter can be viewed as the result of a value adding chain of activities making up the complete or customer's (tourist's) holistic product called "vacation" or "travel." It stretches from first tourism encounters through advertising and/or the provision of tourism information to after sales services.

This paper will take such a market or microeconomic view of innovation behaviour (Scherer and Ross, 1990). The market forces are postulated to take precedence in shaping innovation behaviour at the level of the tourism enterprise. Structure, conduct and performance of markets in general and tourism markets in particular in turn have been greatly conditioned by the twin forces of globalisation and heightened technological change (particularly in the field of information and communication technologies) (Smeral, 2004; Weiermair, 2001a). On the demand side a number of secular changes in tourism behaviour have taken place which have called for and created an innovative response in terms of product-, process-or marketing innovation. The latter include such phenomena as trends towards individualized tourism products, -services and -experiences, towards greater speed and mobility of services, towards animation and/or emotionalisation of products and experiences, towards greater convenience and/or towards more choice (multioption customer) and greater authenticity to name only the most dominant changes in customer choice and behaviour induced innovations (Weiermair and Peters, 2002).

While most innovation research concludes that over 80% of innovation takes place in response to market pull, i.e., is customer driven (Porter, 1990), there nevertheless exist varying inter-firm and inter-branch differences in production, investment and marketing conditions which are more or less conducive to innovation and hence help explain innovation behaviour of firms. This paper will pursue the latter supply side focus and investigate the innovation potential in terms of the innovation dividend to be expected in different parts and places of the tourism value chain.

Furthermore, the author provides, after a brief review of existing innovation models in the tourism literature, the theoretical framework for the modelling of innovation potential across different tourism branches and/or "clusters." The following part of the paper describes in greater detail the environmental or market conditions for innovation across the tourism value chain which is translated into a set of formalised propositions and hypotheses in the following chapter.

A POSSIBLE POINT OF DEPARTURE FOR MODELLING INNOVATION AND INNOVATION BEHAVIOUR IN TOURISM

Although the rise of the new or knowledge economy (Acs et al., 2002) generally has also increased its importance to the services and in particular to the tourism industry, its relevance in terms of new product and/or process development still needs to be ascertained. Not surprisingly innovation management in the service sector in general and tourism in particular have received so far much less scientific and practical attention when compared for instance to manufacturing (Edgell, 1994; Kelly and Stavy, 2000).

In part this can be explained by a lack of innovation activities in many parts of the tourism industry, particularly those which are populated and dominated by small and medium sized enterprises operating in fragmented markets (Peters and Weiermair, 2002). There are very few studies available which have attempted to model innovation behaviour in specific tourism industries (Sancho et al., 2004). Most of what is available are comprehensive typologies of innovation in tourism or descriptive case studies (Hjalager, 2002; Keller and Smeral, 2001).

As a point of departure we choose analytical/empirical economic models of general innovation behaviour as applicable to other industries (see Hauschildt, 1997) and modify such modelling with the characteristics of tourism services production/marketing as well as with behavioural insights from the innovation management literature (Drucker, 1985; Hjalager, 1997; Hübner, 2002; Metcalfe and Miles, 2000). At least in mainstream economics there is agreement that innovation activities are undertaken for the sole purpose of securing long-term survival thorough a sustainable level of profits. Put differently for an optimal "innovation dividend" (Mansfield, 1961). This suggests that innovation activities will be undertaken if expected returns from innovation more than cover all associated and expected cost of developing and exploiting new ideas, products, services or processes. Typical expected increases in sales and revenues can come from new markets and customers or from increased sales and revenues in established markets. Furthermore increased revenue from new products may also compensate or make up for otherwise declining or dying markets. In forecasting sales and revenue from new products or processes all multiplier and/or indirect sales effects have to be included. Also expected future revenues have to be expressed in probabilistic terms. Revenue generation from new product/processes will undoubtedly also depend on the firms' management and marketing capabilities, skills and associated expenditures. In this context marketing expenditures are reckoned as part of the total expected cost associated with the research, development and marketing of new products, services and other types and forms of innovation. It is important to notice that all factors which either ease or impede innovation activities are analytically closely related to the cost-revenue-yield construct of innovation and can thus either be expressed as a cost, revenue or, net revenue function.

In reduced form such an innovation yield function and its attempted maximization through management may look as follows:

$$NPVI = f\left(\frac{ExpTotalEarnings}{1+r^{x-n}} - \frac{ExpTotalCost}{1+r^{n}} \right)$$

where

NPVI is the **net pr**esent **v**alue of **i**nnovation and where

$r = $ is the discount factor or opportunity cost of capital

Exp. Total Earnings are the probable total earnings associated with the innovation for the economic life of the innovation after its completion in year x to period n (end of the innovation life cycle).

Exp. Total Cost are all cost associated with the research, development and commercialisation of the innovation over the period 0 to n and the operating production and marketing cost of producing and selling new goods and services or old goods/services with new production/ marketing processes over the period x-n.

Costs of research and development (R&D) are likely to vary with the (non-)availability and cost of resources needed for R&D. A firm which has a good location in terms of R&D (e.g., close contacts with universities, research institutes) or because of its size or specialization has economies of scale or scope in innovation activities, will likely have lower costs of innovation and hence a competitive advantage over other firms, which do not have theses characteristics. Similarly innovation earnings will depend greatly on the difficulty or ease with which competitors can imitate innovation and the period over which the innovating firm can enjoy USP (unique selling proposition) advantages before competitors imitate and hence put competitive pressure on prices. These competitive advantages have become labelled "first mover advantages" (Agarwal and Gort, 2001).

The potential to innovate, according to our economic model above, will therefore depend on the expected innovation yield which because of different cost and revenue structure across tourism firms, clusters, markets and sub-branches is likely to vary across the tourism value chain. In the next section we shall for demonstration purposes investigate the innovation potential in selected parts of the tourism value chain and analyse the associated cost and revenue determinants.

INNOVATION BY TOURISM STAKEHOLDERS ACROSS DIFFERENT TOURISM SUB-BRANCHES AND/OR THE TOURISM VALUE CHAIN

To advance the analysis of innovation potential across the tourism value chain we may want to choose a specific example involving i.e., a two-season alpine tourism destination. Apriori and using Porter's path-breaking work on value chains (Porter, 1984; Porter, 1990) we could build a hypothetical tourism value chain which would look something like that shown in Figure 1.

The big advantage of the tourism value chain is the fact that while "manufacturing" or "staging" a tourism product which is holistically perceived and consumed by the tourist, it helps to analyse in detail the various steps of a tourism product including, all service providers. To assess the innovation potential at each stage of the tourism value chain or for a re-configured (i.e., integrated) tourism value chain we can employ the same tools which also help analyse market entry or investment decision (e.g., Porter's four market forces of competition explaining "market attractiveness" Porter, 1984).

Taking the first value creating activity in the tourism value chain, i.e., information provision and reservation & booking, we first note the plasticity and immateriality of travel information varying with the type of tourism product/service involved and the complexity of travel information for certain types of travel. At the same time cost and revenue function associated with innovation investments can vary greatly (Weigand, 1996) depending on the structure of the travel intermediary market (in terms of size and number of firms providing information, reservation and booking, in terms of the degree of forward integration of firms towards the vacation core product and/or the degree of specialisation). Economies of scale for R&D costs are likely to exist where markets are

FIGURE 1. The Tourism Value Chain

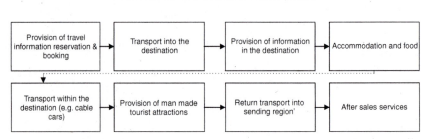

Source: Bieger 2001, Weiermair 2001b

highly concentrated and the average size of firms is large, where market entry barriers exist, where travel information can easily be standardized or configured through appropriate information technologies, and where positive information network effects can be achieved. At the same time firms can enjoy absolute cost advantages through superior location (proximity to and low cost of research facilities, such as e.g., call centres or software houses in Third-World-Countries). Mitigating forces against innovation investments creating mass standardized information, reservation and booking systems are lacking customer trust in travel information and/or difficulties in transforming highly opaque, complex and highly qualitative travel information through appropriate ICT (information and communication technologies) into easily consumable and understandable pieces of travel/vacation information (Schaffer, 2003).

With regard to earnings expectation for individual firms associated with the development and commercialisation of novel information processing, reservation and booking systems, these will vary greatly with the size of the expected market to be served, the expected lead time and hence first mover advantage for innovation returns to accrue before rivals in the industry will imitate innovations and/or retaliate with newer and more up-to-date technology (Rogers, 1995). Size of firms and quality of management will likely be another important dimension for innovation decisions, with small firms and non-professional, non-entrepreneurial or not-strategically oriented management tending to show either negative biases towards innovative technological changes or postponing innovation decisions altogether (Acs and Audretsch, 1990; Morrison et al., 2003; Weiermair and Peters, 1998a). Potential first mover advantages in terms of increased earnings through technological forward integration (as was the case with specific reservation/booking systems) through mergers and acquisitions can be larger and the associated market share gains can be very high. But so are the costs and risks of creating USPs through company specific innovations as the resulting rivalry among competing reservation systems such as Amadeus versus Galileo have shown. By calculating out existing and more importantly future market and company configurations in terms of market growth and competition and/or rivalry behaviour of its stakeholders it should nevertheless be possible to assess the innovation potential of this particular tourism sub-branch and/or develop specific testable hypotheses with respect to the likely innovation behaviour of this market.

To further illustrate the analysis of innovation potential in specific tourism branches of economic activity we now turn to the core tourism business: the accommodation and food sector. In many parts of the world, but notably in Europe's alpine regions this is a highly fragmented market populated by a large number of owner managed SMEs (Peters and Buhalis, 2004). Furthermore in many parts of Europe tourism has become a very mature market with many tourist destinations finding themselves in the consolidation and/or stagnation stage of the destination life cycle (Agarwal, 1994; Buhalis, 2000; Peters and Weiermair, 2000). For this very reason the industry finds itself pushed by market forces into the process of business re-engineering which has to be based largely on its innovation potential. The latter can be found in either the development of new processes and products or in the restructuring of their production and marketing organisation. When applying expected the same cost-benefit calculus for innovations to the hotel and restaurant business, we note the following differences in comparison to our previous example of travel intermediaries:

1. Economies of scale for individual hotel business (as plants or establishments) are exhausted relatively fast depending on the type of hotel at around 120-150 beds.
2. On the other hand there are large economies of scope associated with particular hotel types (e.g., Casino hotels, resort hotels, etc.) and with multi-plant hotel chains (Weiermair and Peters, 1998a).
3. Most possible product innovations in the hotel restaurant/restaurant industry represent different types of product differentiation through product improvements, product line extension and the like (Moutinho 1989) which make it easy for market rivals to imitate at low cost. A priori product innovation therefore carries a high level of risk and in some cases (e.g. new spa or golf hotels) also high cost with little enduring first mover advantages.
4. On the other hand there are likely to exist large pay offs (in terms of either cost reduction or revenue increases) associated with innovation in business concepts (Belz and Bieger, 2000), the development of new marketing schemes (Berry and Brock, 2004) or simply hotel internal re-arrangements between high tech/high touch service delivery schemes (Fitzsimmons and Fitzsimmons, 2003).

When contrasting stakeholders across the tourism value chain, e.g. travel intermediaries versus the hotel accommodation and restaurant branch of economic activity, we note the following tendential differences which are likely to impact the innovation potential:

1. Given the higher task complexity, higher level of competition, closer relationship to centers of research and also greater levels of qualification of their human resources (quality of management) the travel intermediation industry is likely to be faster in recognizing and implementing technological changes or other types of innovation.

2. The more innovative the customer base (in the sense of interest in new and innovative products and services) the higher the realisation of innovations (Porter, 1990). The chance of observing and finding innovative customers is a function of the size of the market. While it is an empirical matter to measure the number of conservative versus innovative customers in each branch of economic activity, the travel intermediary industry on account of its size of the market (in a generally much more concentrated marketplace) is likely to be more innovation driven, thus realizing potentials better and faster.

3. Finally one has to evaluate the risk behaviour and/or perception biases concerning expected costs and revenue, which may differ between the two different branches of the tourism value chain. Which firm in which part of the tourism value chain has which type of entrepreneur and/or industry leader resembling either the true Schumpeterian entrepreneur or the opposite (e.g., an administrator administering inherited assets) remains a highly empirical matter, nevertheless there appears to exist some empirical evidence suggesting a larger percentage of innovative tourism enterprises to come from the travel intermediary industry (Peters et al., 2004; Weiermair et al., 1999; Weiermair et al., 2002).

INNOVATION POTENTIAL ACROSS MAJOR SEGMENTS OF THE TOURISM VALUE CHAIN: HYPOTHESES AND PROPOSITIONS

The previous section has already shown as to how one might further refine initial concepts of innovation potential (in the sense of potential or future innovation dividends) by including specific characteristics of tourism stakeholders. In this section an attempt is made to further formalize and operationalize the concept of "innovation potential" so that testable hypotheses can be derived. The previous discussion in chapter III has identified the following intervening variables and has also specified their directional influence upon the dependent variable innovation potential (InnPot):

All of the hypotheses below are based upon theoretical and empirical research results provided in any standard text on industrial organisation (see Scherer and Ross, 1990)

- Expected earnings increases ($\overset{\Delta}{El}$) are positively related to innovation potential.

- Expected earnings increases ($\overset{\Delta}{El}$) show a positive relationship to market size (MS) and a negative relationship to the past rate of innovation diffusion (diffusion saturation) for any given innovation (DIFSAT).

- The relationship between firm size (S_F) and degree of market competition (CompM) is ambivalent according to theory. Both very small and very large firm size and intermediate forms of competition appear positively related to innovation behaviour (Scherer Ross, 1990; Weiermair Peters, 1998b).

- The higher the percentage of conservative (repeat) customers (RatiorepeatC) the lower the expected increases in innovation associated earnings.

- The closer firms and/or industries in tourism subbranches find themselves to related industries and/or suppliers with a scientific or R&D Base (ReltechF) the higher the innovation potential (InnPot).

- Existing economics of scope (EconSc) of tourism firms positively correlate with expected earnings increases ($\overset{\Delta}{El}$) and hence with innovation potential (InnPot).

- The existence of related complementary or substitute goods or services in tourism (RatiorelServ) has a positive relationship with expected earnings increases ($\overset{\Delta}{El}$).

- Innovation potential is positively related to expected decreases in production or marketing cost ($\overset{\Delta}{LowCost}$) as a consequence of innovative activities.

- Lowered cost ($\overset{\Delta}{LowCost}$) on account of innovation are to be expected if related and involved labour costs are high (LabCost) and can be saved through innovative activities, if marketing and/or customer acquisition cost (MarkCost) can be saved through novel or innovative forms of marketing, and if capital costs (CapCost) can be lowered through innovative ways of financing.

- Lowered cost ($\overset{\Delta}{LowCost}$) can also be expected as a consequence of existing tourism clusters (clusterT).

- Firm Internal (behavioural) variable which will positively impact the innovation potential of firms and sub branches in tourism are:
  - firms' positive record of innovation adoption in the past (InnHist)
  - the existence of an innovation organisation (InnOrg)
  - high level of education of its top management (EdulevM)
  - youth of it managerial workforce (YouthM).[1] where education and youth are used as proxies for management quality as discussed above.

Putting together all firm internal and market forces which demonstrate a positive relationship with innovation potential yield the following system of functional relations for innovation potential of tourism firms and/or sub branches:

1. $InnPot = \overset{\Delta}{EI} + \overset{\Delta}{LowCost}$

2. $EI = f(+MS, -DifSat, +ReltechF, +RatiorelServ, \pm S_F,$
$\pm CompM, -RatiorepeatC)$

3. $\overset{\Delta}{LowCost} = f(LabCost, +MarkCost, +CapCost, +ClusterT)$

4. $InnPot_{firms} = f(+InnHist, +InnOrg, +EduLevM, +YouthM)$

Most of these variables can be obtained through secondary market data and additional primary survey firm data for different parts of the tourism value chain. They are likely to vary across firms and branches of economic activity. Put together as a recursive system of equations it should be relatively easy to subsequently determine the innovation potential for each firm, tourism branch or activity and/or the entire tourism industry as a whole. In turn these estimated figures can be used for the controlling and forecasting of actual innovation activity and/or behaviour in tourism.

CONCLUSION AND OUTLOOK

Considering the multinational companies' sources of competitiveness in international tourism markets e.g., economies of scale, economies of scope and innovation and learning the latter have, as of late, become the most important tool of competitive rivalry (Bartlett & Goshal, 1991). The upsurge in competitive rivalry in today's globalized markets through innovation on the one hand and merger activity and market concentration on the other hand forces SMEs in Europe´s fragmented tourism markets to mobilize their resources in order to be able to compete increasingly in terms of quality (Smeral, 2003; Weiermair et al., 2001).

Knowing the factors of innovation potential of tourism firms, destinations or tourism clusters or an entire tourism sub branch not only helps us predict future areas of change in tourism production, product development and marketing but more importantly can guide investment behaviour towards those parts of the tourism value chain with the highest innovation and investment potential. In many traditional tourism regions such as Europe's alpine regions where the destination life cycle appears to be nearing the consolidation and/or stagnation phase (Weiermair, 2001a), such innovation investment now seems to be furthermore most appropriate in reengineering destination revivals.

NOTE

1. Although age and educational background are often cited as important determinants recent empirical studies at the Center of General and Tourism Management of Innsbruck University (Weiermair et al., 2004) have found no stringent relationship between age/education and degree of innovation of a tourism company. Nevertheless, the influence of these variables should be investigated.

REFERENCES

Acs, Z. J., and Audretsch, D. B. (1990). *Innovation in Small Firms*. Cambridge MA: MIT Press.

Acs, Z. J., de Groot, H. L. F., and Nijkamp, P. (Eds.) (2002). *The Emergence of the Knowledge Economy: A Regional Perspective*. Berlin et al., Springer.

Agarwal, S. (1994). The resort cycle revisited: Implications for resorts. In C. P. Cooper and A. Lockwood (Eds.), *Progress in Tourism, Recreation and Hospitality Management, Volume 5* (pp. 194-208). Chichester, Wiley.

Agarwal, R., and Gort, M. (2001). First-Mover Advantage and the Speed of competitive Entry, 1887-1986. *Journal of Law and Economics 44* (1), pp. 161-177.

Bartlett, C. A., and Goshal, S. (1991). *Managing across borders*. Boston, Harvard University Press.

Belz, C., and Bieger, T. (Eds.). (2000). *Dienstleistungskompetenze und innovative Geschäftsmodelle*. St. Gallen, THEXIS.

Berry, M. M. J., and Brock, J. K. (2004). Marketspace and the Internationalisation Process of the Small Firm. *Journal of international Entrepreneurship 2*(3), pp. 187-216.

Bieger, T. (2001). *Management von Destinationen*. München, Oldenbourg.

Buhalis, D. (2000). Marketing the Competitive Destination of the Future. *Tourism Management 21*(1), pp. 97-112.

Drucker, P. F. (1985). *Innovation and Entrepreneurship: Practices and Principles*. New York, The Free Press.

Edgell, S. (1994). The trails of successful new service development. *Journal of Service Marketing 8*(3), pp. 40-49.

Fitzsimmons, J., and Fitzsimmons, M. (2003). *Service Management*. Boston, McGraw Hill.

Foster, R. N. (1986). *Innovation–The Attacker's Advantage*. New York, Summit Books.

Hauschildt, J. (1997). *Innovationsmanagement*. München, Vahlen.

Hjalager, A. M. (1997). Innovation Patterns in Sustainable Tourism–an analytical typology. *Tourism Management 18*(1), pp. 35-41.

Hjalager, A.-M. (2002). Repairing Innovation Defectiveness in Tourism. *Tourism Management 23*(5), pp.465-474.

Hübner, H. (2002). *Integratives Innovationsmanagement*. Berlin: De Gruyter.

Keller, P., & Smeral, E. (2001). InnoTour: ein erfolgreiches touristisches Programm. *Jahrbuch der Schweizer Tourismuswirtschaft 2000/2001* (pp. 141-159). St. Gallen.

Kelly, D., and Stavy, C. (2000). New service development: Imitation strategies. *International Journal of Service Industry Management 11*(1), pp. 55-64.

Mansfield, E. (1961). The Speed of Response of Firms to New Technique. *Econometrica 4*(1), pp. 741-765.

Metcalfe, J. S., and Miles, I. (2000). *Innovation Systems in the Service Economy*. Boston, Kluwer.

Morrison, A., Breen, J., and Ali, S. (2003). Small Business Growth: Intention, Ability, and Opportunity. *Journal of Small Business Management 41*(4), pp. 417-425.

Moutinho, L. (1989). New Product Development in Tourism. In S. Witt and L. Moutinho (Eds.), *Tourism Marketing and Management Handbook* (pp. 291-294). Cambridge, Prentice Hall.

Peters, M., and Buhalis, D. (2004). Family hotel businesses: Strategic planning and the need for education and training. *Education and Training 46*(8/9), pp. 406-415.

Peters, M., and Weiermair, K. (2000). Tourist attractions and attracted Tourists: How to satisfy today's 'fickle' tourist clientele? *The Journal of Tourism Studies 11*(1), pp. 22-29.

Peters, M., and Weiermair, K. (2002). Innovationen und Innovationsverhalten im Tourismus. *Schweizer Jahrbuch für Tourismus 2001/2002* (pp. 157-178). St. Gallen.

Peters, M., Weiermair, K., and Leimegger, R. (2004). Employees' evaluation of entrepreneurial leadership in small tourism businesses. In T. Bieger & P. Keller (Eds.), *Small and Medium Sized Enterprises in Tourism* (pp. 315-333). St. Gallen: AIEST.

Porter, M. E. (1984). *Wettbewerbsstrategie. Methoden zur Analyse von Branchen und Konkurrenten*. Frankfurt, Campus.

Porter, M. E. (1990). The Competitive Advantage of Nations. *Harvard Business Review 68*(2), pp. 73-93.

Sancho, A., Maset, A., and Weiermair, K. (2004). New Technologies and their Relationship with Quality and Human Resources in the Spanish Hotel Industry. *Unpublished.*

Schaffer, S. (2003). *Building Trust in Online 'Environments.' Developing a Model of Trust Creation for eTravel Agents.* Innsbruck: Dissertation at the University of Innsbruck.

Scherer, F. M., and Ross, D. (1990). *Industrial Market Structure and Economic Performance.* Boston: MIT Press.

Schumpeter, J. A. (1934). *The Theory of Economic Development.* New York, Oxford University Press.

Smeral, E. (2003). *Die Zukunft des internationalen Tourismus.* Vienna: Linde.

Smeral, E. (2004). Wachstumsmaschine Tourismus: Semper et ubique? In K. Weiermair, M. Peters, H. Pechlaner and M.-O. Kaiser (Eds.), *Unternehmertum im Tourismus: Führen mit Erneuerungen* (pp. 35-51). Berlin, Erich Schmidt.

Tidd, J., Bessant, J., and Pavitt, K. (2003). *Managing Innovation. Integrating Technological, Market and Organizational Change.* Chichester, John Wiley & Sons.

Weiermair, K. (2001a). The Growth of Tourism Enterprises. *Tourism Review* 56(3/4), pp. 17-25.

Weiermair, K. (2001b). Von der Dienstleistungsökonomie zur Erlebnisökonomie. In H. H. Hinterhuber, H. Pechlaner and K. Matzler (Eds.), *IndustrieErlebnisWelten* (pp. 35-48). Berlin, Erich Schmidt.

Weiermair, K., Fuchs, M., Peters, M., and Rijken, L. (1999). *RETTOURISM III: Innovationsbereiche für das zukünftige touristische Human Resource Management.* University of Innsbruck, Research study. Unpublished.

Weiermair, K., and Peters, M. (1998a). Entrepreneurial Small-and Medium Sized Tourism Enterprises. In K. S. Chon (Ed.), *Tourism and Hotel Industry in Indo-China & Southeast Asia: Development, Marketing and Sustainability* (pp. 235-243). Houston, Conrad N. Hilton College.

Weiermair, K., and Peters, M. (1998b). The internationalization behaviour of service enterprises. *Asia Pacific Journal of Tourism Research* 2(2), pp. 1-14.

Wcicrmair, K., and Peters, M. (2002). *Innovation Behaviour in Hospitality and Tourism: Problems and Prospects.* Paper presented at the Tourism in Asia: Development, Marketing and Sustainability. Fifth Biennial Conference, Hong Kong.

Weiermair, K., Peters, M., and Reiger, E. (Eds.). (2001). *Vom alten zum neuen Tourismus.* Innsbruck, Studia.

Weiermair, K., Pikkemaat, B., Müller, S., and Walder, B. (2004). *Messung des Innovationsgrades touristischer Produkte in ausgewählten alpinen Destination Österreichs-Ein Pilotprojekt.* ÖNB-Endbericht. Innsbruck. Unpublished.

Weigand, J. (1996). *Innovationen, Wettbewerb und Konjunktur. Eine theoretische und empirische Untersuchung von Innovationsdeterminanten unter Berücksichtigung des Konjunkturverlaufs.* Berlin, Duncker & Humblot.

A Consumer-Based Measurement of Tourism Innovation

Serena Volo

SUMMARY. The present paper reviews the innovation literature related to tourism and examines the twin problems of operational definitions and measurement of innovation in the tourism sector. A conceptual model is then proposed by which the most relevant aspects of innovation and the most relevant aspects of the "tourism experience" can be integrated conceptually, and which can guide the development of related operational definitions and measurements and lead to a standardization of, and therefore an ability to aggregate, tourism innovation statistics across products, providers, markets and geopolitical regions. The model first categorizes innovations along two dimensions: an "invention-adoption" continuum and an "impact-on-the-tourism-experience" dimension, which includes accessibility, affective transformation, convenience and value. How the use of these categories can direct attention to important definitional and measurement issues are discussed as is how their use can improve the comparability of tourism innovation data collected from disparate sources. Finally, a third dimension, the economic impact of the innovation, is introduced to the model. The paper concludes with impli-

Serena Volo is Researcher with the Dipartimento di Metodi Quantitativi per le Scienze Umane, Università di Palermo, Italy, Studio Volo, Via Pacinotti 34, 90145 Palermo, Italy (E-mail: serenavolo@unipa.it).

[Haworth co-indexing entry note]: "A Consumer-Based Measurement of Tourism Innovation." Volo, Serena. Co-published simultaneously in *Journal of Quality Assurance in Hospitality & Tourism* (The Haworth Hospitality Press, an imprint of The Haworth Press, Inc.) Vol. 6, No. 3/4, 2005, pp. 73-87; and: *Innovation in Hospitality and Tourism* (ed: Mike Peters, and Birgit Pikkemaat) The Haworth Hospitality Press, an imprint of The Haworth Press, Inc., 2005, pp. 73-87. Single or multiple copies of this article are available for a fee from The Haworth Document Delivery Service [1-800-HAWORTH, 9:00 a.m. - 5:00 p.m. (EST). E-mail address: docdelivery@haworthpress.com].

73

cations and guidelines for future research aimed at validating the model described. *[Article copies available for a fee from The Haworth Document Delivery Service: 1-800-HAWORTH. E-mail address: <docdelivery@haworthpress. com> Website: <http://www.HaworthPress.com> © 2005 by The Haworth Press, Inc. All rights reserved.]*

KEYWORDS. Innovation, tourism, experience, measurement, indicator

INTRODUCTION

Academics, enterprises and governments have paid increasing attention to innovation statistics and measures over the past few decades. From the traditional measures of innovation–e.g., research and development data and patent statistics–the international community has been moving towards micro-data collection and new indicators (Annunziato, 2003; Tsipouri, 2003; Flor and Oltra, 2004). Even within the service sector of the economy, innovation is receiving increased attention (Drejer, 2002; Evangelista and Sirilli, 1998; Metcalfe and Miles, 2000). Indeed the growth of the number of patents awarded for intangible processes, the common operational definition of innovation, would also appear applicable to the service sector. Innovation however, has been largely ignored by local, regional and national tourism authorities, and the application of innovation measures in tourism has been somewhat limited both in the research literature as well in strategic planning (Jacob et al., 2003; Volo, 2004). Current changes in tourism demand, including customers' late bookings, sophistication of tourists' tastes and preferences, the pervasive global competition and the attendant change in tourism enterprises and destinations' strategies, and last but not least, the growing emphasis on tourist's experience, all argue compellingly for a greater emphasis on innovation within the tourism industry.

This study presents a conceptualisation of tourism innovation that facilitates its measurement. A different way of thinking about innovation in hospitality and tourism is described, and more importantly, a different approach to its measurement is proposed. The next section provides an overview of recent innovation studies, and in this review the notions of invention, adoption and innovation have been used as basis for investigating the academics' and practitioners' efforts to study the phenomenon. Service measures and indicators of innovation were analysed with attention paid to some of the components of the tourism industry. By integrating customers' experiences into these more traditional innovation indicators, a consumer-based framework and system of measures of tourism innovation are developed and its application to the measurement of "destination innovativeness" is presented. The theoretical and managerial implications of such proposed measurements are then discussed so as to lay the foundation for operators of tourism destinations and small and medium enterprises to understand the conditions necessary for effective innovation in their businesses. The final section describes the limitations of the study, presents some suggestions for future research, and highlights the contribution of innovation to the long-term profitability and sustainability of tourism destinations and enterprises.

CURRENT INNOVATION RESEARCH AND MEASUREMENT

Schumpeter's (1942, 1965) emphasis on innovation and the role of the entrepreneur as the "promoter of innovations" has been widely acknowledged, and following his idea, innovation has often been described as positioned somewhere on the continuum between invention and adoption. At one end of the continuum, invention can be defined as "major scientific and technological developments brought about without any specified industrial use in mind" Hjalager (1997, p. 35). At the other end, adoption can be defined as an organization's first usage of existing knowledge without modification. The importance that Schumpeter's vision gives to the internal or external realization of ideas allows for the distinction between innovations and inventions. Specifically it distinguishes innovations as those ideas that are visible and of economic value to, any of the company's actors, including customers, suppliers, intermediaries, various publics, whereas inventions are those ideas that are not brought into the market or integrated into the company and are therefore without economic value. Therefore, an innovation can be any expansion or realization of an invention in the market for business purposes (Arundel, 2003; Hjalager, 1997). While these definitions may appear theoretically clear and simple, clarifying its practical dimensions and making the meaning of innovation operational for scientific investigation has been very challenging. So too has been the issue, often faced by researchers, of how to evaluate and deal with the comparability of innovation statistics among different data sources. Moreover, interpretation of the innovation concept, and therefore measures of innovation changes depending on the perspective considered by the firm and the sector in which it operates.

Acknowledging the important role of innovation, a reasonable amount of research has been conducted to measure enterprises, industries' and even countries' ability to be innovative. Moreover, the more traditional measures of innovation, namely R&D data and patent intensity and related macro-data, have recently been joined by innovation indicators that include commercialisation of new products, new design, new training and software information, as well as measures of cooperation among enterprises and the amount of human resources dedicated to innovation creation. It would seem therefore, that surveys are shifting towards micro-data collection methods and new indicators in the effort to improve the measurement of innovation (Flor and Oltra, 2004; Annunziato, 2003; Tsipouri, 2003). The OECD and the European Commission effort to standardise innovation statistics has been confirmed in the Oslo Manual and the Community Innovation Survey (CIS). The first offers a framework to guide countries in their innovation surveys, and the latter is a postal survey launched in 1993 and carried out every four years with the aim of identifying innovations by gathering data from company managers.

The Community Innovation Survey represents the most important initiative to date, collect, harmonize and to disseminate information relevant to innovation. Although it is affected by comparability and timing problems, it does reflect the increased interest in innovation issues on the part of researchers and in the use of innovation statistics on the part of the tourism industry. Moreover, while a great effort has been made to identify and measure technological, product, and process innovation, many researchers still emphasise the unavailability of much relevant information in innovation. For example, excluded from the survey are organizational and management type of innovations (Lambert, 2003). Kleinknecht (2000) observed that companies answering the *CIS* do not properly interpret the R&D definition and that there is a lack of sectoral and regional disaggregation of data. Other researchers emphasize the experimental nature of the survey because it concentrates only on products (Nas, 2003) and technical innovations (Durvy, 2003). It therefore would appear that these innovation measurement initiatives typically ignore many informative constituent dimensions of innovation, and this suggests that much work is needed, especially when looking at the service sectors (Smits, 2002). Indeed, innovation literature presents several simple indicators of innovation, and only a few of these aggregate multiple measures into a single indicator. Nevertheless, to date the Community Innovation Survey and its regular updates and different versions, represents an important starting point for evaluating innovativeness within the countries and economic sectors of the European Union.

The peculiar nature of the tourism sector creates a need for special considerations when conceptualising, defining and measuring innovation. Although several efforts have been made to define the tourism sector, since the tourism product is in fact a bundle of services it becomes difficult to isolate "tourism producers" and therefore difficult to define precisely all relevant industry players. Many countries are working to develop the tourism satellite account, which should allow better identification of the components of the sector, better define their respective contributions to the national economy, and therefore provide a more coherent basis for innovation measurement in which researchers will be interested. Thus, far little effort has been made to analyse the creation and the diffusion of innovation in the tourism sector, but some researchers considering the important role that tourism plays in many countries' national economies have started to pay attention to the issue, and there has been an emergent interest to understand, conceptualise, define and measure innovation (Jacob et al., 2003, Volo, 2004).

The difficulties in applying the innovation concept in the service industry are underlined in a pilot study conducted in the Balearic Islands by Jacob et al. (2003). Innovation in services is defined as "the conversion of ideas into products, processes or services which are evaluated by the market." Although innovation in tourism is not defined, Jacob et al. (2003) applied the Sundbo and Gallouj (1998) typology of service-sector innovation (product, process, organisational and market) to the traditional components of the tourism sector (e.g., accommodations, restaurants, leisure and recreation, transport and travel organisation and other auxiliary activities). Their results highlighted innovativeness in lodging and accommodations, the predominance of technological over non-technological innovation, and the positive effect of innovation on firms' image, profitability and customer satisfaction. Finally, these authors emphasized the inability of the CIS to investigate innovation in the service sectors and especially in tourism due to limitations in operational definitions and consequent measurements problems. Moreover, it has been suggested that customers' experience is the essential basis of the value proposition between tourism service providers and tourists and that the customers' experience varies along an active to passive continuum and the affect varies from absorption to immersion (Pine and Gilmore, 1999). Hjalager (2002) also focuses on clients and markets by looking at the company relationships and competencies dimensions.

Therefore it would seem important, if not essential, that measures of innovativeness somehow capture the degree to which innovations affect the experience of customers. The effect maybe indirect or delayed but the customer must ultimately feel it for an innovation to be relevant.

The Italian version of the CIS, carried out by Italy's National Statistical Institute (ISTAT, 2003), was analysed with reference to tourism by, and in an exploratory investigation undertaken in Sicily, some definitional issues were addressed when measuring the innovativeness of tourism firms (Volo, 2004). A new approach to defining, and therefore to measuring, tourism innovation was applied to small and medium enterprises by investigating the impact that each innovation (product, process, delivery, organization, markets and marketing) had on four dimensions of the "tourism experience": (a) accessibility; (b) affective transformation; (c) convenience; and (d) value. The results revealed the difficulties small and medium Sicilian tourism entrepreneurs have in understanding the innovation concept, thereby further exposing the need for more definitional and measurement studies. The study also revealed the passive and defensive innovation practices in Sicily. Innovations that introduce new products to new markets with a focus on enhanced affective transformation were rare to nonexistent, while those that focus on process or delivery improvements to existing and established clientele were much more common.

TOWARDS A TOURIST-BASED MEASUREMENT OF INNOVATION

A tourism firm's ability to innovate, determines its success in the current highly competitive market. Moreover, innovation can be the driving force for many tourism destinations that are currently suffering the threats of global competition. It is of great interest therefore, for the private and public sectors to undertake innovative actions that can generate and sustain company or destination growth and profitability. By integrating the reflections and proposals from past studies (Pine and Gilmore, 1999; Volo, 2004), and with the aim of improving the measurement and evaluation of innovative behaviour in tourism, the following definitions are proposed:

Tourism sector: all the contributors to the bundling of services necessary to create the final "tourism experience."

Tourism experience: what the tourist is seeking; tourism experience can be characterised by the following four dimensions:

(a) Accessibility dimension–how accessible is the tourism experience to one who may seek it?
(b) Affective transformation dimension–what degree of affective transformation is experienced?
(c) Convenience–what level of effort is required to access the experience?
(d) Value–what is the benefit received per unit of cost? (Volo, 2004)

Tourism innovation: changes in product, process, delivery, organization, markets and marketing that contributors to the bundled product we call the "tourism experience" have introduced within a relevant time period that might be considered to fall on the invention-adoption continuum and that provide a meaningful change, from the point of view of the tourist, in one of the four dimensions mentioned. Consequently, a tourism innovation should not be considered an innovation unless and until it has some effect, no matter how remotely, on the experience of the tourists, e.g., lower price due to increase efficiency, decrease wait in service time.

A Micro-Tourism Innovation Indicator is therefore proposed as a combination of the focal categories of innovation presented in literature, namely product, process, delivery, organization, markets and marketing, and the four categories related to its impact on the clientele, namely accessibility, affective transformation, convenience, value received. In combining these aspects, a two-dimension matrix is created in which one dimension represents the innovation typology and the other clientele impact. Therefore, for a tourism enterprise T at a given time t, the innovation matrix (M) will be a five by four matrix and can be represented as in Figure 1, where the row vectors are constituted by the five innovation foci dimensions and the column vectors are constituted by the four client impact dimensions.

FIGURE 1. Enterprise Innovation Matrix

	Accessibility	Affective transformation	Convenience	Value
Product	$K_{pd,a}$	$K_{pd,at}$	$K_{pd,c}$	$K_{pd,v}$
Process	$K_{pc,a}$	$K_{pc,at}$	$K_{pc,c}$	$K_{pc,v}$
Delivery	$K_{d,a}$	$K_{d,at}$	$K_{d,c}$	$K_{d,v}$
Organisation	$K_{o,a}$	$K_{o,at}$	$K_{o,c}$	$K_{o,v}$
Market and marketing	$K_{mm,a}$	$K_{mm,at}$	$K_{mm,c}$	$K_{mm,v}$

The value of the components K range between 0 and n (10) being the result of the following calculation:

$$K = f(n_i, c_i, i_1)$$

where

n$_i$ = number of novel initiations in a given typology $0 \leq ni < \infty$

c_i = customer impact ranges from 0 to 1 where 0 = total absence and 1 = total presence of an improvement on tourist experience for the given category

i_1 = innovation level ranging from 1 to 10 where 1 is closest to adoption and 10 to invention.

The value of K is given by:

$$K = f(n_i, c_i, i_1) = n_i {}^* c_i {}^* i_1$$

As can be seen from the above function if any of the arguments, n, c or i, are zero, the function returns a value of zero. That is, in order for any innovativeness to be registered there must be at least some level of all three factors: some novel initiations, some customer impact, and some presence of adoption or invention. And if some novel initiations and some customer impact are present, K will have a higher value if they were the result of invention or innovation as opposed to mere adoption. This is an intentional behaviour of the function. That is, it is intended that invention lead to higher values of K.

By using the matrix, the level of innovation within each of the five focal categories can be computed, as can the level of innovation within each of the four dimensions of experience. Additionally, the "Innovation vector scores" can be weighed according to the enterprise priorities or preferences, and an overall Innovation Indicator for the given tourism enterprise, T, at the given time, t, can be defined as:

$$I_{Tt} = \Sigma (K_{\text{innovation foci, client impacts}})$$

At a macro-level, destinations can use the above data matrix to define different functions that could reveal the innovation profile of the city, area or country of interest. Innovation data can be, in this case, collected for all the contributors to the bundling of services and then combined or correlated with the destination's economic growth and other performance measures. Therefore, considering the following *c* constituents of the tourism industry: **L** lodging and accommodations, **I** tourism intermediaries, **R** restaurants, **T** transportation operators, and **A** attractions, and assuming each will be constituted by a sample of *n* enterprises, it would be possible to measure the ability of each constituent *c* to innovate by looking at the series of the *n* innovation matrixes, *M*, for the given constituent *c*, (Figure 2):

otherwise:

$L = (1_{11} 1_{12} 1_{13} .... 1_{1n})$ where 1_{1n} is the innovation matrix *M* of the n enterprise of the L consituent

$I = (i_{11} \ i_{12} \ i_{13} .... i_{1n})$ where i_{1n} is the innovation matrix *M* of the n enterprise of the I constituent

$R = (r_{11} \ r_{12} \ r_{13} .... r_{1n})$ where r_{1n} i sthe innovation matrix *M* of the n enterprise of the R constituent

$T = (t_{11} \ t_{12} \ t_{13} .... t_{1n})$ where t_{1n} is the innvoation matrix *M* of the n enterprise of the T constituent

$A = (a_{11} \ a_{12} \ a_{13} .... a_{1n})$ where a_{1n} is the innovation matrix *M* of the n enterprise of the A constituent

Constituents' Innovativeness Indicators will therefore be computed as:

$$I_{Lt} = \Sigma I_{Lmt} ; \ I_{It} = \Sigma I_{Imt} ; \ I_{Rt} = \Sigma I_{Rmt} ; \ I_{Tt} = \Sigma I_{Tmt} ; \text{ and } I_{At} = \Sigma I_{Amt}$$

FIGURE 2. Enterprises Innovation Matrixes Series

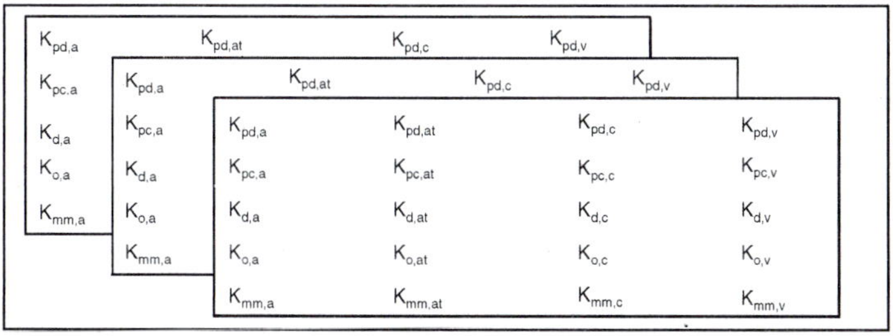

where m varies from 1 to n and the Tourism Destination Innovativeness Indicator at time t will be calculated as function of the constituents' innovativeness indicators

$$I_{Dt} = f(I_{Lt},\ I_{It},\ I_{Rt},\ I_{Tt},\ IA_t)$$

This approach could permit the construction of statistical models for forecasting the economic effects of innovations of various types. In these cases, "innovation vector scores" can be expressed per arrival, per capita, or other economic parameter so as to adjust, by re-scaling, the matrix data for underlying level of economic activity, thus permitting comparisons between large and small destinations or even regional or national comparisons. Moreover, commonly used destination benchmarking instruments can integrate the innovation concept and the ability to innovate as key variables to determine and compare the competitiveness of destinations.

DISCUSSION AND IMPLICATIONS
FOR TOURISM ENTERPRISES AND DESTINATIONS

From a managerial point of view, the proposed method will allow tourism enterprises to look analytically at their ability to enhance the tourism experience by implementing any change lying on the adoption-innovation continuum. By using the following graphical representation, a tourism enterprise could position all the changes in the five potential categories of innovation and have a simple tool to evaluate innovation effectiveness.

For example for the following $K_{o,c}$ (organisation, convenience) entry of the innovation matrix (M) represented in Figure 3 and calculated as follows: $K_{o,c} = n_i {}_* c_i {}_* i_l = -0.7{}^*8 = 11,2$ can be positioned in the following matrix by using the coordinates 0.7 on the y axis and 8 on the x axis, and a larger dimension of the point indicating the organisational innovation will represents the number of innovation implemented (two in this case).

Ideally, a tourism entrepreneur wants to have all the n changes in the five dimensions (product, process, delivery, organisation and market and marketing) located somewhere in the upper right part of the matrix, thus reflecting a radical innovator in all of the dimensions and providing a great change in the customer experience and therefore making it difficult to be imitated by competitors. Changes positioned in the upper left

FIGURE 3. Innovation Matrix: An Entry Example

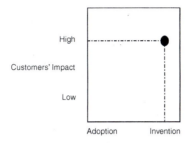

corner would be acceptable in some markets, as they provide improvements in the tourist's experience, although they are not sustainable by the company. On the other hand, for those changes represented by the lower part of the matrix, there is a need to redefine the actions that the company is undertaking as either there is little creative effort on the part of the from company and little improvement from the point of view of the customer. In the worst-case scenario, there is high innovative effort on the part of the company, but very little impact on customers. In such a case there is little or no benefit for any of the players. Furthermore, the ability to innovate needs to be integrated with a firm's economic results, as innovation itself is not a driver for company success unless it stimulates profitability and/or company growth. It is useful therefore, to add an economic impact dimension to the matrix as represented in Figure 4 by the following innovativeness customer impact model.

Similarly destinations can use the taxonomy presented in the present paper to describe the contributors to the bundling of services necessary to create the final "tourism experience." It would be useful to draw the same three-dimension graph and verify the relationship among the three dimensions when the points represent respectively (a) the innovativeness of the destination by looking at the five dimensions and therefore considering the destination similarly to a T tourism enterprise, (b) the innovativeness of the destination' constituents by plotting the "constituents innovativeness" indices, and additionally (c) by looking at only one constituent at time, plotting the constituent' five innovation dimensions. The first graph will allow an understanding of the relationship between innovation and destination profitability and growth, permit life product life cycle analysis and thereby shed light on the question of which typology of innovation is best able to sustain the growth of the

FIGURE 4. Innovativeness Customer Impact Model

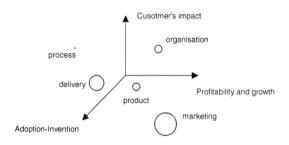

destination over time. Product life cycles could be extended, or at least controlled somewhat, by allocating the right amount of resources to the sustaining-dependent factors. The second proposed graph would reveal the key components of the destination innovativeness success, and the last one would allow the representative of a sub-sector (e.g., accommodations or restaurants) to identify their strength and weaknesses in each of the five dimensions of innovation allowing for, and maybe even provoking, a creative dialogue on the sub-sector innovation.

But the greatest benefit should come from the theoretical contribution of the model. It can serve to overcome the greatest current deficit in the existing research, namely the comparability of concepts, definitions and data. The model presented can serve as a conceptual model for researchers, a prescribed program of needed research. Perhaps more importantly, it is hoped that the model will stimulate discussion in the literature as to what constitutes effective operational definitions of terms and variables and methods of measurement, leading eventually to comparable data across the diverse set of data gatherers and data custodians.

FUTURE RESEARCH POSSIBILITIES

The model presented here needs to be debated and tested empirically for its ability to describe the tourism innovation phenomena with conceptual economy. That is, its performance and simplicity as a meaningful conceptual organizer of the relevant tourism innovation factors and variables needs to be established, and in this regard its ability to relate the interactive effects of innovation among contributions to the bundled set of products that comprise the tourism experience needs to be dissected. These initial research initiatives require mostly descriptive research, but will need to be thorough and preceded by substantial discussion of, and agreement on, operational definitions. Consequently, much of the initial descriptive research needs to be devoted to the proposing, testing and acceptance of operational definitions of key terms.

Once these initial issues of largely a conceptual nature are settled, substantial research is needed to test the model's ability to predict the economic effects of innovation on individual enterprises, destinations and markets, economically linked geographic zones, and eventually to entire countries. After all, it is understanding and controlling the economic consequence of tourism in general, and of tourism innovation in particular, that is practical goal of the research. The utility and acceptance of this research however, will depend in large measure on how well and how meaningfully the definitional and measurement issues are settled, and this is where most of the investment needs to be made initially.

REFERENCES

Annunziato, P. (2003). Indicators of innovation activity–Emerging needs and some proposal. *21st CEIES Seminar: Innovation statistics-more than R & D indicators*, Luxembourg: European Communities.

Arundel, A. (2003). The Knowledge Economy, Innovation Diffusion, and the CIS. *21st CEIES Seminar: Innovation statistics–more than R & D indicators*, Luxembourg: European Communities.

Coombs, R., and I. Miles (2000). Innovation, Measurement and Services: The New Problematique, pp. 85-103 in Metcalfe, J. S. and I. Miles (eds.), *Innovation Systems in the Service Economy. Measurement and Case Study Analysis*, Massachusetts: Kluwer Academic.

Drejer, I. (2002). A Schumpeterian Perspective on Service Innovation. *DRUID Working Paper* n. 02-09.

Drucker, P. F. (1985). *Innovation and Entrepreneurship: Practice and Principles*. New York: Harper & Row.

Durvy, J-N. (2003). User's need for innovation indicators: The experience of the innovation policy unit. *21st CEIES Seminar: Innovation statistics–more than R & D indicators*, Luxembourg: European Communities.

Evangelista, R., Iammarino, S., Mastrostefano, V., and Silvani, A. (2001). Measuring the regional dimension of innovation. Lessons from the Italian Innovation Survey. *Technovation*, 21, pp. 733-745.

Evangelista, R., and Sirilli, G. (1998). Innovation in the service sector. Results from the Italian Statistical Survey. *Technological Forecasting and Social Change 58*, pp. 251-269.

Flor, M.L., and Oltra, M.J. (2004). Identification Of innovating forms through technological innovation indicators: An application to the Spanish ceramic tile industry. *Research Policy*, 33, pp. 323-336.

Foster, R. (1987). *Innovation. Il vantaggio di chi attacca.* Milano: Sperling & Kupfer.

Guellec, D. (2003). Extending and refining the coverage of innovation in innovation surveys. *21st CEIES Seminar: Innovation statistics-more than R & D indicators,* Luxembourg: European Communities.

Hjalager, A-M. (1997). Innovation patterns in sustainable tourism: An analytical typology. *Tourism Management 18*(1), pp. 35-41.

Hjalager, A.-M. (2002). Repairing innovation defectiveness in tourism. *Tourism Management 23*(5), pp. 465-474.

Hughes, A., and Wood. E. (2000). Rethinking Innovation Comparisons between Manufacturing and Services: The Experience of the CBR SME Surveys in the UK, pp. 105-124 in Metcalfe, J. S. and I. Miles (eds.), *Innovation Systems in the Service Economy. Measurement and Case Study Analysis,* Massachusetts: Kluwer Academic.

ISTAT (2003). *L'innovazione nelle imprese italiane negli anni 1998-2000.* Roma: ISTAT.

Jacob, M., Tintoré, J., Aguiló, E., Bravo, A., & Mulet, J. (2003). Innovation in the tourism sector: Results from a pilot study in the Balearic Islands. *Tourism Economics 9*(3), pp. 279-295.

Kleinknecht, A. (2000). Indicators of Manufacturing and Service Innovation: Their Strengths and Weaknesses, pp. 169-186 in Metcalfe, J. S. and I. Miles (eds.), *Innovation Systems in the Service Economy. Measurement and Case Study Analysis,* Massachusetts: Kluwer Academic.

Lambert, R. (2003). UK Users' of innovation data. *21st CEIES Seminar: Innovation statistics–more than R & D indicators,* Luxembourg: European Communities.

Mercury (2003). *Rapporto sul Turismo in Sicilia.* Firenze: Mercuri.

Metcalfe, S., and Miles, I. (eds.) (2000). *Innovation systems in the service economy: Measurement and case study analysis.* Massachusetts: Kluwer Academic.

Nas, S. O. (2003). Different users' needs for innovation indicators: Innovation indicators for economic analysis. *21st CEIES Seminar: Innovation statistics–more than R & D indicators,* Luxembourg: European Communities.

Nonaka, I., and Takeuchi, H. (1995). *The Knowledge-Creating Company.* New York: Oxford University Press.

Page, S. J., Brunt, P., Busby, G., and Connell, J. (2001). *Tourism: A Modern Synthesis.* Italy: Thomson Learning.

Pasetti, P. (2002). *Statistica del Turismo.* Roma: Carocci.

Perroux, F. (1965). *La pensée économique de Joseph Schumpeter. Les dynamiques du capitalisme.* Genève: Librairie Droz.

Pine II, J. B., & Gilmore, J. H. (1999). *The Experience Economy. Work is Theatre & Every Business a Stage: Goods & services are no longer enough.* Boston: Massachusetts Harvard Business School Press.

Rogers, E. M. (1983). *Diffusion of Innovations.* New York: Free Press.

Schumpeter, J. A. (1935). *Théorie de l'évolution économique.* Paris: Librairie Dalloz.

Schumpeter, J. A. (1942). *Capitalism, Socialism and Democracy.* New York: Harper & Row.

Schumpeter, J. A. (1965). *The Theory of Economic Development: An Inquiry into Profit, Credit, Interest, and the Business Cycle* (4th Ed). Oxford: Oxford University Press.

Smits, R. (2002). Innovation studies in the 21st century: Questions from a user's perspective. *Technological Forecasting and Social Change*, 69, pp. 861-883.

Stamboulis, Y., and Skayannis, P. (2003). Innovation strategies and technology for experience-based tourism. *Tourism Management 24*(1), 35-43.

Sundbo, J., and F. Gallouj (1998). 'Innovation in Services,' *SI4S Synthesis Papers* No. S2.

Sundbo, J., and F. Gallouj (2000). 'Innovation as a Loosely Coupled System in Services.' In: Metcalfe, J.S. and I. Miles (eds.) *Innovation Systems in the Service Economy. Measurement and Case Study Analysis*, Massachusetts: Kluwer Academic, pp. 43-68.

Tsipouri, L. (2003). Different Users needs for innovation indicators.' *21st CEIES Seminar: Innovation statistics-more than R & D indicators,* Luxembourg: European Communities.

Volo, S. (2004). Foundation for an innovation indicator for tourism: An application to SME. In P. Keller, and Th. Bieger (Eds.), AIEST 54th Congress: *The Future of Small and Medium Sized Enterprises in Tourism* Vol. 46. St. Gallen, Switzerland: AIEST, pp. 361-376.

von Hippel, E. (1990). *Le fonti dell'innovazione*. Milano: Mc-Graw-Hill.

Towards the Measurement of Innovation– A Pilot Study in the Small and Medium Sized Hotel Industry

Birgit Pikkemaat
Mike Peters

SUMMARY. This paper discusses the importance of innovation as a key component of business strategy in tourism, as well as determinants of innovation processes in the small and medium sized hotel industry in alpine tourism destinations of Europe. Initially, the paper delivers a literature overview on innovations as prerequisites for competitive advantages. Furthermore, the authors shed more light on the measurement of innovation in the tourism industry. The empirical study has been carried out in alpine tourism destinations focusing on the assessment of innovation activities in small and medium sized (SMEs) hotels. Diverse functional areas of hotels have been analysed and the results show rather low degrees of innovation in all areas of the hotel value chain. *[Article copies available for a fee from The Haworth Document Delivery Service: 1-800-HAWORTH. E-mail address: <docdelivery@haworthpress.com> Website: <http://www. HaworthPress.com> © 2005 by The Haworth Press, Inc. All rights reserved.]*

Birgit Pikkemaat (Associate Professor) and Mike Peters (Assistant Professor) are both affiliated with the Center for Tourism and Service Economics, Innsbruck University School of Management, University of Innsbruck, Universitätsstrasse 15, A-6020 Innsbruck (E-mail: birgit.pikkemaat@uibk.ac.at) or (E-mail: mike.peters@uibk.ac.at).

[Haworth co-indexing entry note]: "Towards the Measurement of Innovation–A Pilot Study in the Small and Medium Sized Hotel Industry." Pikkemaat, Birgit, and Mike Peters. Co-published simultaneously in *Journal of Quality Assurance in Hospitality & Tourism* (The Haworth Hospitality Press, an imprint of The Haworth Press, Inc.) Vol. 6, No. 3/4, 2005, pp. 89-112; and: *Innovation in Hospitality and Tourism* (ed: Mike Peters, and Birgit Pikkemaat) The Haworth Hospitality Press, an imprint of The Haworth Press, Inc., 2005, pp. 89-112. Single or multiple copies of this article are available for a fee from The Haworth Document Delivery Service [1-800- HAWORTH, 9:00 a.m. - 5:00 p.m. (EST). E-mail address: docdelivery@haworthpress.com].

Available online at http://www.haworthpress.com/web/JQAHT
© 2005 by The Haworth Press, Inc. All rights reserved.
doi:10.1300/J162v06n03_06

KEYWORDS. Innovation, measurement, alpine tourism, hotel industry .

INNOVATION AS COMPETITIVE ADVANTAGE IN ALPINE TOURISM

Today, especially many alpine tourism destinations in Europe are faced with high competition and mature markets. Starting in the eighties and mid-eighties, a number of dramatic environmental changes occurred which moved the "tourism industry" much closer to the characteristics of the new economy. On the demand side, the undifferentiated conservative and economizing mass customer (tourist) gave way to a much more travelled, experienced and quality conscious individualist: "mass tourism" seemed to have been replaced by the "individualized mass" (Poon, 1993; Opaschowski, 2000). Used to more convenience, faster service and more options from his/her every-day-life, the new tourist also insists on more options, more entertainment and fun, more diversified sports facilities and cultural variety in his/her vacation (Foot, 2002; Bieger and Laesser, 2003). This new consumer thereby puts pressure on the tourism industry and tourism enterprises to develop new products, services and experiences. Global companies very quickly began penetrating formerly fragmented and local tourism markets. Left only with local competitive advantages (Dunning, 1988), and more so competitive disadvantages vis-à-vis the international or transnational tourism enterprise, pressure mounted in many, notably European, regional and local tourist destinations to restructure, reengineer and/or redesign "hard-soft-and human ware" within the core and peripheral tourism businesses.

On the top of the list of newly available factors of production were the new information and communication technologies, often specifically designed for the tourism industry such as CRS (computer reservation systems) or DIS (destination information systems), tourism web-sites on the internet or computer assisted back up systems for complex vacation or business travel packages. Labour in tourism became much more human capital intensive and was generally considered by enlightened management and tourism entrepreneurs as an asset rather than a cost item (Tschurtschenthaler, 1998). As a consequence, there has been a dramatic change in the schooling and training of the tourism labour force (Bieger and Lehar, 1998; Weiermair, 2000). Gradually, the industry also experiences the rise of a new type of entrepreneur who is less operation-and more strategy-oriented, assumes calculated risks, is on average better trained or experienced, more oriented towards prob-lem-solving and assumes more up-to-date styles of leadership. Location and climate, while still remaining important factors of production for tourism products/services, share their importance with other man-made factors such as design features, entertainment content or virtual options of tourism structures and supra-structures (Pine and Gilmore, 1999; Wolf, 1999; Weiermair, 2001). The latter became supplied or otherwise connected through diagonally integrated non tourism firms and indus-tries such as financial services, architecture, design, and real estate de-velopment, sports, culture and entertainment, health care and education, food processing, beverage and agriculture.

These developments show that destinations are permanently forced to create new products and innovations to meet customers' needs and find new solutions for (maybe until today unknown) problems. How-ever, in terms of innovation and creativity the tourism industry is not a best practice industry.

INNOVATION IN THE SMALL AND MEDIUM SIZED HOTEL INDUSTRY

In comparison to other industries, research and development ex-penses or the number of licenses or patents registered are relatively low in the hotel industry. Due to the dominance of small businesses espe-cially in the Alps or rural regions, the tourism industry displays special disadvantages in terms of innovation and product development (Peters and Weiermair, 2002). Basically, small businesses lack economies of scale and are not able to raise profit margins which allow small units to reinvest in research & development, market research, product develop-ment, skill or creativity enhancement. Secondly, small and medium-sized enterprises (SMEs) in tourism are still reluctant in terms of coop-eration or strategic alliances with other competitors: thus, they are not able to gain economies of scope which increases product- and services-variation and thus customers' freedom of choice.

The hotel industry but more so hospitality, traditionally have de-pended on a large supply of semiskilled and cheap manpower (in terms of labour cost) matching relatively low productivity and earning levels of this industry in most jurisdictions. As long as economies in which tourism plays a major role have ample supplies of relatively cheap tour-ism manpower (either through indigenous manpower such as is true in most developing and non-industrial countries or through the import of cheap labour) there will be little need for rationalization-investment and innovation substituting capital for labour. This situation changes however radically when labour costs in the hotel industry begin to rise more rapidly than elsewhere leading to a series of labour saving process innovations such as automated shoe shine, ironing, food preparation services, computerized information processing, etc. By the same token, available and easy access of highly qualified manpower resources and technologies can boost both productivity and the innovative potential of an industry. However, similarly, its absence, as might be the case in tourism and related industries, can do the opposite. Finally, tourism has to be viewed as a holistic value chain of services (Bieger, 2001; Weiermair, 2004) whose innovations cannot only occur at different elements in the value chain (e.g., at the level of travel intermediaries or transportation) but where both the accumulated level of innovation activities and its rate and speed of diffusion within the tourism value chain probably hinge upon strategic places of first innovation investments.

Next, the authors try to throw some more light on the diverse dimensions and types of innovations. Focusing first on the degree of innovation or the question "how new is the innovation?" a useful distinction of innovation types, especially for tourism which is also suitable for hotel services and products has been delivered by Hjalager (2002). Her model categorizes innovation levels in tourism using core competencies as the unit of analysis. This differentiation seems to be appropriate, as innovation in tourism is often based on core competencies. Core competencies may comprise internal or external factors. Internal resources, i.e., resources of the company are the most important determinants regarding positioning and competitive advantages of a company which are difficult to imitate (Gomez and Probst, 1995). Hjalager (2002) distinguishes four types of innovation dealing with either the breaking up or deepening of relationships to clients or to the market and the abandonment or preservation of competencies: regular innovations, niche innovations, architectural innovations, and revolutionary innovations. While niche innovations (e.g., hotel cooperation with a tour operator) emphasize new forms of cooperation and do not touch existing competencies, architectural innovations (e.g., design hotels) introduce new structures and redefine relationships to costumers and existing markets. External branch structures and the target groups keep unchanged when a revolutionary innovation is realized, although services have changed by using new technologies. Regular or incremental innovations are realized with existing competencies and existing relationships, some examples are increased productivity, quality improvements or further training of staff members, e.g., of a hotel (Hjalager, 2002). These systematic categories seem to be useful but the shortened product life cycle noticed in the past decade also has to be recognized. The same is true for innovations, which implies a dynamic change of innovations belonging to one of the four mentioned types (Abernathy and Clark, 1985).

Regarding the object dimension of innovation or answering the question "what is new?" diverse types of innovation have been distinguished in the literature: e.g., product innovations, process innovations, marketing innovations, organisational innovations, social innovations, human resource innovations, technological innovations, etc. (Hausschildt and Schlaak, 2001; Johannessen et al., 2001; Gallouij, 1998; Preissl, 2000; Chapman et al., 2002). A valuable classification for the service sector has been delivered by Tidd et al. (2003) as they focus on technological innovations which has been particular important for the tourism sector over the last decades. Furthermore their concept tries to combine the degree of innovation with the object of innovation which is illustrated in Figure 1.

Similar to Hjalagar (2002) the degree of innovation ranges from only minor continuous innovations which are often associated with process innovations, up to transformational innovations which are often so far-

FIGURE 1. Dimensions of Innovation

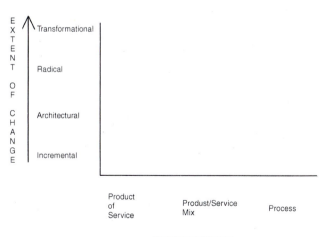

reaching that they are able to change a societies' structure, e.g., mobile phones. The other axis relates to the often used and traditionally so-called distinction of product and process innovations, but delivers a mix of both in the middle of these two extremes. The latter seems to be important for the tourism industry as its product is best characterized as a complex bundle of interwoven products and services.

Discussing types of innovation also the subject dimension has to be mentioned or the question 'to whom is the innovation new?' Traditionally two groups can be addressed: the customers and the company. Discussing this question in detail it is furthermore possible to differentiate subgroups within these two addressees, e.g., is the innovation new in the eyes of all customers or solely for a single target group or is the innovation new in the eyes of all employees in the company or solely for a certain subgroup of employees?

In a next step, the authors attempt to discuss the problems of measuring innovations. To do so, a reasonable number of studies carried out in the tourism industry will be presented.

THE MEASUREMENT OF INNOVATION

A considerable amount of research exists on problems and issues of innovation management and processes in the manufacturing and service industry (e.g., Drucker, 1985; Gallouj, 1998; Kelly and Storey, 2000; Metcalfe and Miles, 2000; Preissl, 2000; Herstatt et al., 2001; Hollenstein, 2001; Afuah, 2003). Less research has been carried out on innovation in the tourism industry (e.g., Hjalager, 2002; Weiermair and Peters, 2002; Keller, 2004; Pikkemaat, 2005) as well as on the measurement of innovation (e.g., Coombs and Miles, 2000; Hauschildt and Schlaak, 2001; Johannessen et al., 2001; Pikkemaat and Weiermair, 2004). From the authors' point of view recently only two studies combined both empirical measurement of innovation and specifics of the tourism industry (Weiermair, 2003; Volo, 2004). Before these studies are discussed, some specifics of the tourism industry which are relevant for the measurement of innovation are presented.

Analyzing the literature about the measurement of innovation in the manufacturing and the service industry, it becomes obvious that, due to the characteristics of the destination product, a new approach is required for measuring innovation in tourism industry. From customers' perspective, the destination product is a rather expensive credence product without a possibility to test before consuming (Zeithaml, 1991). Thus, the consumers' risk is high and trust and personal services are key success factors for gaining tourist's loyalty and competitive advantage. Additionally, tourists demand one holistic tourism experience and don't care about the highly complex production and linkage of single products and services along the tourism value chain. Although, this bundle of tangible products and intangible services demands cooperation and networking of destinations' entrepreneurs, it often is delivered completely independent and uncoordinated. Furthermore, different market segments and different tourists have different travel experiences influencing personal quality judgements about specific products in specific destinations. For example, a tourist travelling to the Italian seaside for the first time may be excited by the Italian way of living and the landscape whereas loyal customers are looking for new attractions as they are already familiar with the destination. Due to the characteristics of the tourism product, measuring innovation in tourism must include a variety of providers from diverse branches, such as accommodation, restaurants, transport, animation, attraction, shopping, or public services. The latter may be one important argument why the European Commission still lacks the conceptualisation of a tourism innovation indicator for measuring innovation in tourism industry, although in many other branches innovation indicators have been developed and used successfully.

Understanding the features of the tourism product is crucial when analyzing the literature about the measurement of innovation. According to Coombs and Miles (2000, 85) there are three choices of how research should proceed on defining and measuring innovation in a "service-rich-world." Assimilation is the idea that service innovation is fundamental similar to manufacturing innovation and can be studied with the same methods and concepts. The demarcation approach argues that service innovation is highly distinctive and requires novel theories and instruments. Finally, the synthesis approach suggests that service innovation reveals the neglected aspects of the innovation process which assumes in its extreme form that material products are only physical embodiments of the services they deliver (Coombs and Miles, 2000, p. 97). The latter seems to hold true for many tourism products. Dimensions of measurement range from single innovation subjects to objects and branches up to regions and whole nations. As evaluation criteria the literature reports technical (such as learning, promotion effects, know how, or information about weak points), market and economical (such as lower costs, increasing sales, or furtherance) as well as system related dimensions (for example social or environmental effects) (Gallouj, 1998; Coombs and Miles, 2000; King, 2000; Johannessen et al., 2001; Chapman et al., 2002).

Although researchers propose and discuss different approaches to define and measure innovation, they agree that methodology and instruments always have to be selected and developed in relation to the specific research question. Johannessen et al. (2001) suggest that, in order to isolate a useful definition and measure of innovation, three newness-related questions have to be asked: "what is new," "how new is it," and "to whom is it new?" However, due to the complex and networked characteristics of the tourism product, at least fours aspects should be considered when starting to define and measure innovation in tourism: (1) What is the focus of the study? e.g., the measurement of innovation intensity, number of successful innovations and number of flops, degree of product and process innovation, intensity of new products and imitations? (2) Which elements of the tourism product should be included? e.g., hotels, restaurants, public services, transport, skiing facilities, and cultural attractions? (3) Who is interviewed? e.g., consumers' perspective or entrepreneur's perspective, market segments, owners or managing directors. (4) Which instruments are suitable? e.g., primary or secondary data, questionnaire, interviews, and focus groups?

In the following the most important results of two empirical studies which have recently been carried out on the measurement of innovation in tourism are presented (Weiermair, 2003; Volo, 2004). Answering the questions above, the first study was conducted in Italy (Sicily) and focussed on small and medium sized enterprises in tourism. The analysis tried to measure entrepreneurs' interpretation of the term "innovation" by carrying out focus groups with lodging and accommodation providers, tourism intermediaries, restaurant and transportation operators and attractions (Volo, 2004). The most important results are listed in Table 1.

The second study carried out personal interviews with larger national and global tourism companies (tour operators, travel agencies, individual hotels, hotel chains, cable car companies, theme parks, a provider of e-tourism (databases), restaurants, and charter airlines) in North America and Western Europe (Weiermair, 2003).

A comparison of these two studies' results seem to be fruitful as the first study focussed on SMEs and the second one on larger national and global acting tourism firms. As we can see in Table 1 and 2, the results highlight the importance of carrying out more empirical research on innovation in tourism. Although both studies used qualitative interview techniques, they are not easily to compare due to different aims and samples. Thus, what seems to be obvious so far for both SMEs and large tourism companies is that:

- most entrepreneurs recognize the importance of innovation.
- instead of 'new to world' products, adoptions are the more favored kind of innovation.
- information technology is closely connected with innovation.

Reviewing and summarizing the present literature about innovation, some hypotheses for the alpine hotel industry can be derived. The empirical study presented in the following chapter will refer to the following postulations:

H_1: The larger the more innovative is the hotel enterprise (Hollenstein, 2001; Avermaete et al., 2002; Weiermair, 2003; Volo, 2004; Keller, 2004).

H_2: The higher qualified the hotel entrepreneur or (owner) manager the more innovative the hotel enterprise (Kelly and Storey, 2000; Kandampully, 2002; Avermaete et al., 2002).

H_3: The younger the entrepreneur or (owner) manager the more innovative the hotel enterprise (Hollenstein, 2001; Avermaete et al., 2002).

H_4: The larger the amount of loyal customers the more innovative the hotel enterprise (Preissl, 2000; Wöhler, 2005).

H_5: The more innovative the hotel enterprise the more satisfied the entrepreneur with the revenue/profit (Kelly and Storey, 2000; Avermaete et al., 2002; Volo, 2004)

H_6: The higher the quality level of the hotel the more innovative the hotel (Hjalager, 2002; Weiermair, 2004).

H_7: A positive significant relationship exists between differentiation on target segments and the degree of innovation (Kelly and Storey, 2000; Hollenstein, 2001).

TABLE 1. Results of an Innovation Study in SMEs

Innovation in SMEs (Volo, 2004)
Innovation is not a concept clearly comprehended as applied tourism. Micro entrepreneurs are not able to discriminate among different kinds of innovation, such as product, process, delivery, organisation, and markets and marketing.
On the adoption-invention continuum adoptions are the more favoured innovation type. Most innovations are adoptions that originate as new technologies suggested by suppliers.
The most common kind of innovation associated with novelty is information technology.
The most common novelty implementation is acquisition of machinery as well as upgrading of the facilities in general.
The main outcomes of innovations have no effect on customer satisfaction, noticeable benefit on process and productivity, weak effect on revenue or attraction of new customers, and high level of improvement in enterprise image.
Innovations are most often reactive in nature as opposed to proactive innovations. The first are changes undertaken to solve an existing problem whereas the latter introduce a new capability or new experience for tourists.
Most innovations appear to score highest on the process and delivery categories and lowest on the product and marketing categories.
Most innovations scored low on all client impact categories, such as accessibility, affective transformation, convenience and value received, a possible exception being convenience.
Entrepreneurs are often not willing to deliver financial information about the enterprise, such as size, turnover, and percentage of turnover dedicated to new activities or number of employees. Almost 60% have a budget designated for innovation but typically it is not a large amount of money.

Used with permission AIEST. (Volo, 2004)

EMPIRICAL STUDY

Methodology

The findings reported in this paper are based on a research project which has been carried out in Tyrol (Austria) in 2003.[1] The aim of this pilot project was the measurement of innovation in alpine tourism destinations for gaining some more insights into the innovation activities carried out by small and medium sized alpine tourism organisation. Additionally, for benchmarking purposes an innovation degree should be calculated. For this purpose, a field survey was designed and survey data were collected.

Thereby, a more qualitative research approach seemed to be more sufficient to assess small business entrepreneurs or owner/managers in-

TABLE 2. Results of an Innovation Study in Large Tourism Firms

Innovation in large tourism firms (Weiermair, 2003)
Most firms recognize the importance of product development. Competition in mature markets (particularly skiing and golf) leads to pressure to add more experience to products.
Innovation rarely involves entirely new products or new markets but rather a process of individualizing mass market (products) by product differentiation, product line extension by branding policies or by changing the cost (price)-quality-ratio of the product. Other reasons are the availability of firm specific technologies and supplier relationships.
Information Technology and its use in e-tourism are seen as a major change although nobody sees it as an innovation (as it comes from outside the industry). The second forms of innovation are new forms of business alliances and cooperative marketing.
Quality assurance, marketing practices, and customer and employee satisfaction are among the most important areas for innovation.
In North America, major objectives are cost reduction followed by revenue generation, while in Europe increasing customer value followed by profit maximisation can be seen as the most important incentive for innovation.
Major movers of innovation are customers followed by competition and the ambition to be the leader in the industry.
Typical product innovations are new products in catering, trendy/more comfortable hardware in the hotel room, new wellness hardware and applications new architecture/design, customer loyalty programmes and price innovations. Typical process innovations are IT (Internet, B2B information & reservation systems), new controlling systems, restructuring of the company, new distribution and marketing systems, collaboration in various fields, further training of the staff members, and service optimisation.
Major barriers are the lack of time, money or know-how, and risk aversion which were all internal factors. As regards outside forces, particularly in Europe bureaucracy and politics were pointed out as barriers for the realisation of innovation activities.
All experts agree on the most promising vehicle for innovation which is cooperation, alliances and/or networks in various fields such as technology, marketing, distribution, and human resources sharing.

Used with permission. Weiermair, K., Professor and Head of Centre for Tourism and Service Economics University of Innsbruck, Empirical evidence gathered so far, " Product Improvement or Innovation: What is the Key to Success in Tourism?", Conference on Innovation and Growth in Tourism Hosted by the Swiss State Secretariat for Economic Affairs (SECO) Lugano, Switzerland 18-19 September 2003, ©OECD 2004

terpretation of innovation management (Volo, 2004). An open structured questionnaire has at least one great advantage when asking small and medium sized entrepreneurs: entrepreneurs are not forced to answer questions which are not relevant for the size of their business.

In total, 107 entrepreneurs/managers of hotels, 65 of restaurants/bars, 11 of transport and 6 of tourism boards could be interviewed. These interviews were carried out between July and September 2003 in six alpine tourism destinations. In this paper, we solely focus on the sample of 107 hotel interviews.

Empirical data were gathered by entrepreneurs' self-evaluation of innovation activities in diverse functional areas, such as quality assurance, gastronomy, marketing, human resources, product bundling, wellness, information technology, operational procedures, strategy development, and animation. Due to the explorative character of this pilot study and the non-existence of patents and copyrights in the small and medium sized alpine tourism industry, the personal interviews were open-structured and varied in length as well as in depth. Thus, in a first step of data analysis these unstructured and non systemized answers of the interviewees had to be listed and categorized as demonstrated in Table 3.

As the aim of this study was the measurement and consequently the benchmarking of innovation activities in tourism organisations, entrepreneurs' open and unstructured statements had to be evaluated. Due to the fact that this study was a pilot project and thus, can be interpreted as a first attempt to measure innovation with qualitative interview techniques for gaining an innovation degree, it was difficult to find an appropriate procedure. After analysing the literature in vain and listing the whole data set, it was decided to rank the diverse single innovation activities of hotel entrepreneurs according to researchers' former experiences with innovation activities and innovation types in alpine tourism destinations. The data are ranked from 0 to 3 innovation points, whereby 0 point stands for *totally not innovative activities* and 3 points for *very innovative activities*. Following this procedure, a maximum degree of innovation of 3 points and a minimum of 0 point becomes possible. E.g., if a hotel entrepreneur is an active member of a know-how network, he/she will gain 3 innovation points but if he/she only buys new

TABLE 3. Examples of Innovation Measures for Hotels in Alpine Tourism Destinations

Functional Variables	Indicators
Quality Assurance	Cachets, quality marks
Gastronomy	Know-how networks, complaint box for customers, after sale services Eating hours, possibilities to get food the whole day long.
Marketing	Specialisation/special interest groups, newsletter and guest journals, new distribution channels, new technological supported marketing strategies.

flower arrangements for the reception desk, he/she will not gain any innovation point. Additionally, we categorize the reported innovation activities according to functional areas of hotels as demonstrated in Table 4. As an advantage we can derive innovation degrees for the functional areas of the hotels as listed in Table 6. After a first analysis and ranking procedure it can be shown that the majority of data reveals only incremental innovations. Consequently, many activities carried out by the hotels gain at least one innovation point although the activity rather tends to be a cosmetic change than a real innovation. Table 4 illustrates this ranking process with some examples.

Findings

At the beginning of the interviews, we asked hotel entrepreneurs about the targeted aim of their innovation activities. Most of them wanted to improve quality (35%), to increase customer satisfaction (21%),

TABLE 4. Ranking of Diverse Innovation Activities Reported by Hotel Entrepreneurs

	1 Innovation Point	2 Innovation Points	3 Innovation Points
Quality Assurance	Quality of Employees (Education)	Specific equipment of hotel rooms, Questionnaire for customers satisfaction	Quality controlling, Payment with foreign currency or charge on the bill, know how co-operation
Marketing	Cooperation with tour operators, Existence of a homepage, Cultural and sport events	International promotion strategies, Promotion within chain hotels or marketing groups, organisation of journalists travel groups	Strategies and actions for customer retention, Mega events with supra-regional importance
Information Technology	Conversion to PC, Member of IT-supported booking systems (e.g., Tiscover)	Internet terminals, new e mail system, hotel TV channel, Internet access in the room, new homepage design, Cooperation with databases	A hotel CD for the customers
Human Resource Management		New concept for employees, employee training, sommelier training	Diet assistance

and to enhance capacity (20%). Only one entrepreneur wanted to become a first mover in the market. Asking them about problems during their innovation processes, the majority of entrepreneurs stated to have no problems at all (73%). Only a minority claimed financial (6.6%), human resource (5.7%), public authority (5.2%), and technical (3.8%) problems. As mentioned above, only very few hotels have already registered patents, licenses, brands, or copyrights. In total, only two entrepreneurs have registered a brand name but 26 have registered the hotels' name or the logo. During the last five years, many of the hotel entrepreneurs have made hardware investments, such as conversion, new facilities or buildings, wellness areas, improved accommodation for employees, or wine cellars. Only a few entrepreneurs have focussed on process innovations. Furthermore, only a minority of innovation activities in the alpine hotel industry can be interpreted as others than incremental innovations.

The innovation degrees of single hotels vary between a minimum of 0.14 and a maximum of 2.14. On average all hotels show an innovation degree of 0.8875. More than the half of all hotels (59.89%) does not achieve an innovation degree of 1. Interestingly, results show that the smaller destinations are the lower the degree of innovation in the hotels. In the smallest destination D 14 of 20 hotels and in the second smallest destination C 14 of 16 hotels show an innovation degree below 1. Table 5 shows the aggregated arithmetic mean of innovation degrees of hotels in the alpine tourism destinations.

In a next step, the survey assessed innovation activities within the hotels during the last five years. Table 6 shows that most innovation activities took place in the area of architecture and design. Unfortunately, these activities are mostly redecoration and renovations instead of major innovations, such as modernisation of a dining room, installation of an elevator, modification of the entrance hall, and renovation of hotel rooms. The maintenance of a certain degree of quality (in terms of national hotel classifications, such as "stars") seems to be the main motivation for these renovation and modernisation activities. As these activities can hardly be interpreted as innovation, the architectural area has to be neglected and the degree of innovation is not calculated for this area.

Few and far between very innovative entrepreneurs exist but they are too few in order to have an impact on the total result. Analyzing the degrees of innovation, the highest innovation score can be reported for *information technology*. Innovative hotels are cooperating with CRS or other databanks. The implementation of the hotel homepage (probably

TABLE 5. Innovation Degree for Hotels

Destination	Innovation Degree of Hotels	Number of Interviews	Standard Deviation
Destination A	1.1322	18	0.47284
Destination B	0.8946	18	0.36483
Destination C	0.5733	16	0.27611
Destination D	0.7310	20	0.42330
Destination E	1.1586	15	0.37949
Destination F	0.8655	20	0.48119
Total	0.8875	107	0.44813

TABLE 6. Innovation Activities and Degree in Functional Areas

Functional Area	% of Innovation Activities	Innovation Degree (Mean)
Information technology	9.07%	1.1963
Gastronomy	9.30%	1.0421
Operational Procedures	3.17%	1.0377
Quality Assurance	2.04%	0.8726
Wellness	1.36%	0.8364
Product Bundling	5.22%	0.7804
HRM	4.76%	0.7788
Animation	4.08%	0.7570
Marketing	1.13%	0.7752
Architecture/Design	57.14%	-
Total	100.00%	0.8875

with the option of online-booking) is often mentioned as innovative activity in the area of *information technology.*

The following part of the statistical analysis presents the testing of the above formulated hypotheses.

Hypothesis 1: The larger the more innovative is the hotel enterprise. Table 7 shows a significant positive correlation between the size of hotels (measured in number of beds) and innovation degree. The hypothesis seems to be confirmed: the larger the hotel the higher the innovation degree.

Hypothesis 2: The higher qualified the hotel entrepreneur or (owner) manager the more innovative the hotel enterprise. Surprisingly, the tests

TABLE 7. Correlation Between Size of Hotel and Innovation Degree

Number of beds	Innovation Degree (Mean)	N	Standard Deviation
1-10	0.4138	2	0.19506
11-30	0.4888	17	0.27158
31-60	0.7629	32	0.28202
61-100	0.7716	24	0.32536
> 100	1.3405	32	0.38655
	Spearman Rho	0.646**	
	Significance (2 tail)	0.000	
	N	107	

** The correlation is significant on 0.01 (two-side)

below show no significant correlation between the education of the hotel manager/entrepreneur (measured as the highest education they have passed) and the innovation degree (see Table 8).

The following hypotheses focus on entrepreneur's demographics, age and sex.

Hypothesis 3: The younger the entrepreneur or (owner) manager the more innovative the hotel enterprise. The innovation degrees of the age groups do not vary much. The youngest group shows the lowest innovation degree and the oldest group the highest. However, this tendency does not hold true for the middle age groups. Thus, a very low correlation exists which is not significant. H_3 cannot be confirmed (see Table 9).

Hypothesis 4: The larger the amount of loyal customers the more innovative the hotel enterprise. The innovation degrees are relatively similar and a low correlation value together with the non-significance shows that this hypothesis cannot be confirmed. There is no correlation between the proportion of loyal customers (measured as % of total customers) and innovation activities of the hotel at all (see Table 10).

Hypothesis 5: The more innovative a hotel enterprise the more satisfied the entrepreneur with the revenue/profit. Analyzing the correlation between entrepreneurs' satisfaction with the hotel's revenue (measured on a 5 point Likert-scale) and the innovation degree, the results don't support the hypothesis (Spearman Rho-0.003 and significance of 0.977). As already stated in other studies (Volo, 2004), some entrepreneurs were not willing to answer the question about the hotel's revenue. Eighty-six persons answered, while 21 refused the question.

TABLE 8. Correlation Between Education of the Hotel Entrepreneur/Manager and Innovation Degree

Education	Innovation Degree (Mean)	N	Standard Deviation
Commercial College	0.6897	1	0.43567
Apprenticeship in other industries than Tourism	0.8138	5	0.35993
Technical College	1.0034	20	0.42506
Apprenticeship in Tourism	0.7615	12	0.49201
Part time courses	0.8227	49	0.40763
Academic Tourism Course	0.9690	10	0.45574
University (Master/Bachelor)	1.2414	7	0.56257
	Spearman Rho		−0.055
	Significance (2 tail)		0.580
	N		104

TABLE 9. Correlation Between Age of the Hotel Entrepreneur/Manager and Innovation Degree

	Innovation Degree (Mean)	N	Standard Deviation
21-30	0.9655	7	0.36656
31-40	0.8513	45	0.39630
41-50	0.9103	30	0.45761
51-60	0.9452	17	0.56910
Over 60	0.8414	5	0.42415
	Spearman Rho		−0.011
	Significance (2-tail)		0.911
	N		104

Hypothesis 6: The higher the quality level of the hotel the more innovative the hotel. The correlation coefficient is significant and thus, we can assume a positive correlation between the quality of the hotel (measured as degree of Austria's national "star" classification of hotels) and the degree of innovation. Hypothesis 6 can be confirmed.

TABLE 10. Correlation Between Proportion of Loyal Customers and Innovation Degree

Percentage of loyal customers	Innovation Degree (Mean)	N	Standard Deviation
0-20%	0.8966	7	0.49412
21-40%	0.9023	30	0.49310
41-60%	0.8977	29	0.43720
61-80%	0.8811	29	0.41834
Over 80%	0.9724	5	0.39946
	Spearman Rho		0.036
	Significance (2-tail)		0.722
	N		100

Hypothesis 7: A positive significant relationship exists between the target segment and the degree of innovation. Additionally, entrepreneurs were asked about their strategies to target special segments of customers, such as families/kids, seniors, wellness tourists, active tourists, and the youth tourists. Multiple answers were possible. Crossing this information with the innovation degree the following results arise.

The t-tests show significant differences for hotels focusing on family/kids or wellness tourists. Thus, hotels which concentrate on one of this target groups show a higher degree of innovation. Obviously, entrepreneurs who offer differentiated products and services have a clearer picture about their target segments' needs and thus are more innovative in creating new customer values. It can be assumed that Austrian hotel entrepreneurs are well informed about these customer segments because both the family segment as well as (Alpine) wellness is high on the agenda of the Austrian Tourism Board who provide tourism entrepreneurs with up-to-date information and trends (Steinhauser et al., 2005).

CONCLUSION

It is obvious that until today, there are still no sufficient empirical research results available. Thus, this pilot project was a first step towards trying to measure innovation in tourism firms. According to the literature the empirical results underline the following types of innovation

TABLE 11. Correlation Between Quality of Hotels and Innovation Degree

Hotel	Innovation Degree (Mean)	N	Standard Deviaton
2 stars	0.3966	4	0.05973
3 stars	0.6594	33	0.23887
4 stars	1.0739	49	0.41169
5 stars	1.5134	9	0.27231
	Spearman Rho		0.703**
	Significance (2-tail)		0.000
	N		95

** The correlation is significant on 0.01 (two-side).

TABLE 12. Correlation Between Special Target Groups and Innovation Degree

Target Group	N	Innovation Degree (Mean)	Levene Test	T-Test
Family/Kids				
Yes	66	2.3939	0.853	0.013
No	35	1.9429		0.019
Youth tourists				
Yes	48	0.7083	0.821	0.884
No	54	0.6852		0.884
Active tourists				
Yes	91	0.7582	0.836	0.884
No	10	0.7000		0.884
Seniors				
Yes	64	0.7813	0.644	0.843
No	37	0.6486		0.856
Wellness-tourists				
Yes	43	1.5581		0.000
No	59	0.3305	0.000	0.000

and innovation activities in tourism organisations (Johannessen et al., 2001; Tidd et al., 2003; Chapman et al., 2002). First, the innovation degree in tourism organisations seems to be low or, to put it in other words, the majority of innovation activities are only minor cosmetic changes not even incremental innovations. Second, referring to the subject of innovation, the data shows that the innovation is most often either new for a target group of customers or for the organisation but neither for the market nor for the hotel industry. Third, process innovations are the dominant type of innovation activities and product innovations can hardly be found.

Furthermore, the results have shown that especially market differentiators pursuit innovation activities. Thus, entrepreneurs who focus on clearly defined target markets seem to be more innovative and in the long run more successful. Recently, this aspect was discussed in detail as "the way out of the middle" in terms of undifferentiated services or products or quality in general (Weiermair and Kronenberg, 2004). In addition, it could be interesting to undertake more research regarding the question whether these innovative entrepreneurs invest more in their software capabilities too. On the other hand a high and stable percentage of loyal conservative customers seem to hinder innovation activities and thus Porters' argument (1990) may be supported: innovative and thus flexible customers force markets and entrepreneurs to be innovative and creative. The focus on the German market segment in the Austrian alpine winter tourism led to a slow adoption processes starting in the 90s in terms of innovation. The literature often reports competition to be the second important factor influencing innovation and it seems as neither too much nor too little competition is a driving force for innovation activities (Keller, 2002; Peters and Weiermair, 2002). Since the beginning of the nineties the Alpine tourism market was characterized as a buyer market and thus competition and innovation activities were rather low.

The demographic variable age seems to have no significant influence on the degree of innovation. It can be assumed that besides age and socialisation, the context of entrepreneurial decision making and the psychographics of entrepreneurs have a strong influence on the degree of innovation in tourism. Interestingly enough, education seems to have no influence on the degree of innovation. However, the average professionalism degree of entrepreneurs in alpine tourism is low all over the industry. In addition, the content of existent tourism curricula has not been analysed and it remains unclear to which extent innovation management plays a dominant role in Austria's educational systems. It seems that experience in the tourism business is still a more important determinant for innovation than entrepreneurial education. But the most important determinant may still be the risk aversion of entrepreneurs. Thus, once more the claim for Schumpeterian entrepreneurs in tourism arises (Weiermair, 2001).

It is necessary to state some limitations of the study. On the one hand some functional areas display low rates of respondents, which may be due to the open structured interviews. On the other hand one main focus of this pilot project was the derivation of innovation areas which are important in the eyes of small business owners and thus a qualitative design seemed to be most appropriate. The survey highlights that from entrepreneurs' view only incremental service and product improvements, such as the extension of the menu, are already interpreted as innovations. Additionally, small and medium sized entrepreneurs intuitively associate hardware instead of software improvements with innovations, such as the renovation of the hotel building or the rooms. However, this is surprising as SMEs suffer from lacking economies of scale. As a consequence, SMEs should focus on the enhancement of software skills and individual tailor-made services. As all interviews have been carried out in the alpine area of Tyrol, the question about regional influences such as political or socio-economic factors arises. Therefore, it may be of interest for further research to comprehensively analyze innovations along the tourism value chain in diversified others than Alpine tourism destinations (e.g., adventure tourism, city tourism). It may be also fruitful to use the results of this pilot study to design quantitative questionnaires, in particular to structure standardized questions according to the innovation activities reported in this study. In addition, another recommendation addresses the need to assess the customers' view of innovation activities. This could be of benefit for future innovation research in tourism as gaps between entrepreneurs' and customers' perception of innovations can be analysed in a next step. Nevertheless, the study was able to empirically validate a low degree of innovation in Alpine tourism destinations as theoretically assumed by a number of former research studies (Keller, 2004; Peters and Weiermair, 2002; Weiermair, 2003).

NOTE

1. We gratefully acknowledge the Austrian National Bank funding the project (no. 10078)

REFERENCES

Abernathy, W., and K. Clark (1985). Innovation: Mapping the Winds of Creative Destruction. *Research Policy 13*(1), pp. 3-22.
Afuah, A. (2003). *Innovation Management: Strategies, Implementation and Profit.* New York: Oxford University Press.

Amt der Tiroler Landesregierung (2004). *Tourismusstatistik.* Innsbruck: Tiroler Landesregierung.

Avermaete, T. J., Viene, E.J. Morgan, and Crawford, N. (2003). Determinants of innovation in small food firms. *European Journal of Innovation Management 6*(1), pp. 8-17.

Bieger, T. (2001). *Management von Destinationen.* München: Oldenbourg.

Bieger, Th., and Ch. Laesser (2003). Tourismustrends-Eine aktuelle Bestandsaufnahme. In Bieger, T., Ch. Laesser (eds.), *Jahrbuch 2002/2003* (pp. 13-37), Institut für öffentliche Dienstleistungen und Tourismus, Universität St. Gallen: St. Gallen.

Bieger, T., and G. Lehar (1998). Touristische Weiterbildung im Spannungsfeld von unterschiedlichen politischen und wirtschaftlichen Interessenslagen und Weiterbildungsangeboten am Beispiel Österreich und der Schweiz. In Weiermair, K. and M. Fuchs (eds.), *Rettoursim II: Strategiekonferenz* (pp. 113-148), Innsbruck: Studia.

Chapman, R. L., S. Soosay, and J. Kandampully (2002). Innovation in logistic Services and the New Business Model: A conceptual Framework. *Managing Service Quality 12*(6), pp. 358-371.

Coombs, R., and I. Miles (2000). Innovation, Measurement and Services: The new Problematique. In Metcalfe, J. S. and I. Miles (eds.), *Innovation Systems in the Service Economy* (pp. 85-103), Boston, Mass. et al.: Kluwer Academic Publ.

Drucker, P. F. (1985). *Innovation and Entrepreneurship: Practices and Principles.* New York: The Free Press.

Dunning, J. H. (1988). *Explaining International Production.* London: Unwin.

Foot, D. (2002). Leisure Futures: A Change in Demography? In Weiermair, K./ Mathies, C. (Eds.) *The Tourism and Leisure Industry: Shaping the Future* (pp. 21- 34), Haworth Press: New York et al.

Gallouj, F. (1998). Innovating in Reverse: Services and the Reverse Product Cycle. *European Journal of Innovation Management 1*(3), pp. 123-138.

Gomez, P., and G. Probst (1995). *Die Praxis des ganzheitlichen Problemlösens.* Bern et al.: Haupt.

Hauschildt, J., and T. Schlaak (2001). Zur Messung des Innovationsgrades neuartiger Produkte. *Zeitschrift für Betriebswirtschaft 71*(2), pp. 161-182.

Herstatt, C., C. Lüthje and C. Leitl (2001). Wie fortschrittliche Kunden zu Innovationen stimulieren. *Harvard Business Manager 24*(1), pp. 60-78.

Hjalager, A.-M. (2002). Repairing Innovation Defectiveness in Tourism. *Tourism Management 23*(4), pp. 465-474.

Hollenstein, H. (2001). *Innovation Modes in the Swiss Service Sector.* Wien: WIFO Working Papers, Nr. 156.

Johannessen, J.-A., B. Olsen and G.T. Lumpkin (2001). Innovation as newness: what is new, how new, and new to whom? *European Journal of Innovation Management 4*(1), pp. 20-30.

Kandampully, J. (2002). Innovation as the Core Competency of a Service Organisation: The Role of Technology, Knowledge and Networks. *European Journal of Innovation Management 5*(1), pp 18-26.

Keller, P. (2004). Innovationen und Tourismus. In Weiermair, K., M. Peters, H. Pechlaner, M. Kaiser, (eds.), *Unternehmertum im Tourismus: Führen mit Erneuerungen* (pp. 203-216), Berlin: Erich Schmidt.

Kelly, D., and C. Storey (2000). New service development: imitation strategies. *International Journal of Service Industry Management 11*(1), pp. 55-64.

King, W. R. (2000). Measuring Police Innovation: Issues and Measurement Policing. *International Journal of Police Strategies and Management* 23(3), pp. 303-317.

Metcalfe, J. S., and I. Miles (2000). *Innovation Systems in the Service Economy*. Boston: Kluwer.

Opaschowski, H. W. (2000). *Kathedralen des 21. Jahrhunderts*. Hamburg: B.A.T Forschungsinstitut.

Peters, M., and K. Weiermair (2002). Innovationen und Innovationsverhalten im Tourismus. In Bieger, T. and Ch. Laesser (eds.), *Schweizer Jahrbuch für Tourismus 2001/2002* (pp. 157-178), St. Gallen.

Pikkemaat, B. (2005). Zur Empirischen Erforschung von Innovationen im Tourismus. In P. Tschurtschenthaler, H. Pechlaner, M. Peters, B. Pikkemaat and M. Fuchs (eds.), *Erfolg durch Innovation* (pp. 87-102), Wiesbaden: Gabler.

Pikkemaat, B., and K. Weiermair (2004). Zur Problematik der Messung von Innovationen bei komplexen, vernetzten Dienstleistungen-dargestellt am Beispiel der touristischen Dienstleistung. In Bruhn, M. and B. Stauss (eds.), *Dienstleistungsinnovationen-Forum Dienstleistungsmanagement* (pp. 359-379), Wiesbaden: Gabler.

Pine, J. B., and J. H. Gilmore (1999). *The Experience Economy*. Boston, Mass.: Harvard Business School Press.

Poon, A. (1993). *Tourism, Technology and Competitive Strategies*. Wallingford: CAB International.

Preissl, B. (2000). Service Innovation: What makes it different? Empirical Evidence from Germany. In Metcalfe, J. S., I. Miles (eds.), *Innovation Systems in the Service Economy* (pp. 125-148), Boston, Mass.: Kluwer.

Steinhauser, C., B. Theiner, B., and B. Jochum (2005). Schnittstelle Wissenschaft und Praxis: Innovative Produktentwicklung im Tourismus, illustriert am Beispiel "Alpine Wellness." In Pechlaner, H., P. Tschurtschenthaler, M. Peters, B. Pikkemaat and M. Fuchs (eds.), *Erfolg durch Innovation-Perspektiven für den Tourismus und Dienstleistungssektor* (pp. 363-381), Wiesbaden: Gabler.

Tidd, J., J. Bessant, and K. Pavitt (2003). *Managing Innovation: Integrating Technological, Market and Organizational Change*. Chichester et al: Wiley.

Tschurtschenthaler, P. (1998). Humankapitalentwicklung als tourismuspolitisches Instrument zur Bewältigung der Tourismuskrise. In Weiermair, K. and M. Fuchs (eds.), *Zukunftsentwicklung für eine optimale Humankapitalentwicklung/-verwertung in der Tourismuswirtschaft* (pp. 16-39), Innsbruck: Institut für Tourismus und Dienstleistungswirtschaft, Universität Innsbruck.

Volo, S. (2004). Foundation for an innovation indicator for tourism. In Keller, P. and Th. Bieger (eds.), *The Future of Small and Medium Sized Enterprises in Tourism* (pp. 361-376), St. Gallen: AIEST.

Weiermair, K. (2000). Know-how and qualification gaps in the tourism industry: the case of alpine tourism in Austria. *The Tourist Review* 2(1), pp. 45-53.

Weiermair, K. (2001). Von der Dienstleistungsökonomie zur Erlebnisökonomie. In Hinterhuber, H. H., H. Pechlaner and K. Matzler (eds.), *IndustrieErlebnisWelten* (pp. 35-48), Berlin: Erich Schmidt.

Weiermair, K. (2003). *Product improvement or innovation: what is the key to success in tourism?*: OECD Conference in Lugano, Switzerland.

Weiermair, K. (2004). Design und Qualität im Tourismus. In Klaus, W./Pikkemaat, B. (eds.), *Qualitätszeichen im Tourismus* (pp. 171-180), Berlin: Erich Schmidt Verlag.

Weiermair, K., and Ch. Kronenberg (2004). Stuck in the middle: Strategies for improving the market position of SMEs in tourism. *The Poznan University of Economics Review 4*(1), pp.103-112.

Weiermair, K., and M. Peters (2002). Innovation Behaviour in Hospitality and Tourism: Problems and Prospects. *Tourism in Asia: Development, Marketing and Sustainability. Fifth Biennial Conference*Hong Kong, Hong Kong Polytechnic University.

Wöhler, K. (2005). Der Kunde als Innovationsquelle. In H. Pechlaner, Tschurtschenthaler, M. Peters, B. Pikkemaat and M. Fuchs (eds.), *Erfolg durch Innovation* (pp. 243-259), Wiesbaden: Gabler.

Wolf, M. J. (1999). *The Entertainment Economy: How mega-media forces are transforming our lives*. New York: Times Books.

Zeithaml, V. A. (1991). How Consumer Evaluation Processes differ between Goods and Services. In Lovelock, C. H. (ed.), *Services Marketing* (pp. 39-47), New Jersey: Prentice Hall.

An Investigation of the Factors Affecting Innovation Performance in Chain and Independent Hotels

Michael Ottenbacher
Vivienne Shaw
Andrew Lockwood

SUMMARY. The failure rate of new service projects is high, because the knowledge about how innovations should be developed is limited. In the last decade, several studies have investigated the success factors associated with service innovations (e.g., Atuahene-Gima, 1996; de Brentani, 2001; Storey and Easingwood, 1998). However, no research in new service development (NSD) has addressed the question of whether chain affiliated and independently operated service firms have different approaches for developing successful innovations. The majority of past new service development (NSD) success studies have concentrated on

---

Michael Ottenbacher is Assistant Professor, School of Hospitality and Tourism Management, University of Guelph, Guelph, Ontario, N1G 2W1, Canada (E-mail: mottenba@uoguelph.ca).

Vivienne Shaw is Director of Topajka Shaw Consulting Limited, 10 Kiwi Burn Place, RD1 Te Anau, New Zealand (E-mail: viv.shaw@ihug.co.nz).

Andrew Lockwood is Deputy Head of School and Forte Professor of Hospitality Management, University of Surrey, School of Management, Guildford, GU2 7XH, United Kingdom (E-mail: a.lockwood@surrey.ac).

[Haworth co-indexing entry note]: "An Investigation of the Factors Affecting Innovation Performance in Chain and Independent Hotels." Ottenbacher, Michael, Vivienne Shaw, and Andrew Lockwood. Co-published simultaneously in *Journal of Quality Assurance in Hospitality & Tourism* (The Haworth Hospitality Press, an imprint of The Haworth Press, Inc.) Vol. 6, No. 3/4, 2005, pp. 113-128; and: *Innovation in Hospitality and Tourism* (ed: Mike Peters, and Birgit Pikkemaat) The Haworth Hospitality Press, an imprint of The Haworth Press, Inc., 2005, pp. 113-128. Single or multiple copies of this article are available for a fee from The Haworth Document Delivery Service [1-800-HAWORTH, 9:00 a.m. - 5:00 p.m. (EST). E-mail address: docdelivery@haworthpress.com].

Available online at http://www.haworthpress.com/web/JQAHT
© 2005 by The Haworth Press, Inc. All rights reserved.
doi:10.1300/J162v06n03_07

the financial service sector, which is generally represented by large corporate organizations. The findings of this study indicate that the factors which impact on the performance of NSD depend on the organizational relationship of hotels-chain affiliation or independent operation. The study's results suggest that market attractiveness, process management, market responsiveness and empowerment predict NSD success within chain affiliated hotels. While empowerment and market attractiveness are also related to NSD success in independent hotels, this is also linked to effective marketing communication, employee commitment, behaviour based evaluation, training of employees and marketing synergy. *[Article copies available for a fee from The Haworth Document Delivery Service: 1-800-HAWORTH. E-mail address: <docdelivery@haworthpress.com> Website: <http://www.HaworthPress.com> © 2005 by The Haworth Press, Inc. All rights reserved.]*

KEYWORDS. Innovation, new service development (NSD), new product development (NPD), chain and independent hotels

INTRODUCTION

Every two years the Marketing Science Institute updates research priorities for marketing, which leading academics and managers see as important for improving business practice through academic research. The latest top tier priority topics consist of five issues, and one of them relates to innovation activities for new services and products (Marketing Science Institute, 2004). The top priorities were selected because of the importance and relevance of a topic, as well as their researchability and potential to have an impact in the field (Marketing Science Institute, 2004).

In the turbulent hospitality industry, chains and independent enterprises alike are continuously forced to look for ways of improving quality and reputation, cutting costs, and increasing sales and profits. Adding to these challenges, and often precipitating them, is fierce competition among local and international hospitality organizations, technological innovations and changes in customer needs. One way for hospitality organizations to achieve their objectives is through innovation, i.e., the ability to develop and launch new and successful service offers. New service products represent an important resource for survival and growth (de Brentani and Cooper, 1992), hence innovations has become a strategic weapon for both successful chains and independent hospitality enterprises alike.

Despite the crucial importance of being innovative and developing new services, the knowledge about how to achieve success is limited (Johne and Storey, 1998). As a result, managers often rely on gut-feeling, speculation, and their own limited experience about the keys to innovation success. Alas, the failure rate for new services remains high. On average, four out of ten new services fail in the market place (Griffin, 1997). Thus, our understanding of the factors that impact innovation performance has to increase if service firms are to significantly improve their success rate.

It is rather surprising that although innovation in services is an important aspect of hospitality management, intuitively and theoretically, the authors found little published research. For example, Jones (1996) discussed case studies in regard to the innovation process of hospitality organizations. Enz and Siguaw's (2003) study showed that innovations were significantly affected by outstanding hospitality individuals, also called "best practice champions." Such personnel were shown to have leadership qualities in general, problem-solving skills as well as supporting and leading the project.

In the hospitality sector, there has been substantial growth and transformation. In the last two decades, it seems that new hospitality chain operations have mastered the challenging market conditions (Kotler et al., 2002). New chain affiliated hospitality operations have flourished all around the world and continue to build on their position as market leaders in the hospitality sector. What factors influence the innovation success of corporate hospitality organizations? Is it their financial strength, their powerful and sophisticated marketing systems or do they have a more structured approach to innovation? Compared to chain operations, independent hospitality firms are smaller, often have a less hierarchical system, resulting in a less structured approach to innovation. This, however, means that independent firms can be more adaptable to changing conditions, giving them the flexibility to respond more quickly to customer needs and problems (Rueckert et al., 1985). In general, independent hotels are smaller, family owned operations, while chain hotels are larger organizations. Storey (1994) suggests that there are several key differences between small and large firms. For example, smaller firms are likely to face greater uncertainty in terms of the market but will have more internal consistency in their actions and motivations. On the other hand, in larger companies the emphasis on control is vital. Storey (1994) further argues that small and large firms have different approaches to innovation activities. Although small operations make very low investments in research, they are more likely to serve niche markets and are better placed to respond to changing customer needs than the large corporate hospitality firms. The purpose of this article is, therefore, to report on a survey of hotel managers' perceptions of what factors contribute to the success of innovations in corporate versus independent hotels.

What is an innovation?

Schumpeter (1947) was one of the first to develop a theory about innovation. He defines innovations as "new ways of doing things, or [as] better, unique combinations of the factors of production," and identifies them as the core of an entrepreneur's work (McGuire, 1996, p. 2). According to Drucker (1985), innovation should be viewed and implemented as an opportunity, which results in the creation of a new, or a change to a different product or service. An innovation can be an idea, practice, process or product perceived as new by an individual (Rogers, 1983) and that transforms a new problem-solving idea into an application (Kanter, 1983). Following suggestions by Burgelman and Maidique (1996, p. 2) "innovations are the outcome of the innovation process, which can be defined as the combined activities leading to new, marketable products and services and/or new production and delivery systems." New hospitality service developments range from true innovations, which are totally new-to-the-world services with an entirely new market, through to fairly minor modifications of existing services. In this study, the whole range of hospitality innovations has been included, ranging from new-to-the-world innovations through incremental improvements to simple repositioning.

DEVELOPMENT OF SUCCESSFUL INNOVATIONS

When analyzing the development of new service projects in the financial service sector, we learn that success or failure is not the result of managing one or two activities very well. Instead, it is the result of a more comprehensive approach. Success is more likely to be achieved if one manages a large number of aspects competently, and in a balanced manner (Johne and Storey, 1998). The critical dimensions that influence service innovation performance have been separated into four clusters of concerns: (1) service or product related, (2) market-related,

(3) process-related, and (4) organizational-related clusters of items (de Brentani, 2001).

In relation to product-related determinants the relative advantage of a product or service has been recognized as important source of success in new product and service development literatures (Cooper et al., 1994, Cooper and Kleinschmidt, 1987). In addition to product features, tangible quality (de Brentani, 1991), functional quality (Storey and Easigwood, 1998) and, to a lesser extent, innovative technology (Cooper et al., 1994), have also been found to improve the performance of service innovations.

In relation to the market determinants of service innovation success, market synergy (Cooper and de Brentani, 1991) and market attractiveness (de Brentani and Ragot, 1996) are particularly important influences. In terms of process-related determinants, the implementation of a proficient and market-oriented new product development process including pre-launch activities (Atuahene-Gima, 1996), employee involvement in the process (de Brentani, 1991), launch preparation (Cooper and de Brentani, 1991), supporting the new project with excellent communication (Edgett, 1994) and effective process management during the process (de Brentani and Ragot, 1996) have been shown to be important. Finally, organizational-related determinants include synergies between the new service and the marketing, managerial and financial resources (de Brentani, 1991). The reputation of service firms has also been linked to NSD success (Storey and Easingwood, 1998).

Interviews with hospitality managers indicate that the most critical aspect of innovation in the hospitality sector are their employees (Ottenbacher and Shaw, 2002). Hotels often have the same "hardware" so that employees are the ultimate moderators for differentiating services. This means that when assessing the performance of new services, it is essential to include criteria covering employee management. The relevance of employees in service innovation efforts has been alluded to in previous studies (de Brentani, 1991; Storey and Easingwood, 1998), but not with the intensity they deserve for such a highly personalized service offering as hospitality. Korczynski (2002) argues that service management should leave behind the old production line approach and concentrate on the modern application of systematic human resource management. Such a modern application involves careful selection of employees, employee training, empowerment, low formalization, behavior-based evaluation and a strategic approach to human resource management.

The evaluation of new services and products is most frequently based on financial measures of performance (Montoya-Weiss and Calantone, 1994). Nevertheless, using only financial measures is too limited, because it neglects several aspects of benefit to the company. The findings of success studies in innovation have shown that success on one specific dimension of performance does not necessarily mean success on the other performance dimension (de Brentani, 1991). This study, therefore, measures NSD performance along 12 dimensions: total sales, market share, profitability, improved loyalty, improved image, enhanced profitability and sales of other hotel services, new markets opened up, new customers attracted, cost efficiencies, customer satisfaction, positive employee feedback and competencies of employees.

RESEARCH METHODOLOGY

The objective of this research was to compare chain and independent innovations in order to discover what factors impact performance for each type of project. The study used the methodology developed by Cooper (1994) and validated by several innovation researchers doing similar studies (de Brentan, 1991; Storey and Easigwood, 1998), which compares large numbers of actual innovation projects so that the factors which appear to be linked to performance can be identified. The data collection involved a mail survey of the hotel sector in Germany. This was based on a random sample drawn from a list of hotels operating in Germany traced through the "Hotel Guide" from the German Hotel and Restaurant Association. The appropriateness of the questionnaire was confirmed through the evaluation of academics knowledgeable about innovation and pretests with hospitality managers in Germany.

Like other success studies in service innovation (Cooper et al., 1994, de Brentani, 1991), hotels were contacted by telephone to identify potential projects for study and the person best able to respond to the questions. The criterion for inclusion in the study was that the organization had developed new hospitality services over the past three years. Although the research method relies on the knowledge and memory of single respondents, because the projects were relatively recent (last 3 years) and because the managers had been carefully selected (only those with and intimate knowledge of and involvement in the projects), on average, the results should be valid.

The questionnaires that were sent out to hospitality managers in Germany sought information on the following issues: (a) the factors influencing success, (b) the performance of new innovations and (c) background information on the respondents and their hospitality organizations (including whether they are part of a hotel chain or an independent operation). 480 questionnaires were sent out to hospitality managers in Germany. In total, completed questionnaires were received for 180 new hospitality services. This represents a response rate of 37.5%, where 73 were part of a hotel chain and 107 were independent hotels.

Exploratory factor analysis (principal component) was used to simplify the complex sets of data and define the underlying structure. From a total of 105 items, the factor analysis produced 23 dimensions with Cronbach alphas ranging from .59 to .88. Both the Kaiser-Meyer-Olkin (KMO) and the significance of the Bartlett test suggested a highly stable instrument design. The projects were then grouped according to their hotel affiliation-chain or independent. Consequently, two sub samples comprising 73 chain and 107 independent innovation projects were identified. Regression analysis is very useful for making predictions of likely values of the dependent variable and to test whether a specific variable (or set of variables) is important in predicting a dependent variable (Hair et al., 1998). The focus of this study was to investigate the linkages between the success factors and innovation performance. Separate regression analyses were used to highlight the differences between independent hotels and chain affiliated hotels. The two stepwise multiple regression analyses were conducted with the success factors as the independent variable and a summed performance dimension as the dependent variable. This dependent variable consisted of twelve performance measures. These measures were the result of the literature review into performance measures as well as preliminary interviews for the present study. Since these items cover a range of domains (including, financial success, customer satisfaction, employee satisfaction), all indicative of innovation success, the values from the five-point Likert scales have been summed to form one overall dependent variable used in the regression analysis. The advantage of this process is that, through summation, we reduce the statistical error attached to individual items, as well as reducing the variety of foci of how success is measured amongst the sample of managers. The dependent variable thus, measures innovation success per se rather than any distinct aspect of it. The survey used five-point, Likert-type scales measuring levels of agreement with given statements.

FINDINGS

The results of our study reveal that innovation success for chain hospitality services depends on four key factors, while innovation success for independent hospitality services relates to seven key factors. Table 1 shows the results of the two regression analyses that identified the 11 factors, two of them overlapping, which we discuss in the following paragraphs.

Chain Affiliated Hotel Innovation Success

There are four factors that influence the performance of chain affiliated hospitality innovations: *Market attractiveness, NSD process management, market responsiveness and empowerment.*

Market attractiveness: Managers perceive that both the potential and the attractiveness of the target market are crucial parameters for innovation success. The potential relates to both the current and the future size of the market. The current market needs to be large enough to promise a worthwhile return. Yet, this is not the only criterion, as the potential in the future needs to be carefully assessed as well. As hospitality firms often have to make significant financial investments, only those innovations which release an almost immediate ROI as well as promising a long-term volume potential for the new service project, are perceived as successful by managers of chain hotels. This suggests that successful chain hospitality organizations only target innovations that will have a large potential, possibly to satisfy the financial requirements set by the head office.

NSD process management: The results further suggest that successful chain hospitality innovation projects implement a formal and well-planned development process. Successful innovations have significantly higher levels of employee training and employee involvement in the launch activities. Furthermore, successful hospitality chain innovations test their project before they launch it on the marketplace. In addition, successful projects are guided by a clear and well communicated innovation strategy and vision and supported by effective internal marketing to employees which causes higher levels of employee commitment and motivation.

Market responsiveness: Market responsiveness relates to the fit between the new service and the demands of the market. The measurement scale underlying this factor suggests that successful hospitality chain innovations have a higher level of market responsiveness. Such

TABLE 1. Results of Regression Analyses (Standardized Regression Co-Efficients)

Factors of NSD Resulting from the Factor Analysis	Chain Hotels		Independent Hotels	
	Beta	*p*-value	Beta	*p*-value
SERVICE PRODUCT				
Tangible quality	-	-	-	-
Service advantage	-	-	-	-
Consistency service delivery	-	-	-	-
Innovative technology	-	-	-	-
MARKET				
Market responsiveness	.24	.013	-	-
Market attractiveness	.41	.000	.23	.002
Price competition	-	-	-	-
Competitive offerings	-	-	-	-
PROCESS				
Effective marketing communication	-	-	.24	.001
Raise awareness	-	-	-	-
Employee involvement in process	-	-	-	-
NSD pre-launch activities	-	-	-	-
Employee commitment	-	-	.22	.003
NSD process management	.28	.004	-	-
ORGANIZATIONAL				
SHRM	-	-		
Behavior based evaluation	-	-	.24	.002
Training of employees	-	-	.27	.000
Empowerment	.21	.026	.17	.015
Management synergy	-	-	-	-
Reputation	-	-	-	-
Selective staffing	-	-	-	-
Formalization	-	-	-	-
Marketing synergy	-	-	.22	.003
Sample Size	73		107	
No. of factors in equation	4/23		7/23	
F-value (equation)	12.4		17.5	
Adjusted R^2	.38		.52	

innovations are based on active market research and respond to actual as well as anticipated customer demand. This highlights that successful innovations require close customer contact, detailed consumer research and comprehensive understanding to distinguish between what might be a fad, fashion, or indeed, a trend. Effective customer responsiveness thus relies on the ability to comprehend the market, and on competently trained and flexible staff to respond to its challenges. The ability to respond thus underpins market selection.

Empowerment: Empowerment refers to the process by which managers give employees the autonomy to exercise control over job-related situations and decisions. Successful new chain hotel services occur at establishments where managers are more likely to allow employees to use their discretion and own judgment in solving problems. Management is more likely to transfer responsibilities, provide opportunities for personal initiatives and to demonstrate trust in their employees. Empowerment of employees in the service industry is not only sensible but almost unavoidable. Employees need flexibility to adapt their behaviors to the demands of each service encounter, thereby meeting customer needs more effectively (Hartline et al., 2000). Bowen and Lawler (1992) suggest that empowerment is recommended when service delivery involves managing a relationship as opposed to simply performing a transaction. Reasons for establishing a relationship with customers are to increase loyalty and obtain ideas about improving the service delivery system, or to gain new ideas for new services (Chebat and Kollias, 2000).

Independent Hotel Innovation Success

In addition to the two overlapping factors of *market attractiveness* and *empowerment*, five further aspects are key success factors for independent hotel innovations: *Training of employees, behavior based evaluation, effective marketing communication, marketing synergy* and *employee commitment.*

Training of employees: The first key factor for independent hospitality innovation includes planned programs to improve the performance of individuals and/or groups of employees. This in turn, implies changes in employees' knowledge, skills, attitudes and/or social behavior (Cascio, 1989). Training of employees is critical in order to enhance front-line expertise (de Brentani and Cooper, 1992), as well as crucial in the launch preparation stage of the innovation process (Edgett, 1994).

Behavior-based evaluation: Successful new independent hospitality projects evaluate front-line employee performance in relation to employees providing courteous service, having the ability to resolve customer complaints and problems, meeting customer needs and being committed to the operation and to the customers. In other words, management evaluates staff's friendliness and commitment rather than specific work-related outcomes (e.g., quota) (Hartline et al., 2000), as customers would do (Parasuraman et al., 1991). Furthermore, behavior-based evaluation encourages employee performance that is consistent with customer expectation of service quality and is particularly suited to employees with customer contact (Chebat and Kollias, 2000).

Effective marketing: Effective marketing communication comprises effective and well targeted advertising/promotion campaigns, informing journalists, guides and magazines about the new service and achieving a distinct position with the new service. This means that the marketing aspects of the launch were better targeted-at the right customer. Better communication should result in more effective advertising and promotion than competitors, create a brand image and be consistent with the marketing strategy. It is not sufficient simply to create an innovation and announce it exists because even the best products and services "don't sell themselves."

Marketing synergy: A further key aspect for successful new independent hospitality services points to the fit between the innovation, the marketing mix, and the capabilities of the firm. A successful innovation fits into both the existing skills as well as the product and service mix offered by the hotel. In other words, it is appropriately priced, advertised and delivered. Managers perceive the gestalt of the service in its totality rather than merely by concentrating on perfecting the technical aspects of the service. Although there can be no doubt about the need for perfection, synergy refers to the fit, position and level of harmony in the product portfolio.

Employee commitment: While training and empowerment are important aspects of successful innovations, managers expressly distinguish between these facilitating parameters and the desired outcomes in staff's attitudes, particularly during the launch. Managers should not only effectively train their employees involved in the service, but employees also need to understand and support the service so that they are fully committed to it. Internal marketing is critical at this stage because it supports the motivation and commitment of employees towards the project. Personal engagement and "taking ownership" are pre-requisites for bringing new services to success. They help overcome initial difficulties and prevent staff from blaming others for failure, as any innovation requires a change from routine.

CONCLUSIONS AND LIMITATIONS

This research focused on identifying the characteristics that determine the success of chain affiliated versus independent hospitality innovations. In regard to the chain affiliated innovation, market attractiveness, market responsiveness, process management and empowerment are related to success and failure. On the other hand, the results further show that in addition to market attractiveness and empowerment, effective marketing communication, employee commitment, behavior based evaluation and marketing synergy are also critical for independent hospitality innovation success.

Overall, the findings indicate that of the four key groups of determinants of new service performance, the market, process and organizational dimensions are particularly critical. On the service product dimension, no factor significantly impacts hospitality innovation success. This non-significance does not mean that the service product related aspects are not important for hospitality innovations but, for example, the consistency of service delivery might be a basic requirement of any hospitality service and therefore expected under all circumstances. Confirmation of this assumption would require further investigation.

Looking at the success factors found in previous service innovation studies, several have been confirmed, which are: market attractiveness, market responsiveness, effective marketing communication, employee commitment and marketing synergy. On the other hand, in the hotel sector several success factors have not been confirmed, such as service advantage and pre-launch activities. The high degree of intangibility of many hospitality services means that its attributes can be easily copied, and therefore, any service advantage that is derived from them is short lived and difficult to sustain. The limited impact of pre-launch activities could be explained that most hotel innovations are improvements of existing services and involve smaller financial budgets compared to the financial innovations. Therefore, market studies and a competitive analysis are less critical and a less formal process saves valuable time and resources.

However, the main focus of the study was to investigate the influence of success factors on innovation performance and hence whether chain affiliated and independently operated hospitality firms should have different strategic approaches for developing successful innovations. The results show that although chain and independent innovations have some common success characteristics, with two factors overlapping; hotel chains and independent hotels should have different strategies if they would like to achieve success with their innovation projects. Chain innovation relates to only four, while independent hotel innovation success is linked to seven key factors. This might be explained that hotel chains are more experienced and more professional in developing innovations, so only a few factors are critical. On the other hand, independent hotel success might be related to more factors because of their need for flexibility and their focus on niche markets.

Further interesting insight into hospitality innovation success can be gained by focusing on the actual differences between independent and chain projects and speculating on why they exist. The survey results indicated that chains have a more structured approach towards innovation activities. This could be linked to the fact that new services are likely to be launched across the chain and therefore formal planning and evaluation is needed for each project. Chains might also have the necessary knowledge and resources to do market research so that their innovations are responsive to market needs and demands. On the other hand, independent operations might not see the necessity to invest in market research to know how to respond to changes in the market or focus on satisfying unmet customer needs or not have the financial resources available. They might believe that their contact with current customers offers them sufficient insight into future hospitality customer needs. This approach might provide some interesting insights but potentially does not provide adequate information, especially about current non-customers spending their money at competitors.

Independent hospitality innovations success is strongly related to effective marketing communication. Independent hotels have to work harder to inform their potential customers about their innovations. They often don't have the infrastructure of a marketing and public relation department and don't budget at all or only small amounts for a marketing campaign. Although even the best innovations don't sell themselves, hospitality firms often do not adequately resource and have effective marketing communication plans when launching new projects. However, successful independent hospitality innovations do need the support of effective marketing communication in order to be a success.

Training of employees is also more critical for independent innovations success. Chain hotels have in general more professional training structures and also invest more money in training. It seems chain hotels have realized that employee training is important when developing innovations in order to enhance front-line expertise. Enz and Siguaw (2000) argue that employee training has become an increasingly critical aspect in the hotel sector, in order to increase service quality, reduce labor costs and increase productivity. Thus, independent innovations need the support of effective training programs. Small, independent hotels may also have stronger employee loyalty by giving employees the feeling that they are part of the larger family which is why we may see employee commitment during the development process and training being more critical and important.

In addition, hospitality services often have high levels of intangibility and production and consumption is simultaneous. Therefore, hospitality services depend heavily on the skills and experiences of the employees that deliver them. If the innovation project lacks marketing synergy, then these delivery skills and resources are less likely to be adequate, resulting in lower service quality and dissatisfied customers (Cooper and de Brentani, 1991). Every hotel has an image that communicates expectations but also reflects the confidence of customers to try an innovation. It seems that chain hotels communicate a clearer and more positive image about their expertise, probably due to an emphasis on brand strategies; marketing synergy being an essential part of any branding strategy. On the other hand, independent hospitality innovations need to work harder to develop innovations that fit their expertise and portfolio, while creating a specific image for their operation.

Notwithstanding the results of this study, there are a number of possible limitations. The study has been conducted in a national context (Germany). The study included only the view from managers about how they experienced the performance of hospitality innovations. It did not consider staff or customers. It would be of interest to assess whether the results are applicable to other countries and to take a staff or customer perspective.

In summary, these results have important impact for managers who are involved in innovation activities, but also contribute academically, because they provide conceptual and empirically based new knowledge about the success factors that are likely to be linked to NSD projects.

So does the fact that chain operations have had especially strong growth and success in the hospitality industry relate to superior innovation activities? Or is it simply the case that chains have more money and more formal structures? This study suggests that along with the corporate growth in the hospitality sector, there are also many independent hotels that have been very successful with their innovation activities. Therefore, innovation success in the hospitality industry is not only a matter of money and structure. There are a small number of success factors that are common to both chain affiliated and independent hotels, which were empowerment and market attractiveness. However, the secret of successful hospitality innovation appears to be that chain affiliated and independently operated hospitality firms should have different priorities when developing innovations. Hospitality firms should vary their emphasis between the market, process and organizational factors in order to develop successful corporate or independent hospitality innovation and offer the quality products and services that their customers demand.

REFERENCES

Atuahene-Gima, K. (1996). Differential potency of factors affecting innovation performance in manufacturing and services firms in Australia, *Journal of Product Innovation Management 13*(1), pp. 35-52.

Bowen, E., and Lawler, E. (1992). The empowerment of service workers: What, why, how, and when, *Sloan Management Review 33*(3), pp. 31-39.

Burgelmann, R.A., and Maidique, M.A. (1996). *Strategic Management of Technology and Innovation*, Chicago: Irwin.

Cascio, W.F. (1989). *Managing Human Resources: Productivity, Quality of Work Life, Profits*, New York, McGraw-Hill.

Chebat, J.C., and Kollias, P. (2000). The impact of empowerment on customer contact employees' roles in service organizations, *Journal of Service Research 3*(1), pp. 66-81.

Cooper, R.G., and de Brentani, U. (1991). New industrial services: What distinguishes the winners, *Journal of Product Innovation Management 8*(2), pp. 75-90.

Cooper, R.G., Easingwood, C.J., Edgett, S., Kleinschmidt, E.J., and Storey, C. (1994). What distinguishes the top performing new products in financial services, *Journal of Product Innovation Management* 11 (4), pp. 281-299.

Cooper, R.G., and Kleinschmidt, E. (1987) New products: What separates winners from losers, *Journal of Product Innovation Management 4*(3), pp. 169-184.

de Brentani, U. (2001). Innovative versus incremental new business services: Different keys for achieving success, *Journal of Product Innovation Management 18*(3), pp. 169-187.

de Brentani, U. (1991). Success factors in developing new business services, *European Journal of Marketing*, 25 (2), pp. 33-59.

de Brentani, U., and Cooper, R.G. (1992). Developing successful new financial services for businesses, *Industrial Marketing Management 21*(3), pp. 231-241.

de Brentani, U., and Ragot, E. (1996). Developing new business-to-business professional services: What factors impact performance, *Industrial Marketing Management 25*(6), pp. 517-530.

Drucker, P.F. (1985). Innovation and Entrepreneurship: Practice and Principles, London: Heinemann.

Edgett, S.J. (1994). The traits of successful new service development, *Journal of Services Marketing 8* (3), pp. 40-49.

Enz, C., and Siguaw, J. (2000). Best practices in human resources, *Cornell Hotel and Restaurant Administration Quarterly 41*(1), pp. 48-61.

Enz, C., and Siguaw, J. (2003). Revisiting the best of the best: Innovations in hotel practice, Cornell Hotel and Restaurant Administration Quarterly 44(5/6), pp. 115-123.

Griffin, A. (1997). PDMA research on new product development practices: Updating trends and benchmarking best practices, *Journal of Product Innovation Management 14*(6), pp. 429-458.

Hartline, M.D., Maxham J.G., and McKee, D.O. (2000). Corridors of influence in the dissemination of customer-oriented strategy to customer contact employees, *Journal of Marketing 64*(2), pp. 35-50.

Johne, A., and Storey, C. (1998). New service development: A review of literature and annotated bibliography, *European Journal of Marketing 32*(3/4), pp. 184-251.

Jones, P. (1996). Managing hospitality innovation, *Cornell Hotel and Restaurant Administration Quarterly 37*(5), pp. 86-95.

Kanter, R.M. (1983). *The Change Masters,* New York: Simon and Schuster.

Kotler, P., Bowen, J., and Markens, J. (2002). *Marketing for Hospitality and Tourism*, Upper Saddle River: Prentice Hall.

M. Korczynski (2002). *Human Resource Management in Service Work*, New York: Palgrave.

Marketing Science Institute (2004). Online, accessed 5.November 2004, *http://www. msi.org/msi/rp0204.cfm.*

McGuire, J.W. (1996). *Theories of Business Behaviour*, Englewoods: Prentice-Hall, Inc.

Montoya-Weiss, M.M., and Calantone, R. (1994). Determinants of new product performance: A review and meta-analysis, *Journal of Product Innovation Management 11*(5), pp. 397-417.

Ottenbacher, M., and Shaw, V. (2002). The role of employee management in NSD: Preliminary results from a study of the hospitality sector, Proceedings of the 2002 Product Development and Management Association (PDMA) Research Conference, Orlando, USA, pp. 109-133.

Parasuraman, A., Berry, L., and Zeithaml, V. (1991). Understanding customer expectations of services, *Sloan Management Review 32*(3), pp. 39-48.

Rogers, E.M. (1983). *Diffusion of Innovations,* 3rd ed., New York: The Free Press.

Rueckert, R.W., Walker, O.C., and Roering, K.J. (1985). The organization of marketing activities: A contingency theory of structure and performance, *Journal of Marketing 49*(1), pp. 13-25.

Schumpeter, A. (1947). *Capitalism, Socialism and Democracy,* 2nd ed., New York: Harper & Row Publishers.

Storey, C., and Easingwood, C.J. (1998). The augmented service offering: A conceptualization and study of its impact on new service success. *Journal of Product Innovation Management 15*(4), pp. 335-351.

Storey, D.J. (1994). *Understanding the Small Business Sector,* London: Routledge.

Innovative Product Development in Hotel Operations

Joerg Frehse

SUMMARY. The hotel industry has a hard time resisting the continued globalization pressure. In order to survive the fierce international competition, even hotel chains need to offer their potential customers an added value that they do not receive from their competitors. The product development offers promising integrated solution approaches. Numerous unique characteristics can be established through entrepreneurial implementation of innovative product concepts in hotel operations. Indicating that this can occur in the fullest sense, this theoretical article concludes with an actual product development. Its objective is to demonstrate that the integration of the resource-based view in the product development processes in hospitality and tourism is necessary to generate competitive differentiation opportunities. Environment-based and resource-based views are no longer interpreted as monistic and mutually exclusive, but as complementary management approaches. A practical example underlines the fact that such considerations are already being implemented in hotel chains although they still tend to be neglected in tourism-scientific research. *[Article copies available for a fee from The Haworth Document Delivery Service: 1-800-HAWORTH. E-mail address: <docdelivery@ haworthpress.com> Website: <http://www.HaworthPress.com> © 2005 by The Haworth Press, Inc. All rights reserved.]*

Joerg Frehse, Dr., is Director, Business Development, Arabella Sheraton, Hotel Management, GmbH Arabellastrasse 13, D-81925 München (E-mail: joerg.frehse@ arabella.sheraton. com).

[Haworth co-indexing entry note]: "Innovative Product Development in Hotel Operations." Frehse, Joerg. Co-published simultaneously in *Journal of Quality Assurance in Hospitality & Tourism* (The Haworth Hospitality Press, an imprint of The Haworth Press, Inc.) Vol. 6, No. 3/4, 2005, pp. 129-146; and: *Innovation in Hospitality and Tourism* (ed: Mike Peters, and Birgit Pikkemaat) The Haworth Hospitality Press, an imprint of The Haworth Press, Inc., 2005, pp. 129-146. Single or multiple copies of this article are available for a fee from The Haworth Document Delivery Service [1-800-HAWORTH, 9:00 a.m. - 5:00 p.m. (EST). E-mail address: docdelivery@haworthpress.com].

Available online at http://www.haworthpress.com/web/JQAHT
© 2005 by The Haworth Press, Inc. All rights reserved.
doi:10.1300/J162v06n03_08

KEYWORDS. Product development, innovation, hotel industry, hotel operations, resource-based view

INTRODUCTION

Weak worldwide economic activity, military conflicts, terrorist attacks as well as new viral diseases led to profitability declines in the European hotel industry for the fourth time in a row by the end of 2004. The aggressive expansion of international hotel chains is continuing as well (Peters and Frehse, 2005). Market liberalization and deregulation also increase competition and lead to more and more homogenous service packaging in the hotel industry. Furthermore, the growing flood of information decreases the efficacy of classical market-development instruments. Potential guests are increasingly looking for hotel offers with unique characteristics (Hinterhuber, 2001).

Therefore, the product development departments of international hotel chains face three new core challenges:

1. They must take account of continuously changing trends in the market and requirement in their planning processes.
2. They must constantly find new ways and methods to attract guests with innovative offerings as well as increase their quality of life in the short term during their hotel stay.
3. They must create instruments that differentiate them from their competitors.

Integrated product development offers promising solution approaches. However, the few explanation approaches to be found in tourism-science literature, such as how competitive advantages evolve under current market conditions and how these can be used by the company in the long term–also in regard to the hotel business–are mainly based on an outside-in perspective and the associated positioning of service offerings in existing markets (Frazer, 1961; Baumol, 1968; Weiermair and Peters, 1998; Reis, 1999). A comprehensive consideration of the competition, industry, and environmental situation is considered to be the basic element of any strategic plan.

In principle, the tourism research community is in agreement that within the scope of international service activities the origin of market success should be seen in the development, accumulation and maintenance of permanent competitive advantages over the strongest competitor. However, its evolution is explained with contrary thought models.

It is almost regrettable that the integrated concepts of the environment-based view and the resource-based view that are especially demanded in the tourism-science discussion have seldom been applied to date (Bieger, 1998, p. 2; Weiermair, 2001, p. 13). Also in respect of product developments, the disregard for the inside-out perspective, in other words, the company's own problem resolution expertise is lamented from many sides, since ultimately, pure orientation to the mainstream market will not be sufficient (Rühli, 2000, p. 73; Meffert, 2002, p. 671).

But while in the broad-based scientific discussion the two conventional concepts of the "Environment-Based View" and the "Resource-Based View" are increasingly interpreted not as monistic, as mutually excluding alternatives, but as complementary strategy approaches (Hinterhuber and Friedrich, 1997; Ossadnik, 2000), tourism research and practice has been very reluctant to take up resource-based recommendations for action.

This article takes up the discussion about this research deficit. Within the scope of a practical example the product development process is built on a foundation extended by resource perspectives. Drawing heavily on the AltiraSPA[1] wellness concept of the ArabellaSheraton hotel group,[2] this article documents the fact that innovative product developments, which link the external environmental, market and industry conditions with company-internal and service-specific competencies offer a winning strategic approach to successfully face the demands mentioned at the start-also in the hospitality and tourism industry.

For this purpose it would seem obvious to focus on the search for discriminating models based on resource-based considerations and to derive the perspectives of integrated product development for research and practice. In a further step the innovative product development process and the contents of the AltiraSPA wellness concept are outlined. In order to obtain general implications for successful product development in business practice, it is also essential to explain the underlying understanding of innovations as well as the special features of hotel services. Moreover, the common feature of the prevailing theoretical trends of consolidating new product concepts is the attempt to explain the cause-effect relationship between observable consumer behavior and its determining factors. By proceeding in this manner not only is the necessary integration consolidated but the degree of innovation of AltiraSPA as a new product development of ArabellaSheraton in hotel operations is also highlighted. The main findings of this article as well as starting points for further research in the field of tourism science are a basis for the fifth chapter.

THE RESOURCE-BASED VIEW
AS A THEORETICAL REFERENCE FRAMEWORK

The introductory remarks have already illustrated that consumers in the high quality segment are not only concerned with the price and material elements but also with additional emotional elements of hotel services. Also from a resource-based view, the success potential of a company is marked by material and immaterial production factors that contain a business-specific element (Penrose, 1959; Grant, 1991; Hall, 1992). Thus, only resource heterogeneity based on factor imperfection enables the construction, accumulation and achievement of competitive advantages.

The imperfection of factor markets is particularly high at the cross-border level. This enables hotel companies with their traditionally high level of internationalization to make higher-than-average profits by acquiring an important resource to the service-provision process for a price considerably below their potential added value for the customer. This low price results either from not noticing the special features shown in the previous section or from misinterpreting the performance potential of the resource.

A hotel company that recognizes the strategic success potential of a material or immaterial resource that distinguishes it from its competitors and integrating it into the system of general business marketing and sales activities in terms of the product development understanding applied in this article is generally able to establish material and immaterial resources on easy terms (Frehse and Peters, 2004). However, long-term competitive advantages can only be achieved and covered within service policy if all marketing activities are based on business-specific resources that meet the principal requirements outlined below.

Non-imitability: Success potential generating resources are distinguished by the fact that rival businesses are not able to imitate them within a short time. A promising imitation is, for instance, not possible if success potentials are neither as a whole nor separately available on the market (Handlbauer, 2000, p. 127). Thus, the less a package of resources can be protected against possible attempts of imitation from competitors, the lower the strategic success potential.

Company specificity: Resources must be integrated into a hotel company in such a way that only there can they develop their full value. It is basically assumed that every company can be distinguished by an individual, distinct package of resources (Peteraf, 1993, p. 180).

Non-substitutability: Non-imitability and company specificity of resources on their own are not sufficient to realize long-term competitive advantages. Thus, innovative product development processes resulting in an extra feature for the customer also harbor an omnipresent danger of substitution against which no resource can be completely protected (Collis, 1991, p. 12). In the final analysis, specific advantage-generating features of a substitute decide on the residual value of the original resource, regardless of the form of substitution. If a substitute resource is easily imitable, not particularly business-specific, and easily available, it can be assumed that neither the substitute resource nor the original resource threatened by substitution will play a competition-deciding role (Barney, 1991, p. 111).

Utility-making ability on the market: The requirements on a strategically valuable resource discussed so far are almost entirely founded on the internal orientation of the resource-based view. However, there is no doubt that the realization of long-term competitive advantage also requires the integration of an external environmental, market and sector-oriented view. In order to classify a resource as strategically relevant in terms of generating advantages, it must have a value-generating character on the market, which is reflected in extra utility regarding the distinct hotel service perceived by the customers.

Resources can mainly be distinguished by specificity if they are not traded on the factor markets (Dierickx and Cool, 1989, p. 1505). The AltiraSPA concept, which will be highlighted below, represents such a factor in terms of the definition explained in the fourth chapter. It forms the capital of confidence that ArabellaSheraton has gained from consumers for its wellness competency and with which the hotel group finally reduces insecurity in the process of choosing accommodation.

In the luxury segment in particular, the business arrangement of such capital of confidence requires the use of appropriate material and immaterial business-internal resources and it is lived and communicated by the product concept as a result of this combination of resources towards the demand side. There is an almost unlimited factor market for material service potentials but only the combination and accumulation of these factors by immaterial resources within the innovative concept of the "seven pillars" enables the development of the competitive advantage-generating product development AltiraSPA.

DECISIONS AND DEVELOPMENT PROCESS
OF THE INNOVATIVE ALTIRASPA CONCEPT

In literature innovations are often distinguished by personnel, social, structural, procurement, and also marketing innovations, according to the functional structure within the company (Barney, 1991; de Brentani, 2001; Hübner, 2002). But as hotel services usually combine potential, process, and result elements and, consequently generate them as a complex, networked cluster of service offerings and service production processes, the above dimensions from the traditional goods area do not appear very helpful (Pikkemaat and Weiermair, 2004).

Therefore, in this article innovative product developments are deemed to be the result of a process (Cooper, 1993; Atuahene-Gima, 1996; Burgelmann and Maidique, 1996). They are innovations which, in terms of strengthening competitiveness, provide an effective contribution for the creation of customer value and, hence, the market success of the hotel company. Accordingly, innovations refer to everything that can be connected to a clear core benefit for all consumers and the resulting competitive advantages.

Market innovations are understood to be solutions that either resolves an existing problem in a completely new way or which satisfy customers' needs for which there was previously no solution. They are clearly distinguished from previous offerings according to the subjective attitude of the potential users. One example of a market innovation is the continuing creation of high-quality hotel offerings in remote corners of the world, such as deserts, solitary islands, under water, and secluded valleys, etc.

In regard to operational innovations, hotel companies develop specific service concepts, although under certain circumstances this could be an imitation of a competitor's service that is already available on the market. Continuous improvement and the adoption of good ideas from the competition in terms of "benchmarking" are now also standard in the hotel industry. On the other hand, the continuous development of market innovations cannot be expected (Fitzsimmons and Fitzsimmons, 2003). Accordingly, this article and the following case examples also concentrate solely on the introduction of operating innovations.

But independent of market innovations or operating innovations extensive customer acceptance is also always the key to entrepreneurial success in the area of product development (Haedrich and Jeschke, 1993). Consequently, a strategic planning process must always precede the development of new operating concepts. Ultimately the quality of this depends on the international competitiveness of the company (Kaplan and Murdock, 1991). In regard to the hotel industry, a systematic strategic plan such as this, which especially involves the continuous further development of some product concepts that have already been introduced to the market, can be deduced from the typical new product planning process (Haedrich and Jeschke, 1993).

According to this process, on the basis of the defined corporate and marketing goals, the central task of management is to recognize the market opportunities of operating innovations at an early stage. On the one hand, a continuous search for new service concepts and the associated market opportunities could be defined in the hotel company's vision, but on the other hand, certain events, such as legal conditions, could trigger a planning process for innovative product developments (Koppelmann, 1993).

But in both cases a promising search for new entrepreneurial fields of activity assumes that the search field is adequately marked out. Apart from the fact that search fields must be compatible with the strategic corporate and marketing goals, in general they should be in areas in which the hotel company wants to play out its strengths over the competition, so that strategic success factors can actually have an effect. This particularly relates to the guest and quality segments in which the hotel company is active.

For a search field analysis economic literature contains various approaches and methods for analyzing the company's market environment, many of which can, in principle, be applied to the hotel industry (Griffin, 1997). An analysis of needs trends, changes in the age and education structures of consumers, shifts in the size of households, technological developments, changing lifestyles and changes in competitive strategies and conditions are just some examples. A comprehensive, environment and market-oriented early clarification system such as this also ensures that the relevant company-policy signals are picked up at an early stage. This puts the hotel company in a position where it can recognize opportunities and trends for the development of new products and identify the risks that exist–also taking account of the existing offering.

In this connection, during the last few years the ArabellaSheraton hotel group has also realized that spa and wellness as a megatrend would enhance the portfolio of four and five star properties of the brands "ArabellaSheraton" and "The Luxury Collection" and contribute to higher occupancy rates with the hotel, as international clientele in particular demand wellness facilities. As a result, the chain's upscale city hotels and resort destinations have established first-rate wellness facilities over the last few years. But the hotels designated their wellness and spa facilities as part of the hotel property. Names like "Aquabella" or "Mind & Motion" were created but these did not represent entities separate from the hotels or spas, which meant that they did not create a significant differentiation from the main competitors nor attract many new clients.

Because of these deficits, the decision to create a separate wellness concept in order to demonstrate the competence of ArabellaSheraton in the spa field was made during preparations for the opening of the Mardavall Hotel & Spa in Majorca/Spain in May 2002. Consequently, the product development department had the task of developing the basic idea, the philosophy, and the future direction for the wellness concept, reaching its decision after an analysis of the present situation, trends and changes in the spa industry, existing wellness facilities, and the activities of the competition.

Based on a German Trend Study (Horx-Strathern et al., 2001), the product development department agreed that the pertinent six sigma trends were essential to the creation of the future wellness concept of ArabellaSheraton. Furthermore, it agreed that wellness is a fashionable term lacking in clear content and definition and that the current wellness trend is similar to the eco movement or convenience movement, where we can already see a blurring of the traditional borders between cosmetics, body care, pharmaceuticals, medicine, sports and nutrition. After a thorough review of all wellness and spa areas in the entire Arabella-Sheraton hotel group, it was determined that not all 21 spa and wellness areas would be suitable for marketing under the product.

The decision that hotel spas would in fact be considered was postponed until after the concept had been created. Some hotels, however, such as Mardavall, Western Cape and Schloss Fuschl, played an important role in the consideration that the product concept should fulfill high leverage quality and core standards. The product development department justified the decision for a spa concept according to the following six standards and criteria:

1. The concept is a commitment to the customer, standing for consistent high quality and reliability as a guaranteed basis for customer loyalty.
2. The concept comprised clearly defined characteristics, unmistakably separating it from competing companies, products or services.

3. The concept helps customers to orient themselves and avoid mistakes in buying decisions, thus earning their confidence.
4. The concept is associated with a certain image, which serves to position the given company in its socio-economic environment while representing an image that the customer identifies with.
5. The customer is willing to pay a higher price for a well-managed offering than for a comparable product.
6. Unbranded products will increasingly become unsustainable. Today, product branding is necessary to participate viably in the market.

In consideration of the above-mentioned criteria, the product development department identified the following six advantages for the wellness concept:

1. A wellness concept provides a clear differentiation from the competitors.
2. The consumer is willing to pay a higher price for the same product
3. A wellness concept creates loyalty.
4. A wellness concept makes possible the use of more effective communication measures.
5. A wellness concept creates a positive image for the individual hotel.
6. A unique wellness concept attracts new guests.

Subsequent to the situation analysis and the decision to proceed, it was essential to define the identity that would serve as the foundation of the concept, comprising unique features and creating the spa's image. The identity should define the values that impart the new concept to the customer. The identity should reach the selected luxury target group and differentiate the ArabellaSheraton hotel group from the competition. Based on the information listed above, the product development department identified the following seven central pillars essential to the AltiraSPA wellness concept.

1. "Beauty"   (beauty treatments for face, body and skin)
2. "Life balance"   (treatments such as Yoga, Tai Chi and Meditation)
3. "Aqua"   (sauna, passive water use)
4. "Vitality"   (fitness)
5. "Harmony"   (massages)
6. "Nature"   (activities in nature)
7. "Nutrition"   (balanced cuisine)

As the ArabellaSheraton hotels are based in five different countries, the group decided to create an international wellness concept that focuses more on regional strengths than, for example, Asian rituals, with every spa under the umbrella concept offering unique features rooted in its local surroundings. Furthermore, a key element of the wellness concept is the unique service provided to the customer as immediate reflection, the luxuriousness and transparency of the wellness area. The AltiraSPA philosophy with the seven pillars should provide the transparency that potential hotel guests are always looking for.

CHARACTERISTICS, MECHANISMS AND UNDERLYING PRODUCT CONCEPT UNDERSTANDING

In the turbulent market environment outlined in the first section, hotel companies have to know what customers are looking for and what their thoughts are, in particular with regard to the fine tuning and characterization of hotel-business product or service packages. For a service sector strongly determined by immaterial elements, like the hotel industry, an important operative instrument like AltiraSPA is more likely to attract and win over customers with a consistent product strategy than for instance in the consumer goods and capital goods industries.

However, the service sector still features relatively few renowned products (Richter and Werner, 1998, p. 29). Basically, this is surprising because for the market success of service providers in particular, the functions of information, orientation, confidence building, risk-reduction, quality assurance and emotionalization are coexistent core functions of a product concept (Kernstock, 2004, p. 190). Moreover, established markets contain a preference-building function, especially saturated markets (Esch and Wicke, 2001, p. 6).

Firstly, the initial processes of booking accommodation are based on insecurity from the consumers' point of view. There is an imbalance of information between supplier and consumer. Accordingly, in principle the consumer would already like some subjective security as the hotel stay approaches. Hotel companies that develop innovative and strong product packages for parts of their service offerings satisfy these customers' needs in their own interest because in the hotel industry the consumers' product orientation is decisive for their choice of hotels. In this context, the customers' orientation is higher the more often they use a service concept function to make their decision on insecurity (l Altobelli and Sander, 2001, p. 9).

Different empirical investigations document that especiall ArabellaSheraton hotel group's luxury segment, potential guests generally do not only choose their hotel on the basis of price and the presence of material performance components but that they are also concerned with the quality of immaterial, emotional elements of the services offered (Saleh and Ryan, 1991; Teas, 1993). As a result of the special features of hotel services as well as the synergetic intertwining of their sub-components in the hotel-business value-added process, the individual performance components cannot simply be decomposed and recomposed. Hence, AltiraSPA also represents more than the total of the aggregated individual values of its service components.

• Due to the cross-section function of hotel service, the presence of well-trained internal resources enables the simultaneous performance of several activities with regard to international guests, particularly in the wellness sector. Especially in this context, various interdependencies facilitate a general expertise diffusion that in the end promotes a consolidation of wellness-specific service elements along with a product concept. Thus, the AltiraSPA wellness concept also represents more than the sum of its parts. In the end, the seven supporting pillars form the basis of the concept but the strategic success potential of international competition results solely from the quality perceived by international guests.

Due to complexity and lack of transparency, consumers–especially in the luxury segment–are normally unsure of the success of the arrangements in the pre-contact phase, at least in the case of initial purchase processes. Figure 1 shows that both expectancy and insecurity in regard to quality increase analogous to the quality of hotel services requested. Consequently, potential guests get information, pass on information, take measures to prevent insecurities and revise their booking plans in case of unexpected events.

In order to successfully meet such considerations in terms of business, marketing science is primarily concerned with analyzing the exchange processes between supplier and consumer and giving advice for their marketing-policy development. From that point of view, the product development of ArabellaSheraton must always guarantee that its own product concept meets the target system of consumers in their subjective perception more than comparable competitors' offers.

Following this approach, the AltiraSPA is the result of internal and external marketing activities and its main function is to efficiently and

FIGURE 1. The Brand as a Medium to Mediate an Extra Utility Perceived

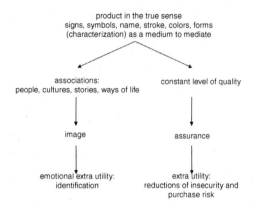

product in the true sense
signs, symbols, name, stroke, colors, forms
(characterization) as a medium to mediate

associations: constant level of quality
people, cultures, stories, ways of life

image   assurance

emotional extra utility: extra utility:
identification   reductions of insecurity and
                                    purchase risk

Used with permission. (Tomczak and Brockdorff 2000, p. 489)

effectively communicate all material and immaterial performance features of wellness offerings. Only then does the innovative product concept allow potential guests to identify with a particular performance offer and arouse certain associations. AltiraSPA should represent a special image, a quality of life, a culture or a clientele which the customer feels part of.

Thus, strong immaterial key information primarily offers the hotel guest an extra emotional feature (Zeithaml, 1991). Accordingly, within this article, innovative service concepts are performances that make a quality promise in addition to a distinguishable characterization by a systematic and, in particular, customer-oriented sales concept; this quality promise achieves–a long-term valuable, utility-making effect and can realize a sustainable success in fulfilling customer expectations in the relevant target group.

Conversely, hotel companies can benefit from such customer advantages, as consumers are generally willing to pay a higher price for those advantages (Oelsnitz, 1997, p. 71). If the product development can succeed in satisfying the needs of international guests in such a way that the evaluation of the particular hotel services is already positive in the pre-contact phase, demand is unrealistic despite higher prices. The more unique a new product is presented from the customers' point of view, the greater the company's scope in terms of pricing and the less the costs of the actual hotel stay matter on the consumer-side.

Furthermore, a service concept can increase the involvement of consumers through emotionalization and thus lead to increased brand loyalty (Haedrich and Tomczak, 1996, p. 42). It is an instrument of differentiation and distinction, especially in markets with homogenous offer structures (Stauss, 1998, p. 13). Moreover, newly developed products represent a constant quality level of the hotel service in question, which clearly reduces the customer's feeling of insecurity. In its function of characterizing service, it forms the basis of a market and target group-oriented creation of image and preference in favor of its own product offer (Becker, 1998, p. 501). In this context, AltiraSPA, representing all material and immaterial key information, is a medium that helps to implement and realize the positioning of all services in the wellness sector. To summarize, Figure 2 shows that in such a case the brand makes it possible to realize and communicate the hotel service in its entirety.

PERSPECTIVES OF AN INTEGRATED PRODUCT DEVELOPMENT AND MANAGEMENT APPROACH FOR RESEARCH AND PRACTICE

A service concept's fascination and magnetism in the hotel industry is greater the more clearly and uniquely the product is developed and the more distinct its rough edges appear. Moreover, there is no doubt that all potential customer-attracting features in the market must be formed and cultivated internally because individual development of services is much more difficult than contributions in kind. Not least, the way in which guests find themselves included in the service-provision process of wellness services in a hotel is decisive for their final judgment of quality. Therefore, the design of a business-internal process can become a success factor, if not the most essential success factor, as soon as the provider wants to strategically position its service (Meyer and Tostmann, 1995, p. 15).

In addition to the outside-in perspective and due to its concentration on internal success potentials in particular, the resource-based view offers a theoretical addition even for product development and management in the hotel industry. The consistent integration of the inside-out perspective represented in this context requires the construction, accumulation and achievement of business-specific resources for achieving

FIGURE 2. Expectancy and Insecurity of Quality of the International Hotel Industry

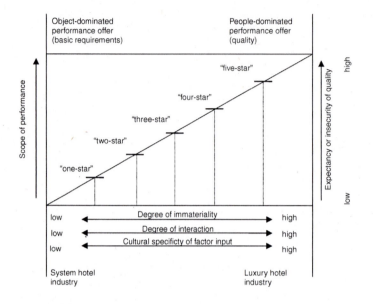

(Source: own illustration based on Faust 1993, p. 15 and Stauss 1994, p. 224)

competitive advantages by a cross-border product policy. Illustrated by the innovative and integrative development of the wellness concept of the ArabellaSheraton hotel group, this article shows how this can also be planned and managed in hotel operations.

With regard to the future of a wellness and spa product for a hotel chain, there seems to be little question that the increasing introduction of wellness and spa facilities will influence almost every aspect of business in both resort hotels and city hotels. As a mega trend, wellness and spa have survived their initial stage and have now entered a significant growth stage as more and more individuals and organizations are recognizing their importance for future life and health. However, in combination with innovative internal product development, the wellness and spa hotel competency must offer target-group adapted solutions for individual problems. The focus is certainly on integrated aspects. Hotel service offerings like AltiraSPA must be transparent and measurable and must provide a clear benefit for the customer.

In this context, consistent adherence to quality standards that must be applied to the service potential, the service providing process, and the result is the only way to offer a promising solution approach. With its innovative "pillar-philosophy" AltiraSPA wants to cover the market factors mentioned above and attempt to differentiate them in a transparent way. The seven pillars and the core standards that are connected with them provide the basis for the implementation and the success of AltiraSPA. In the meantime the concept has found worldwide recognition in more than thirty hotels under the umbrella of the Starwood Spa Collection. Only by developing products with business-internal immaterial and material resources and external market situations can an insecurity-reducing effect be achieved and can the potential of acquisition and customer loyalty of its own performance offering be clearly raised.

Besides, on the basis of the practical example discussed here it has been made clear that in the tourism-scientific discussion it is no longer practical to consider the traditional strategy approaches in international management as mutually exclusive theory strings. Rather, research can only make statements that serve as an implication for specific design parameters in the hotel industry with the complementary and, at the same time, supplementary consideration that has been implemented within the scope of AltiraSpa.

NOTES

1. The "AltiraSPA" name stems from the ancient Greek names "Althea," she who heals, and "Saphira," the beautiful.

2. The ArabellaSheraton hotel group is a joint venture between the Munich-based Schoerghuber Corporate Group and Starwood Hotels & Resorts Worldwide Inc. formed in 1998. The company currently manages 33 establishments in Germany, Austria, Switzerland, Majorca and South Africa under "The Luxury Collection," "ArabellaSheraton Hotels & Resorts" and "Four Points Hotels" brands.

3. The detailed standards could not be attached to this paper due to the enormous size of the document.

REFERENCES

Atuahene-Gima, K. (1996). Differential potency of factors affecting innovation performance in manufacturing and services firms in Australia, *Journal of Product Innovation Management 13* (1), pp. 35-52.

Barney, J.B. (1991). Firm Resources and Sustained Competitive Advantage, *Journal of Management* 17 (1), 99-120.

Baumol, W.J. (1968). Entrepreneurship in Economic Theory, *American Economic Review 58*, 64-71.

Becker, J. (1998). *Marketing-Konzeption: Grundlagen des strategischen und operativen Marketing-Managements*, Muenchen, Vahlen.

Bieger, T. (1998). Tourismusmarketing im Umfeld der Globalisierung: Aktuelle Herausforderungen, innovative Lösungen und neue Strukturen, *Thexis 15* (3), 2-13.

Burgelmann, R.A. and Maidique, M.A. (1996). *Strategic Management of Technology and Innovation*, Chicago, Irwin.

Collis, D.J. (1991). *Organizational Capability as a Source of Profit*, Working Paper, Harvard Business School.

Cooper, R.G. (1993). *Winning at New Products. Accelerating the Process from Idea to Launch*, Massachusetts, Perseus.

de Brentani, U. (2001). Innovative versus incremental new business services: Different keys for achieving success, *Journal of Product Innovation Management, 18* (3), 169-187.

Dierickx, I., and Cool, K. (1990). *A Resource Based Perspective on Competitive Strategy*, Working Paper, Insead.

Esch, F. R., and Wicke, A. (2001). Herausforderungen und Aufgaben des Markenmanagements. In Esch, F.-R. (Eds.), *Moderne Markenführung, Grundlagen– Innovative Ansätze–Praktische Umsetzungen* (pp. 3-59), Wiesbaden, Gabler.

Fantapié Altobelli, C., and Sander, M. (2001). *Internet Branding: Marketing und Markenführung im Internet*, Stuttgart, Lucius & Lucius.

Faust, T. (1993), *Qualitätsmanagement von Hotels. Theoretische Ansätze und praktizierte Formen*, Forschungsbeitrag, Universität Mainz.

Fitzsimmons, J., and Fitzsimmons, M. (2003). *Service Management*, Boston, McGraw-Hill.

Frazer, H.W. (1961). *A Theory of the Optimum Time Rate of Growth of the Firm*, Princeton.

Frehse, J., and Peters, M. (2004). A multiple-item scale for measuring international service competencies in the hotel industry, *HOTELLINK–Journal for Theory and Practice of Hotel Industry 2* (4), 31-45.

Grant, R.M. (1991). The Resource Based Theory of Competitive Advantage: Implications for Strategy Formulation, *California Management Review 33*, Spring, 114-135.

Griffin, A. (1997). PDMA research on new product development practices: Updating trends and benchmarking best practices, *Journal of Product Innovation Management 14* (6), 429-458.

Haedrich, G., and Jeschke, B. G. (1993), Zur Integration sozio-politischer Interessen beim Innovationsmanagement, *Thexis 5* (6), 8-13.

Haedrich, G., and Tomczak, T. (1996). *Strategische Markenführung*, Bern et al.

Hall, R. (1992). The Strategic Analysis of Intangible Resources, *Strategic Management Journal 13* (2), 135-144.

Handlbauer, G. (2000). Competing on Cognition? Möglichkeiten und Grenzen einer konstruktivistischen Orientierung der Strategischen Unternehmensführung. In Hinterhuber, H.H. and Friedrich, St.A. and Al-Ani, A. and Handlbauer, G. (Eds.), *Das Neue Strategische Management* (pp. 73-90), Wiesbaden, Gabler.

Hinterhuber, H.H. (2001). Wie führe ich mein Hotel in die Einzigartigkeit?, In Weiermair, K. and Peters, M. and Reiger, E. (Eds.), *Vom alten zum neuen Tourismus* (pp. 102-107), Innsbruck, Studia.

Hinterhuber, H.H., and Friedrich, St. A (1997). Markt- und ressourcenorientierte Sichtweite zur Steigerung des Unternehmenswertes, in: Hahn, D. and Taylor, B. (Eds.), *Strategische Unternehmensplanung, strategische Unternehmensführung,* (pp. 988-1016), Heidelberg, Physica.

Horx-Strathern, O., Horx, M., and Gaspar, C. (2001). *Was ist Wellness? Anatomie und Zukunftsperspektiven des Wohlfühltrends,* Wellness-Dossier des Zukunftsinstituts und der GfK, Frankfurt.

Hübner, H. (2002). *Integratives Innovationsmanagement,* Berlin, Schmidt.

Kaplan, R.B., and Murdock, L. (1991). Core process redesign, *The McKinsey Quarterly,* No. 2, 27-43.

Kernstock, J. (2004). Möglichkeiten und Grenzen des Corporate Brand Management. In Weiermair, K. and Peters, M. and Pechlaner, H. and Kaiser, M.O. (Eds.), *Unternehmertum im Tourismus. Führen mit Erneuerungen* (pp. 187-202), Berlin, Schmidt.

Koppelmann, U. (1993). *Produktmarketing, Entscheidungsgrundlage für Produktmanager,* Berlin, Springer.

Meffert, H. (2002). Zukunftsperspektiven der Markenführung–zusammenfassende Thesen. In Meffert, H. and Burmann, C. and Koers, M. (Eds.), *Markenmanagement. Grundfragen der identitätsorientierten Markenführung* (pp. 671-673), Wiesbaden, Gabler.

Meyer, A., and Tostmann, T. (1995). Die nur erlebbare Markenpersönlichkeit, *Harvard Business Manager 17* (4), 9-15.

Oelsnitz, D. von der (1997). Dienstleistungsmarken: Konzepte und Möglichkeiten einer markengestützten Serviceprofilierung, *Jahrbuch der Absatz-und Verbrauchsforschung 43* (1), 66-89.

Ossadnik, W. (2000). Markt-versus ressourcenorientiertes Management-alternative oder einander ergänzende Konzeptionen einer strategischen Unternehmensführung, *Die Unternehmung 54* (4), 273-287.

Penrose, E.T. (1959). *The Theory of Growth of the Firm,* Oxford.

Peteraf, M.A. (1993). The Cornerstones of Competitive Advantage: A Resource-Based View, *Strategic Management Journal 14* (3), S. 179-191.

Peters, M., and Frehse, J. (2005). The internationalization of the European hotel industry in the light of competition theories, *Tourism 53* (1), 55-65.

Pikkemaat, B., and Weiermair, K. (2004). Zur Problematik der Messung von Innovationen bei komplexen, vernetzten Dienstleistungen–dargestellt am Beispiel der touristischen Dienstleistung. In Bruhn, M. and Stauss, B. (Eds.), *Dienstleistungsinnovationen–Forum Dienstleistungsmanagement* (pp. 359-379), Wiesbaden, Gabler.

Reis, T. (1999). *Globales Marketing im Dienstleistungssektor: Determinanten-Ansatzpunkte–Erfolgsträchtigkeit,* Wiesbaden, Gabler.

Richter, M., and Werner, G. (1998). Marken im Bereich Dienstleistungen: Gibt es das überhaupt? In Tomczak, T. and Schögel, M. and Ludwig, E. (Eds.), *Markenmanagement für Dienstleistungen* (pp. 24-36), St. Gallen, Thexis.

Rühli, E. (2000). Strategie ist tot. Es lebe das neue Strategische Management. In Hinterhuber, H.H. and Friedrich, St.A. and Al-Ani, A. and Handlbauer, G. (Eds.), *Das Neue Strategische Management* (pp. 73-90), Wiesbaden, Gabler.

Teas, R. (1993). Expectations, Performance, Evaluation and Customers' Perceptions of Quality, *Journal of Marketing 57* (10), 18-34.

Saleh, F., and Ryan, Ch. (1991). Analysing Service Quality in the Hospitality Industry Using the SERVQUAL Model, *The Service Industries Journal*, 11 (3), 324-343.

Scheuing, E.E. (1989). *New product management*, Columbus, Sra.

Stauss, B. (1994). Dienstleistungstypologie und Markteintrittsstrategien im internationalen Dienstleistungsmarketing. In Schuster, L. (Eds.), *Die Unternehmung im internationalen Wettbewerb* (pp. 213-231), Berlin, Schmidt.

Stauss, B. (1998). Dienstleistungen als Markenartikel–etwas Besonderes? In Tomczak, T. and Schögel, M. and Ludwig, E. (Eds.), *Markenmanagement für Dienstleistungen* (pp. 10-23), St. Gallen, Thexis.

Tomczak, T., and Brockdorff, B. (2000). Bedeutung und Besonderheiten des Markenmanagements für Dienstleistungen. In Belz, Ch. and Bieger, Th. (Eds.), *Dienstleistungskompetenz und innovative Geschäftsmodelle* (pp. 486-502), St. Gallen, Thexis.

Weiermair, K. (2001): Wie kann die Wissenschaft die Praxis unterstützen? In Weiermair, K. and Peters, M. and Reiger, E. (Eds.), *Vom alten zum neuen Tourismus* (pp. 108-116), Innsbruck, Studia.

Weiermair, K., and Peters, M. (1998). The internationalization behaviour of service enterprises, *Asia Pacific Journal of Tourism Research* 2 (2), 1-14.

Zeithaml, V.A. (1981). How Consumer Evaluation Processes Differ Between Goods and Services. In Donnelly, J.H./George, W.R. (Eds.), *Marketing of Services, Proceeding Series, American Marketing Association* (pp.186-190), Chicago, Amer.

Challenges in Mobile Business Solutions for Tourist Destinations– The Trial Case of St. Moritz

Pietro Beritelli
Matthias Schuppisser

SUMMARY. Mobile business applications in tourism have been developed in the last years for various platforms and services. However, most of the applications have been tested in lab-like conditions. The article describes the trial case of St. Moritz, Switzerland. With the help of the Destination-Pilot acceptability, usability, and market potential for mobile information services have been tested in a real environment situation. The trial involves numerous visitors and tourist enterprises. The paper presents opportunities and limitations to so called mobile travel recommender systems. Strong emphasis is put on the methodical and technical challenges in the set up trial phase as well as on potential business models for exploitation. *[Article copies available for a fee from The Haworth Document Delivery Service: 1-800-HAWORTH. E-mail address: <docdelivery@haworthpress.com> Website: <http://www.HaworthPress.com> © 2005 by The Haworth Press, Inc. All rights reserved.]*

Pietro Beritelli is Assistant Professor and Deputy Director, Institute for Public Services and Tourism, University of St. Gallen, Dufourstrasse 40a, CH-9000 St. Gallen, Switzerland (E-mail: pietro.beritelli@unisg.ch).

Matthias Schuppisser is Project Manager, Institute for Tourism and Hospitality, University of Applied Sciences, CH-7000 Chur, Switzerland (E-mail: matthias.schuppisser@fh-htwchur.ch).

[Haworth co-indexing entry note]: "Challenges in Mobile Business Solutions for Tourist Destinations–The Trial Case of St. Moritz." Beritelli, Pietro, and Matthias Schuppisser. Co-published simultaneously in *Journal of Quality Assurance in Hospitality & Tourism* (The Haworth Hospitality Press, an imprint of The Haworth Press, Inc.) Vol. 6, No. 3/4, 2005, pp. 147-162; and: *Innovation in Hospitality and Tourism* (ed: Mike Peters, and Birgit Pikkemaat) The Haworth Hospitality Press, an imprint of The Haworth Press, Inc., 2005, pp. 147-162. Single or multiple copies of this article are available for a fee from The Haworth Document Delivery Service [1-800-HAWORTH, 9:00 a.m. - 5:00 p.m. (EST). E-mail address: docdelivery@haworthpress.com].

KEYWORDS. Mobile business, travel recommender systems, push and pull strategy, SMS, WAP, destination management

INTRODUCTION

Tourist Services and Their Relevance for Mobile Business Solutions

Today, competition among tourist destinations is fierce. Increasingly, destinations place the individual guest and his needs at the centre of their strategic priorities. Mobile business solutions could play in the future an important role in this war for customers. Especially, if we look at the particularities of tourist services (Mazanec, 1994), there are four basic considerations for the case of mobile business to make.

First, tourist services are strongly seasonal. This leads suppliers to constantly adapt, reshape, and re-price their offers and to take various customer segments into account during the business year. Tourist enterprises need an operating system, which is able to increase flexibility in combining services in accordance to changing customers and their needs. Customer relationship management solutions target this necessity, and mobile business solutions leverage their value on this need (Poslad et al., 2001; Malaka and Zipf, 2000). Second, a tourist follows the residence principle, in the sense that she has to move to the destination by means of transportation. Tourist services imply mobility of demand, and mobile business solutions address this feature (Estevez and Fernandez, 2002; Andrade et al., 2002). Third, the uno acto-principle leads to simultaneity between presence of the tourist and the service delivery. A guest is therefore part of the tourist experience himself, by deciding which service to consume at which moment and by acting on the stage of the travel experience as the protagonist. Mobile business solutions could facilitate service delivery and consequently service quality by catching this simultaneity through situation marketing (Bristow et al., 2002; Schmidt-Belz et al., 2002). Fourth, the travel experience from the visitor's point of view is a chain of events and interactions delivered by numerous suppliers and private persons. The complementarity of all these elements leads to an incontrollable supply chain. Therefore, the coordination between potential suppliers and actors is the key to a successful travel experience. Destination management, understood as an organisational approach which among others increases coordination and effectiveness for tourist places and regions requires (1) the engagement of an organisation dedicated to this challenge (in many cases the tourist office) and (2) the support of information technology (Bieger, 2002). For alpine destinations, only a small part of tourist services is bundled into tour packages or integrated within all-inclusive resorts. Still today, the usual visitor is an individual tourist. Mobile business solutions enable this type of traveller to organise his travel not only before, but also during his journey (Cheverst et al., 2002; Kulju and Kaasinen, 2002).

Travel Recommender Systems

Today, there are several models how a visitor chooses the services before, during, and after the trip (Moutinho, 1987; Ankomah et al., 1996; Fesenmaier and Jeng, 2000). Travel recommender systems are based on these models. They propose with the help of various information and communication technology applications information and services (Burke, 2000) that hopefully lead the visitor to a more valuable trip. Mobile travel recommender systems, in particular, have clear benefits: (1) the visitor receives filtered and suitable suggestions, and destinations impede an annoying information overload during his stay (Good et al., 1999; Hibbard, 1997), (2) cross-selling increases sales volume, (3) the tourist's location can be identified and based on the visitor's contextual needs (Zipf and Malaka, 2001; Abowd and Mynatt, 2000; OpenLs, 2000) matching services could be proposed (e.g., early works from Lenz, 1996; and further developed by Delgado and Davidson, 2002).

Transportation companies already capitalise on the use of mobile commerce applications by delivering SMS or WAP services for online information (railways and airlines) and for reservation and sales (airlines) (Marcussen, 2002). However, for mobile travel recommender systems in a complex environment, namely where numerous SMEs and public services create together an integrated travel experience, practical solutions have been implemented only in few cases and are still tested under lab-like conditions. There have been made tests in museums (Oppermann and Specht, 1999), leisure parks (Bellotti et al., 2001) exhibition centres (Mathes et al., 2001), conferences (Sumi and Mase, 2001) cities (Cheverst et al., 2002; Rakkolainen and Vainio, 2001), and with different platforms like web sites (Estevez & Fernandez, 2002), GPS supported PDAs (TourServ, 2002; Kulju and Kaasinen, 2002; Löhnert et al., 2001), as well as the whole range of mobile terminals including PDAs and 2G+ phones, PC and ISDN card phones and digital TV (Andrade et al., 2002). Today, independently of the technological progress, a shift towards large-scale, representative, and more complex studies for mobile travel recommender systems is in course (e.g., Schmidt-Belz et al., 2002).

This article presents the trial case study of a mobile travel recommender system for St. Moritz. It follows three objectives:

1. To present methodological and technological limitations to mobile travel recommender systems when tested in a real life environment and with real visitors.
2. To analyse the specific case of St. Moritz and to define future perspectives of mobile business for the destination.
3. To describe further work and challenges.

PROJECT AND METHODOLOGY

Technical Background

The project was set up as a trial to gain both, academic research and business related results, based on a newly developed system called Destination-Pilot. The project aimed at evaluating the benefits of mobile travel recommender systems for tourist offices and tourist destinations. Technical feasibility and usability as well as the potential for exploitation were additional goals which should help define a plan for realisation at large scale for the whole destination. The core piece of the Destination-Pilot consists of the Business Rule Engine, a software application, which uses four different types of impulses released by the visitor and the suppliers in the destination to optimally match the personal and situational profile of a guest with the service portfolio of a destination. The use of the Destination-Pilot is expected to be a profitable business for tourist organisations, hotels, tour operators, event organisations and many other service providers in the destination. Specifically, it leverages on the following six principles.

(1) Mobile tourism: Today, many guests use the Internet to obtain information that helps them to book and plan a journey at home, whereas the possibilities of the new generations of mobile communication are scarcely used (Tjostheim and Boge, 2001). Especially these new communication channels open up new opportunities to meet guest's requirements in offering situation-based services. *(2) Customized solution:* The Destination-Pilot combines data of the personal and situational profile in order to propose tailor-made service offers. *(3) Situation-Based*

Services: The service portfolio of a tourist region can be marketed accordingly because the Destination-Pilot places virtually any service offer that matches the situational and individual needs of a guest. *(4) New Business Potential:* The solution addresses enterprises and organisations of the tourism and telecommunication industry that intend to gain access to new revenue opportunities. *(5) Mobile Cross Selling:* The Destination-Pilot anticipates needs and enables cross selling (e.g., golfers receive an invitation to an evening concert). The guest will be pro-actively informed about the services adequate to his situational context. Either through SMS, E-mail, MMS or through his individual and personalised portal the guest is provided with the necessary information that enables him to make his best choice. *(6) One-to-one Marketing:* The information about the guest is stored in a database. The continually updated and refined individual profile of the guest's requirements serves to satisfy his needs more precisely in the future.

The Destination-Pilot consists of a Business Rules Engine (BRE), a front-end and a back-end-system. All interactions between the sub-systems are controlled by business rules. The BRE is the core information and control-system of the Destination-Pilot. The BRE works on the basis of impulses which are generated by either visitors or suppliers. Depending on the impulse it generates two types of actions: push-action (information is delivered to the visitor), pull-action (visitor generates an enquiry).

There are four impulses which trigger the BRE: two impulses which are based on information stored in the back-end-system "location" (where is the visitor currently?) and "CRM" (which profile does the visitor have?) and two impulses located in the front-end-system "visitor" (enquiry generated by the visitor), "offer" (information delivered to the visitor). The system allows a fine tuned push- and pull- marketing: the impulse types "location," "CRM" and "offer" trigger push-actions, whereas the impulse type "visitor" activates additionally a pull process, eventually leading to a further pull- and push- interaction and therefore to a chat between visitor and suppliers. The latter enables processes based on assumptions on guest behaviour, customer segments and available customer data. It continuously improves the quality of push-actions through the learning aptitude of the BRE and permanent increasing knowledge of the guest (see also Ricci et al., 2002).

Figure 1 shows schematically the mechanism between impulse types, BRE, and push- and pull-actions.

Besides the four impulses described above, the Destination-Pilot uses the so-called Intelligent Pull, because it induces the visitor to do the

FIGURE 1. Impulse Types, BRE, and Push- and Pull-Actions

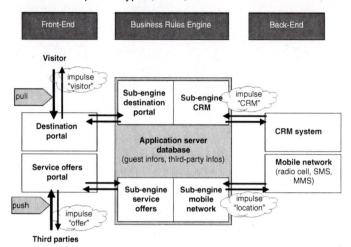

first step. It informs the Destination-Pilot of the visitor's location and his needs, without infringing personal data protection. The Intelligent-Pull is either based on an SMS sent by the visitor or on retrievable information from a WAP page. Placards, billboards or other visual displays positioned at convenient places in the tourist destination could motivate the guest to send an SMS and make full use of the mobile portal of the destination. To attain the desired information the guest is invited to send an SMS or to submit a particular address in his WAP portal. The SMS number is distinctive and guarantees a location-based, customer-related service; no other billboard with the same content positioned at a different place has the same number. The guest sends an SMS and the Destination-Pilot immediately transmits the requested details about the services like time and place of a certain events or about the tourist companies like their address and their opening hours (either by SMS or MMS). If the guest decides to submit his WAP address he receives in return a WAP page containing the desired information. After these transactions the Destination-Pilot knows the location of the guest and has detailed information with regard to his preferences and his needs in a given situation. This information together with the mobile network number is deposited in the database. A guest who has informed himself by means of an SMS on a billboard about e.g., the condition of the skiing slopes, will receive more "push"-offers during his stay corresponding to his cluster of requirements, such as the offers from discotheques, or fashion boutiques.

Application of the Trial

St. Moritz is a large (approximately 1 million overnights per year) tourist resort in the Swiss Alps. It is internationally well known and offers a wide range of services, including summer and winter leisure and sports activities, such as e.g., cultural events, conference, exhibitions facilities, and spa areas. The destination comprises one central town and eleven mid-sized and small villages. It attracts varied target groups, and despite the image of a luxurious place, it offers a wide price and quality range, which makes it a suitable trial place. The tourist office of the St. Moritz is IT-friendly, innovative, and has the critical size (approximately 30 employees) to implement such a case. The IT system is state-of-the-art, from the reservation system, to the web–accessible information database, to the company intranet. But the most convincing and synergetic fact for this project is the current implementation of a smart customer card for visitors and locals, which includes services from hotels, mountain railways, restaurants, rental shops, and leisure services. Hence, for this trial, only customer card holders were included. This gives a good basis for gaining first customer data sets. To reach the trial objectives a series of main challenges have been addressed. Figure 2 depicts the complexity of flows to be tracked and evaluated during the trial as well as the associated challenges.

The main data and actions generated in the trial will come through SMS. WAP and other platforms have proved to be technically still in development, limited in use, too uncertain in their benefit and therefore unsuitable for the trial (Tjostheim and Boge, 2001; Carroll and Coladon, 2002; Ejiogu and Jordan, 2002). The available SMS-Service during the trial included information for the categories accommodation, restaurants, winter sports, entertainment, shopping and transportation. The guests needed to send the keyword through SMS to the number +41 78MYSTMOR(itz) (pull-service). Additionally, they were delivered up to date information and offers by the tourist companies in the destination (push-service). The following specific cases were tested and evaluated.

- Info service selection (pull): This function displayed the various main and sub-categories of offers in the destination. Main categories were accommodation, restaurants, winter sports, entertainment, shopping, and transport. Subcategories for accommodation were e.g., 5*, 4*, ... , holiday apartment, subcategories for winter sports were e.g. cable-cars, rental shops, weather, slope condition, etc. For some subcategories further subdivisions were delivered. For 5* hotels, for example, the subcategories Boston, Alpenblick, Schlossgarten, etc. were available. The subdivisions ended with the specific company or service containing a rather fix information (address) and a variable part (update).

- Info service address (pull): The addresses of all participating tourist enterprises were retrievable, according to their categories. A total of 250 addresses were included in the project. Thus, guests could not only see which services were offered but also where they were located and which general information was given (e.g., opening hours for cable-cars and restaurants).
- Info service update (pull): Up to date information on services and events have been submitted through a specific supplier portal on the internet (e.g., Update Hotel Boston on +41 78MYSTMOR(itz): *"Today, starting at 7 p.m. live New Orleans Jazz at the piano bar. Entrance free."*)
- Free subscriber service (push): The tourist suppliers had the opportunity to send SMS to individual guests. The messages were based on the visitor's profile. Previously, guests could enter their interests in a login-protected area on www.mystmoritz.ch, which could be adapted anytime by the guest himself (e.g., Free subscriber service music: *"Today, starting at 7 p.m. live New Orleans Jazz at the piano bar, Hotel Boston, Via Badrutt 1. Entrance and welcome drink free."*)

A total of 241 requests by visitors (push) have been recorded. Specific information on visitors generated by these interactions has been stored by the BRE the CRM sub-engine (see Figure 1). The following chapter is based on the evaluation of the amount of data generated as well as on its quality. Additionally, in order to draw general conclusions and implications for practice and theory, the results have been compared to the expected objectives of the project.

RESULTS

There are seven areas of qualitative and quantitative research leading to the final conclusions: (1) technical aspects, (2) cost and revenue model, (3) involvement of local tourism enterprises, (4) involvement of guests,

FIGURE 2. Activities and Challenges of the Project

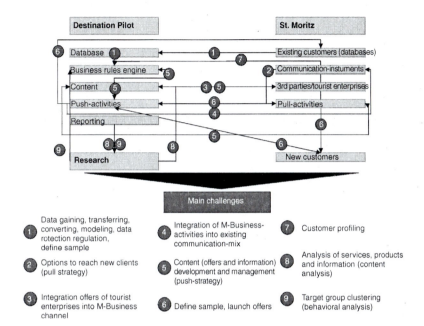

(5) content quantity and quality, (6) communication, and (7) volume and potential.

1. Technical Aspects

The SMS technology is mature and can be exploited. However, there is a considerable mismatch between the need for volume in mobile business and the options offered by the telecommunication provider, especially in respect of the price for business or quick dial numbers. The alternative, namely the installation of an ordinary mobile number, is much cheaper. But for that case, no useful pricing can be achieved (see next point).

2. Cost and Revenue Model

There have been two basic options for the implementation of a business model and derived pricing strategy. On the one hand, the supplying tourism enterprise should pay every time it gained some benefit. That would occur when the end-users requested through mobile phone any kind of information on the specific enterprise. The costs for every transaction were charged to the enterprise. On the other hand, the end-user should pay every time he requested information that were only to his personal benefit (e.g., snow conditions, slope conditions, weather reports). For the trial, the involved companies decided to bear all the charges and to evaluate at a later time the introduction of an extended subscriber service paid by the users. Every company has been charged a fix price of 200.-CHF. The additional costs to send SMS (push services) amounted to 0.20-0.60 CHF per SMS.

3. Involvement of Local Tourism Enterprises

Despite the existence of loose networks among the tourist enterprises, due partly to the need for cooperation, there was no juridical obligation to join the project. Costs and effort to convince the enterprises to engage in the project were accordingly high. The bottom-up approach with the goal to involve as many enterprises as possible was the most difficult challenge. The project responsible was confronted with the need to acquire a critical mass of enterprises, which in return increases the incentive for other enterprises to join the project. A total of around 250 enterprises have been included in the trial.

4. Involvement of Guests

An additional challenge was given by the critical mass of visitors potentially using the system. The more were presumed to make use of the services (market potential), the higher was the incentive for the enterprises to join, the higher was the attractiveness of the system (in terms of optional variety), the higher in return was the attractiveness for the users to use the system. Furthermore, the guests had to be acquired under the circumstance that they might stay only a short period of time in the destination (usually, three-four overnights). The benefit of such a system increases with the willingness to stay longer and/or repeat the visit to the destination.

5. Content Quantity and Quality

Basic information about the destination, its enterprises and services as well as addresses and locations were available. The guest could know weather and slope conditions, the address and location of a hotel, the location and opening hours of services like fashion shops, flower shops, hairdressers, etc. However, it was difficult to add up to date information on daily events and offers in order to "push" bookable or at least valuable content. Reason for this was the earlier mentioned challenge to get as many enterprises on the boat as possible. Looking back, the project responsible assume that despite around 250 enterprises included in the trial, the volume and quality (especially "pushable" offers) of content did not surpass the critical mass for success. Reason for this was the lack of effort by the participating companies. They needed not only to think of which offers could be adequate to be sent through this system and therefore decide rather quickly on the according action. They also had to take their time to put up a short but persuasive text. These might be rather simple tasks but if we consider a hotel manager dealing the first time with these new options of marketing, it is possible that despite the delivered examples by the project partners the uncertainty of the outcome leads him to abstain from it.

6. Communication

The project has been announced locally and to visitors early through various media and informative events. The St. Moritz tourist board could additionally leverage on its home printed lifestyle magazines and brochures which are sent to their repeat visitors as well as to various sponsoring enterprises and business partners. During the trial season the project has been explained in detail to locals and guests. Among other communication media, web banners have been placed on the destination's homepage. The communication efforts and the resulting costs have been so high that it is difficult to justify, especially during the initializing phase, the benefit of such an undertaking.

7. Volume and Potential

Due to the limited volume of requests and offers, some basic key figures could be reported. Among others the number of accesses (Figure 3) and the type of information (Figure 4) present a good overview of the volume caught during the trial phase. Considering the strong seasonality of St. Moritz during the winter, it is no surprise that January was a very strong month. However, as the season starts one-two weeks before Christmas, December is somewhat an important period. Moreover, February is a strong month for family holidays. The project consortium

FIGURE 3. Accesses by Visitor

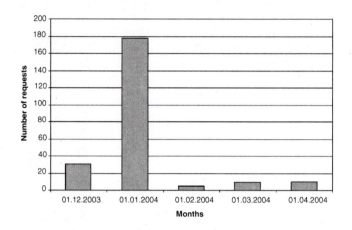

FIGURE 4. Type of Services

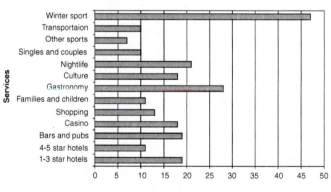

expected more frequencies in these two months. It is possible that for December the service was not well known, yet and that for February fewer events and a different clientele (more families, less young segments) have led to a rapid decrease.

As communication measures for the project started during December, and January is a strong month for St. Moritz, interested users made use of the system especially during January. As expected, information about winter sports and offers (ski area tickets, slope conditions, ski rentals etc.) were the most requested ones. The very limited volume of requests for singles and couples as well as for families and children is due to the lesser than expected interaction between visitor and BRE, which led to a limited profiling. Basically, there were three reasons for the modest volume of users. (1) The visitors have not been informed thoroughly about the project. With reference to content and to the choice of the communication channels, the project responsible implemented a convincing concept. However, the costs resulting from all these activities, led the decision makers to choose a "medium intensity." (2) The benefit for the users has not been made clear enough. Due to a limited volume of offers and information, the customer value of the system was limited. (3) The costs arising from the initialization phase were not only high for the local tourist office but also for the enterprises willing to push specific offers. The time and effort necessary for this work was at least as hindering as the financial burden.

CONCLUSION AND FURTHER RESEARCH

Based on the experiences of the trial in St. Moritz, for the introduction of mobile business solutions in tourist destinations four conclusions can be drawn.

(1) The starting phase is mostly critical. The more services are offered, the higher the potential of users. First condition is the cohesion and coordination of the tourist enterprises in the destination. An effective network is more capable to collect the critical mass of services. For the case of St. Moritz we think that the cohesion among the enterprises and the coordination efforts delivered by the tourist office were extraordinary. However, even such a large tourist office like St. Moritz with an effective information platform for the destination could not convince and include all the possible partners at once.

(2) The local enterprises must be willing to develop bookable or at least valuable offers (push). A passive behaviour (pull strategy) does not differentiate them from the competition. The limited number of push offers developed by the tourist enterprises shows that there are probably difficulties in dealing with such a new distribution channel, namely an uncertain efficiency of the platform (are the efforts worthwhile?), the necessary flexibility in deciding on a short term basis (especially during the high season) which offers are adequate, the lack of acquaintance in formulating the offers and dealing with possible requests by the visitors, etc.

(3) Communication efforts must address the supply and the demand side, before, during, and after the critical season. If mobile business solutions want to be successful, they have to be treated like current traditional operative work (e.g., booking centre, advertising department) and therefore staffed and equipped with the according personnel and resources. The tourist office was accordingly staffed for the project. However, the trial was limited to one season, so that possible improvements for further seasons could not be implemented. Even though the project was highly prioritized in the tourist office, the costs to carry on for the following seasons were too high. Consequently, it will be difficult to justify the implementation of this solution at a local level (local tourist office) for the long-term without providing quick profitable results.

(4) The current pricing conditions, strongly affected by the prices set by telecommunication companies, allow only large tourist destinations, with an overnight size of at least 1 million to finance such an endeavour. Further research must address the following areas. (1) Affordable financing models and therefore general business models have to be tested. Costs are currently too high to justify mobile business systems for destinations. Therefore, new approaches for financing must be found and successfully implemented. (2) Incentives for basic interest and frequent use on the demand side must be developed and evaluated. Still today, we don't really know which mechanisms lead consumer groups to adopt a specific technology or not. Concepts and models for usability could be helpful. (3) Models for technology diffusion should be adopted and verified for the case of mobile business in order to identify the critical mass at the demand and supply side.

REFERENCES

Abowd, G. D., and Mynatt, E. D. (2000). Charting Past, Present, and Future Research in *Ubiquitous Computing. ACM Transactions on Computer-Human Interaction 7*(1), pp. 29-58.

Andrade, M.T., Santos, E., Livaditi, J., and Tsakali, M. (2002). Managing multimedia content and delivering services across multiple client platforms using XML. Presentation at the Workshop Mobile Tourism Support Systems, Pisa, 17 September 2002.

Ankomah, P.K., Crompton, J.L., and Baker, D. (1996). Influence of cognitive distance in vacation choice. *Annals of Tourism Research 23*(1), pp.138-150.

Bellotti, F., Berta, R., De Gloria, A., Margarone, M., and Gabrieli, A. (2001). E-Tour: Multimedia Mobile Guides to Enhance Fruition of the Heritage. *Conference pro-*

ceedings of the EU-IST E-Business and E-Work Congress 2001, Venice 17-19 October 2001.

Bieger, T. (2002). *Management von Destinationen*. 5. ed. Munich/Vienna: Oldenbourg.

Bristow, H., Baber, C., Cross, J., Woolley, S., and Jones, M. (2002). Minimal Interaction for Mobile Tourism Computers. Presentation at the Workshop, *Mobile Tourism Support Systems*, Pisa, 17 September 2002.

Burke, R. (2000). Knowledge-based Recommender Systems. in: Dekker, M. (ed.), *Encyclopaedia of Library and Information Science, volume 69* (32), pp. 1-23.

Carroll, R., and Coladon, M. (2002). What works with Mobile Internet—Lessons from Japan. *Conference proceedings of the EU-IST E-Business and E-Work Congress 2002*, Prague 16-18 October 2002.

Cheverst, K., Davies, N., and Mitchell, K. (2002) A reflective study of the GUIDE system. Presentation at the Workshop *Mobile Tourism Support Systems*, Pisa, 17 September 2002.

Delgado, J., and Davidson, R. (2002). Knowledge bases and user profiling in travel and hospitality recommender systems. In *Proceedings of the ENTER 2002 Conference*, Innsbruck, Austria, Springer: Vienna et al., January 22-25 2002, pp. 1-16.

Ejiogu, C., and Jordan, P. (2002). Revolutionizing the pre-flight Experience. Presentation at the Workshop *Mobile Tourism Support Systems*, Pisa, 17 September 2002.

Estevez Garcia, J.A., & Fernandez Ortiz, G. (2002). ESTIA: Efficient electronic Services for Tourists In Action. *Conference proceedings of the EU-IST E-Business and E-Work Congress 2002*, Prague 16-18 October 2002, pp. 669-684.

Fesenmaier, D.R., and Jeng, J. (2000). Assessing structure in the pleasure trip planning process. *Tourism Analysis 5* (1), pp. 13-29.

Good, N., Schafer, J.B., Konstan, J., Borchers, A., Sarwar, B., Herlocker, J., and Riedl, J. (1999). Combining Collaborative Filtering with Personal Agents for Better Recommendations. *Proceedings of the 1999 Conference of the American Association for Artificial Intelligence (AAAI-99)*, pp. 439-446.

Hibbard, J. (1997). Straight line to relevant data. *Informationweek, 657*, pp. 21-25.

Kulju, M., and Kaasinen, E. (2002). Route Guidance Using a 3D City Model on a Mobile Device. Presentation at the *Workshop Mobile Tourism Support Systems*, Pisa, 17 September 2002.

Lenz, M. (1996). Imtas-intelligent multimedia travel agent system. In Information and Communication Technologies in Tourism. *Proceedings of the ENTER 1996 Conference*, Springer: Vienna et al., 1996, pp. 11-17.

Löhnert, E., Wittman, E., Pielmeier J., and Sayda F. (2001). VISP-A Mobile Digital Tour Guide for Mountaineers. 7th EC-GI & GIS Workshop EG II-Managing the mosaic, Potsdam, Germany, 13-15 June 2001.

Malaka, R., and Zipf, A. (2000). DEEP MAP-Challenging IT research in the framework of a tourist information system. pp. 15-27 In: Fesenmaier, D. Klein, S. and Buhalis, D.: Information and Communication Technologies in Tourism 2000. *Proceedings of ENTER 2000*, Barcelona. Wien, New York.

Marcussen, C. (2002). SMS, WAP, m-commerce-opportunities for travel and tourism services. Presented at the *22nd "Electronics in Tourism" ITB Congress*, Berlin 17-20 March 2002.

Mathes, I., Pateli, A., Tsamakos, A., and Spinellis, D. (2001). Context Aware Services in Exhibition Environment-The mEXPRESS approach. *Conference proceedings of the EU-IST E-Business and E-Work Congress* 2001, Venice 17-19 October 2001, pp. 685-692.

Mazanec, J. (1994). Consumer, behaviour, marketing research, and segmentation. In Witt, S. and Moutinho, L. (eds.), *Tourism marketing and management handbook. 2. edition*, Hempstead, 1994. Prentice Hall, pp. 293-299.

Moutinho, L. (1987). Consumer behaviour in tourism. *European Journal of Marketing, 21*(10), pp. 5-44.

Open Location Initiative (OpenLS) (2000). *Open Location Initiative, http://www.openls.com/*

Oppermann, R., and Specht, M. (1999). A Nomadic Information System for Adaptive Exhibition Guidance. *Proceedings of the International Conference on Hypermedia and Interactivity in Museums (ICHIM 99)*. Washington, USA, 23 –September 1999, pp. 103-109.

Poslad, S., Laamanen, H., Malaka, R., Nick, A., Buckle, P., and Zipf, A. (2001). CRUMPET: Creation of User-friendly Mobile services Personalised for Tourism. In: *3G 2001. Second International Conference on 3G Mobile Communication Technologies*. London, 2001, pp. 26-29.

Rakkolainen, I., and Vainio, T. (2001). A 3D City Info for Mobile Users. Computers & Graphics, *Special Issue on Multimedia Appliances 25*(4), pp. 619-625.

Ricci, F., Arslan, B., Mirzadeh, N., and Venturini, A. (2002) Itr: A case-based travel advisory system. In S. Craw, *6th European Conference on Case Based Reasoning, ECCBR 2002*, Aberdeen, 4-7 September 2002, pp. 613-627.

Schmidt-Belz, B., Poslad, S., and Zipf, A. (2002). Creation of User-friendly Mobile Tourism Services. Presentation at the *Workshop Mobile Tourism Support Systems*, Pisa, 17 September 2002.

Sumi, Y., and Masc, K. (2001). Digital Assistant for Supporting Conference Participants: An Attempt to Combine Mobile, Ubiquitous and Web Computing. *Proceedings of Ubicomp 2001–Ubiquitous Computing, Third International Conference*, September 30–October 2, Atlanta, Georgia, USA, pp. 156- 175.

Tjostheim, I., and Boge, K. (2001). Mobile Commerce–Who are the potential customers. Presentation at the COTIM, *Conference on telecommunications and information markets*.

TourServ (2002). EU project IST-1999-20414. Personalised Tourist Services Using Geographic Information Systems via Internet. *Final Report covering period 1.09.2000–30.11.2002.*

Zipf, A., and Malaka, R. (2001). Developing "Location based Services" (LBS) for Tourism-The service providers view. *ENTER 2001, Proceedings of the 8th International Congress on Tourism and Communications Technologies in Tourism*. Montreal, Canada, pp. 24-27 April.

Evaluating Internet Portals–
An Empirical Study
of Acceptance Measurement Based
on the Austrian
National Tourist Office's Service Portal

Claudia Klausegger

SUMMARY. Due to the great importance of the "information business" in the tourism industry, the Internet has seen increasing use in this field. This paper deals with the evaluation of Internet portals based on the example of the Austrian National Tourist Office, Austria's largest tourism service organization. The empirical analyses performed on the basis of 172 useable questionnaires demonstrate the high significance of the Internet in the work processes of tourism professionals. In this context, significant differences were identified between the four user groups examined in the B2B field (provincial tourism organizations, hotels, travel agencies/operators and associations) and between age groups and genders in the various dimensions of Internet portal evaluation. Usability and content play the most critical role as factors influencing the appeal

Claudia Klausegger is Assistant Professor of Marketing, Vienna University of Economics and Business Administration, Department of Marketing, Augasse 2-6 A-1090 Vienna, Austria (E-mail: claudia.klausegger@wu-wien.ac.at).

[Haworth co-indexing entry note]: "Evaluating Internet Portals–An Empirical Study of Acceptance Measurement Based on the Austrian National Tourist Office's Service Portal." Klausegger, Claudia. Co-published simultaneously in *Journal of Quality Assurance in Hospitality & Tourism* (The Haworth Hospitality Press, an imprint of The Haworth Press, Inc.) Vol. 6, No. 3/4, 2005, pp. 163-183; and: *Innovation in Hospitality and Tourism* (ed: Mike Peters, and Birgit Pikkemaat) The Haworth Hospitality Press, an imprint of The Haworth Press, Inc., 2005, pp. 163-183. Single or multiple copies of this article are available for a fee from The Haworth Document Delivery Service [1-800-HAWORTH, 9:00 a.m. - 5:00 p.m. (EST). E-mail address: docdelivery@ haworthpress.com].

of Internet portals, the users' satisfaction with them, and their frequency of return visits to a portal. The design of a portal has a significantly lower influence. *[Article copies available for a fee from The Haworth Document Delivery Service: 1-800-HAWORTH. E-mail address: <docdelivery@haworthpress.com> Website: <http://www.HaworthPress.com> © 2005 by The Haworth Press, Inc. All rights reserved.]*

KEYWORDS. Acceptance measurement, internet portals, satisfaction measurement, e-tourism, Austrian National Tourist Office

RESEARCH QUESTION AND OBJECTIVES

In recent decades, tourism has become a crucial, fast-growing sector of the Austrian economy (Pringlhuber, 2002, p. 3). Austria's GDP, balance of payments and employment levels are heavily dependent on the development of the Austrian tourism industry. For this reason, there are numerous organizations at the national and provincial level whose task is to promote Austrian tourism (BMWA, 2001, p. 1). At the national level, these organizations include the Federal Ministry of Economics and Labor (abbreviated BMWA), the Austrian Federal Economic Chamber (WKÖ), the Austrian Hotel Association (ÖHV), the Austrian Association of Travel Agents (ÖRV) and the Austrian National Tourist Office (ÖW). The Austrian National Tourist Office, which was set up in 1946, is the largest service organization in Austria's tourism industry and was thus chosen as the subject of this empirical study.

Information plays a significant role in the tourism industry, which is why the Internet is seeing increased use in this area. The term 'e-tourism' is no longer a mere buzzword, and numerous initiatives have been launched to promote electronic business in the tourism industry throughout Europe (Werthner, 2000, p. 3ff). In Austria as well, a majority of tourism enterprises have Internet access as well as their own web sites (Werthner, 2000, p. 4ff). For Austria's tourism organizations, there is no longer any question of *whether* they should go online, rather the problem is *how* to present their Internet content (Vogel, 2001, p. 5).

In line with this trend (and in the course of its organizational development into a contemporary, market-driven tourism marketing organization), the Austrian National Tourist Office has been expanding its "information business" via the Internet aggressively for both customer acquisition and support since 1996. In 2001, the previous web site was replaced with a portal site consisting of a B2C portal (for tourists and people interested in Austria) and a separate B2B portal (for tourism professionals, decision makers and journalists). The Austrian National Tourist Office's B2B portal is currently being redesigned and expanded to create a comprehensive information and marketing platform. The basic information required to develop this modified concept includes customer data with regard to the need for Internet portals, satisfaction with the current state of the Austrian National Tourist Office's web site, as well as the most important factors influencing acceptance.

The objective pursued in this paper consists of two parts: The theoretical, conceptual part deals with a brief description of the object of the empirical study (the Austrian National Tourist Office) and a delineation of the term "Internet portal." This is followed by a brief overview of existing models of acceptance measurement for Internet portals in the literature, after which the model underlying this empirical project is presented. The main part of this paper is an empirical study based on the Austrian National Tourist Office as an example. This is meant to address the fundamental question of the need for Internet portals among tourism professionals as well as the current and future importance of portals in work processes. In addition, the Austrian National Tourist Office's Internet portal is used as an example to measure the importance/relevance of the information provided as well as satisfaction with its current offerings. The second empirical objective deals with the extent to which differences in perception exist among the various user groups of the Austrian National Tourist Office's B2B portal (provincial tourism organizations, hotels, travel agencies/operators and tourism associations). In addition, the results are examined for demographic, segment-specific differences. The final part of the empirical investigation reviews the acceptance measurement model underlying this study, that is, the most essential factors influencing satisfaction with the web portal and intentions to use the portal again.

THEORETICAL CONCEPTUAL DISCUSSION

Brief Description of the Austrian National Tourist Office and Its Internet Portal

Since 2001, 75% of the Austrian National Tourist Office has been owned by the Republic of Austria and 25% by the Federal Economic Chamber (WKÖ). The principal objective of the Austrian National

Tourist Office is to promote the Austrian tourism industry. The agency's most important tasks are as follows:

- to position, maintain and develop "Austria as a holiday destination" as a blanket brand in line with the agency's public mandate.
- to conduct market research.
- to recognize trends and develop specific focus areas.
- to supply tourists and people interested in Austria from various markets with information on Austria's tourism offerings.
- to supply Austrian tourism professionals with market-driven services.

The Austrian National Tourist Office addresses each target group with special services. Since 1996, the agency has operated an Internet portal which was originally designed as a joint platform for B2C and B2B services. In 2001, the platform was separated into as the B2C portal and as the B2B portal. The portal is produced by the Austrian National Tourist Office as well as external partners such as TIScover, Feratell, Net Hotels, the Austrian Federal Economic Chamber as well as provincial tourism organizations.

The B2B portal was set up for the purpose of providing tourism professionals, decision makers and journalists with information on the Austrian tourism industry and on the Austrian National Tourist Office, which offers its products and services via this platform. At the same time, tourism professionals can use the portal to plan and prepare the activities they wish to carry out in cooperation with the agency.

Definition of Internet Portals

Internet portals are relatively new business models on the Internet and e-business around the world. The term "portal" was first used in 1998. The relevant literature also mentions synonymous terms such as web portal, Internet portal, portal site, doorway page, gateway site, entry page, start page, personal page, personal portal or hub (Schumacher et al., 1999, p. 6).

There is no uniform academic definition of the term "portal" in the literature (Stampfli-Marzaroli, 2000, p. 9), but numerous attempts have been made to explain the term (Bauer, 2001, p. 19). The term "portal" is rooted in the Latin word "porta," which means door, gate or entrance (Risak, 2001; Pöhlsen, 2000, p. 1). Frischmutz et al. (2001) thus define portals as entrances to the web which support a large number of visitors with various needs in their search for information and services. "A portal makes it easier for the user to search the Internet; it bundles and catalogs information" (p. 101). Aside from this broad definition of portals, there are also narrower interpretations which require the site to be capable of personalization as an additional criterion. Personalization refers to the ability to tailor a web site to the preferences and interests of the individual user (Frenko, 2002). The basic difference between a portal and a web site is that a web site is a graphic representation of statistical information on the Internet and, in contrast to portals, does not offer additional functions (net4eyes, 2002).

In this study, we use a broader working definition of the term "portal": A portal is defined here as a means of accessing a certain area of the Internet or web which is able to provide an overview and orientation aid and to make information and services available to the user in structured form.

Models for Measuring the Acceptance of Internet Portals, Description of the Working Model

The literature on evaluating Internet portals distinguishes between quantitative and qualitative evaluation approaches (Kurz, 1998, p. 216ff). In quantitative approaches, a web site is appraised by analyzing log files stored on the provider's server. These log files contain quantitative indicators such as hits, page impressions and visits (Ganglmair, 2000, p. 30ff.; Preim, 1999; Wenzel, 2001; Hoffmann and Novak, 1996; Inan, 2002). One major disadvantage of these approaches is that log file analyses can not be used to draw immediate conclusions as to satisfaction, and that it is not possible to derive information on the (socio-demographic) characteristics of the web site's users using this approach (Preim, 1997; Grösswang, 2000, p. 9). Therefore, this study is based on a qualitative approach in which acceptance is measured using a multidimensional construct and in which (socio-demographic) differences between user groups can be investigated.

In addition to the wide variety of definitions of the term "portal," there is also a broad range of models which attempt to identify the predominant influencing factors using structural analysis (Kollmann, 1998, p. 73; Mills and Morrison, 2003). In this study, an input/output model has been chosen (see Figure 1). Input/output models depict acceptance on the basis of certain influencing factors. In contrast to pure input models (e.g., the acceptance models developed by Allerbeck and Helmreich, 1984; Schönecker, 1985; Eidenmüller, 1986; Joseph, 1980),

FIGURE 1. Working Model for Acceptance Measurement

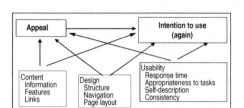

the behavior of the users is taken into account as a result of acceptance (e.g., the acceptance models of Helmreich, 1980; Hilbig, 1984; Wallau, 1990; Swoboda, 1996). In input/output models, the attitude, behavior and satisfaction of the user are taken into consideration as elements of acceptance. These models are only criticized for their failure to account for feedback processes between acceptance and the original influencing factors (for example, the feedback models presented by Reichwald, 1978; Kredel, 1988; Schönecker, 1980).

The model used in this study is based on the input/output model of acceptance measurement developed by Wallau (Kollmann, 1998, p. 82ff.), the empirical model for measuring the acceptance of multimedia customer information systems developed by Swoboda (1996, p. 38ff.), and the studies carried out by Erber and Grösswang (Kurz, 1998, p. 219, Grösswang, 2000, p. 70ff.) to identify the determinants of web site acceptance.

In this paper, acceptance measurement establishes a connection between general attitude judgments and the future use of the medium. In the model approach selected for the empirical study, acceptance is defined as the interplay between attitude and use behavior, as postulated by Swoboda (1996, p. 22) and Wagner (2002, p. 55).

Transposed onto the specific applied case of the Austrian National Tourist Office's portal, this means that the acceptance of the Internet portals is defined as the interplay of a positive attitude regarding the agency's portal and the intention to use this portal again (or the actual use of the portal). The user's attitude, behavioral intentions and satisfaction are used as dimensions determining acceptance. Attitude is measured on the basis of the model developed by Grösswang (2000, p. 209ff.) using the 'appeal/overall impression' indicator, and the behavioral intentions are measured by "use" and "intention to use the portal again." In the evaluation of web sites and portals, three crucial areas can be queried: content, design and usability (Stampfli-Marzaroli, 2000, p. 3ff.). These three areas are also investigated empirically in this paper. They are included in the model by means of individual questions and subjected to evaluation by core B2B users. Content is evaluated in the basis of the dimensions "information," "features" and "links"; design is assessed on the basis of "structure," "navigation" and "page layout"; and usability is measured in terms of "appropriateness to purpose," "self-description" and "consistency."

EMPIRICAL DISCUSSION

Central Research Questions

For the empirical section, the Austrian National Tourist Office's B2B portal has been chosen as the example for the study. The research questions in the empirical study focus on the following areas:

- How significant are Internet portals in the work processes of tourism professionals today, and how significant will they be in the future?
- What features do tourism professionals expect of Internet portals?
- How satisfied are Austrian tourism professionals with the Austrian National Tourist Office's existing Internet portal?
- Are there segment-specific differences between the core user groups of the agency's B2B portal in terms of Internet portal acceptance?
- What are the most important factors influencing the acceptance of Internet portals?

In the first step, the analyses are descriptive with regard to the significance, need for and expectations imposed on tourism portals, as well as satisfaction with the Austrian National Tourist Office's B2B portal. In the next step, the research hypotheses regarding existing segment-specific differences and the acceptance measurement concept underlying the study are reviewed by statistical means.

Survey Design for the Empirical Study

The empirical data was collected by telephone using a standardized questionnaire. This survey was carried out between 9:00 a.m. and 4:00

p.m. on a total of seven business days between June 17, 2002, and June 28, 2002.

The population was defined in line with the core target groups of the agency's B2B portal and includes Austria's provincial tourism organizations, regional and tourism associations within the individual provinces and regions of Austria, hotels (limited to 3, 4 and 5-star establishments) as well as travel agencies/operators (with the exception of businesses dealing entirely in outgoing tourism).

As regards sample selection, it appeared sensible to perform a full survey of the provincial tourism organizations, as there are only nine of them in all of Austria. With regard to the other three groups–associations, hotels, and travel agencies/operators–the decision was made to conduct a partial survey. These samples were drawn by means of quota sampling. The core target group features which were considered relevant in this context included the following:

- The category to which the organization belongs (associations: regional or tourism association; hotels: 3, 4, 5-star hotel; travel agency/operator).
- The size or capital strength of the tourism associations, measured on the basis of the number of overnight stays in the relevant reporting area.
- The province in which the organization is based.

The data required in order to calculate the contingents was acquired from the Austrian National Tourist Office, the Austrian Federal Economic Chamber and the Austrian Association of Travel Agents. A pre-test was carried out by means of six interviews (three in person, three by telephone). The results led to a number of minor changes in the questionnaire with regard to the comprehensibility of the questions.

Results of the Empirical Study

Description of the Sample (Distribution)

A total of 172 valid questionnaires could be included in the analysis. Table 1 shows the distribution of the respondents across the four core target groups.

The personal information collected from the respondents included their professional functions within the relevant organization as well as their gender and age. As regards professional functions, more than half

TABLE 1. Sample Distribution Across the Four Core Target Groups of the Austrian National Tourist Office's B2B Portal

Category	Sample (number)
• Provincial tourism organizations	7
• Hotels	60
° 5-star	10
° 4-star	33
° 3-star	17
• Travel agencies/operators	44
• Associations	61
° Regional associations	22
° Tourism associations	39
• > 100,000 overnight stays	13
• 10,000-100,000 overnight stays	19
• < 10,000 overnight stays	7
Total	172

of the respondents worked in a management position, and 18% of the respondents were employed exclusively in the field of "marketing & sales." With regard to gender distribution, 90 (52.3%) of respondents were male and 82 (47.7%) were female. The distribution of ages shows that the 30-39 age group was the largest in the sample (35.7%), followed by the 40-49 age group (26.8%) and the 20-29 group (22%).

Selected Descriptive Analyses

Frequency of Use, Areas of Use and the Current and Future Importance of the Internet

In the first part of the questionnaire, respondents were asked about the importance of the Internet. When asked about the frequency with which they used the Internet in their work processes (using a 5-point Likert scale, 1 = daily, 5 = never), 156 respondents (90.7% of the sample) indicated that they used the Internet on a daily basis. 15 respondents (8.7%) indicated that they used the Internet in their work processes several times per week. Only one person (0.6%) used the Internet once per week. None of the respondents selected the options "infrequently" or "never."

As regards the importance of the Internet in their work processes (closed-end question with a 6-point Likert scale, 1 = very low, 6 = very high), 81.9% indicated that the Internet is of "rather high" to "very high" importance to their work processes. Only 18.1% of the respondents estimate the importance of the Internet to be "rather low" to "very low."

With regard to the specific areas in which the Internet is used (the question indicated three pre-defined areas of use with a 6-point scale, 1 = never, 6 = very often), the tourism professionals indicated that they use the Internet most frequently for communication purposes (mean = 5.15). The second most frequent use of the Internet was for acquiring information (mean = 4.86). Respondents indicated that they used the Internet rather infrequently for the purpose of purchasing goods and services (mean = 2.20).

When respondents were asked about the future significance of the Internet (with 3 possible answers) the frequency distribution showed that 80.8% of them believed that the Internet would gain importance in their work processes. 19.2% of the interviewees agreed with the statement that the importance of the Internet would remain approximately the same in their work processes. None of the respondents agreed with the statement that the Internet would lose importance in their work processes in the future.

When asked about the areas in which they use the Internet (the question indicated three pre-defined areas of use with a 6-point scale, 1 = never, 6 = very often), the respondents believed that the "use of the Internet for acquiring information" (mean = 5.02) and the "use of the Internet for communication" (mean = 5.34) would tend to increase in importance in the next five years. In contrast, the "use of the Internet for shopping" was appraised more cautiously by the respondents (mean = 3.74).

Relevance of Specific Content, Design Elements

When asked about the importance of the information in an Internet portal (without specific reference to the Austrian National Tourist Office's portal; 6-point Likert scale, 1= completely unimportant, 6 = very important), respondents indicated that they considered the availability of "current information from the tourism industry such as trends and new developments" (mean = 5.32), "links to the most important institutions and organizations in the tourism industry" (mean = 5.14), an "event calendar" (mean = 4.98), and "information on products and services in the tourism marketing field" (mean = 5.96) to be substantially more important than the availability of "yellow pages" (mean = 3.71) or "discussion forums or chat rooms" (mean = 3.32).

In order to assess the presentation characteristics of a tourism portal, respondents were asked to rate the four dimensions "general clarity," "clear structure," "easy orientation" and "highly up-to-date content" on the basis of a six-point Likert scale (1 = "completely unimportant" to 6 = "very important"). As the average values for all four characteristics were above 5.5, we can assume that all four are considered very important by the potential users of a tourism portal.

In order to assess which qualities are considered important to the user friendliness of a portal, another four characteristics were chosen (easy-to-understand operation, short loading times, easy interaction possibilities and uniform, standardized page design) and presented for the respondents to rate using a six-point scale (1 = "completely unimportant" to 6 = "very important"). As the mean values for the characteristics "easy-to-understand operation" and "short loading times" were 5.62, we can assume that the respondents regard these two portal characteristics as very important. With its mean score of 5.18, the "easy interaction possibilities" characteristic is less important than the first two characteristics but still more important on average than the "uniform, standardized page design" (mean = 4.84).

In response to the open-ended question regarding an ideal tourism portal, the TIScover portal was named most frequently by far (mentioned 26 times), followed by the Austrian National Tourist Office's Portal (6 times) and various search engines such as the Yahoo! and "www.salzburgerland.at" portals.

Satisfaction and the Importance of Individual Elements in the Austrian National Tourist Office's Portal

The specific satisfaction and acceptance scores for the Austrian National Tourist Office's B2B portals are presented here in abbreviated form only. In general, users are very satisfied with the Austrian National Tourist Office's B2B portal; 70% of current portal users intend to continue using the portal in the future as well. The reasons against using the portal again were related to the complexity of the portals or a lack of need for the portal's offerings. As far as satisfaction with the individual functions of the Austrian National Tourist Office's B2B portal was concerned, scores were consistently above 4 (on a six-point satisfaction scale) with the exception of the video archive. The corresponding importance/performance matrix is depicted in Figure 2.

None of the assessment characteristics specified for the agency's portal are located in the "high importance and low satisfaction" quadrant; this means that there is no urgent need for change in any of the cri-

FIGURE 2. Importance/Performance Matrix

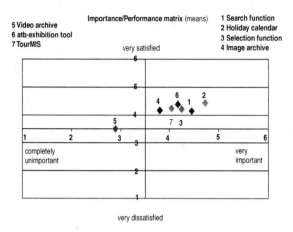

very dissatisfied

teria. The respondents were most dissatisfied with the video archive (mean = 3.50), indicating reasons such as "logging in is a nuisance" and "could not find anything." However, at the same time the video archive element received a rather low mean rating of 2.90 in terms of importance. The quality of the holiday calendar (rated highest in terms of importance with a mean of 4.73 and highest in terms of satisfaction with a mean of 4.44) should most certainly be maintained. Due to their importance from the users' point of view, the other criteria in the upper right quadrant (search function, atb exhibition tool, selection function, TourMIS, image archive) should also be subjected to critical observation and further development.

Analysis of Segment-Specific Differences Between User Groups

In the next step of analysis, the data was examined for significant evaluation differences between user groups and on the basis of demographic criteria (age and gender).

Evaluation Differences Between the Four Categories (Provincial Tourism Organizations, Associations, Hotels, Travel Agencies/ Operators)

One significant result could be derived by reviewing the differences in evaluations based on a comparison of mean scores from the four user groups in question: Employees of provincial tourism organizations estimated the importance of the Internet to be significantly higher than marketing employees in the other categories. The other categories do not differ significantly. In the non-parametric tests performed here, no significant differences between the categories were identified with regard to the future importance of the Internet. In the individual areas of use, there were entirely significant differences between the provincial tourism organizations and the remaining categories. Provincial tourism organizations use the Internet significantly more frequently for communication purposes and information acquisition. Hardly any differences arose in the evaluation of the information's importance (exception: information on products and links to important organizations are significantly more important to provincial tourism organizations). Evaluations of the design of the tourism portal showed no significant differences, nor did the figures indicating acceptance (purpose of use, frequency of use). Only the probability of using the portal again is rated lower by hotels than by associations, travel agencies and travel operators.

Evaluation Differences Between Hotel Classes, Hotel Types and Regions

As far as they could be calculated given the fairly small quantity of category data, no significant differences were detected between the various hotel classes (3, 4, and 5 stars), nor were the differences in evaluations among hotel types significant. Finally, as the Chi^2 test (p = 0.267) shows, no differences in the use of the B2B portal could be detected between regions.

Evaluation Differences Between Genders, Age Groups and Management Levels

In order to review differences in evaluations based on gender, T-tests and U-tests (after Mann and Whitney) were carried out. The analysis results show no significant differences in the importance of the Internet, the purpose of use, the need for tourism portal or user friendliness. This was also the case with the frequency of use and the importance of the elements of the B2B portal. In the evaluation of the Internet portal's presentation, significant differences did arise in the "general clarity." "easy orientation" and "highly current information" characteristics. Women rated the importance of these characteristics significantly higher than their male colleagues. There were also differences in the individual dimensions of satisfaction with the Austrian National Tourist Office's B2B portal. Women were significantly more satisfied than men with the search function and the selection function. No significant differences were found for the holiday calendar, image archive, video archive, atb exhibition tool and TourMIS database elements. Women rated the individual presentation elements (general clarity, clear structure, easy orientation, legible font) significantly higher.

In the analysis of evaluation differences based on age, the correlation coefficient (r) of -0.197 (p = 0.011) shows a slightly significant connection between age and the importance of the Internet, that is, the importance of the Internet decreases significantly for older age groups. The areas in which the Internet is used differ significantly, in particular the use of the Internet to acquire information (r = -0.251, p = 0.001) and to communicate (r = -0.201, 0.009). With regard to the need for an Internet portal for the tourism industry, the Chi^2 test and the contingency coefficient (C = 0.109) did not show significant results (p = 0.364) for different age groups, nor did the use of the B2B portal.

In order to review the extent to which significant evaluations difference exist in relation to the employees' management levels, an H-test (after Kruskal and Wallis) and one-factor variance analyses were performed. These tests showed no significant difference in the frequency of use between management levels. Moreover, all three levels assessed the importance of the Internet without significant differences (one-factor variance analysis, p = 0.945). Likewise, there were no significant differences between management levels in the areas of Internet use or in their assessments of the need for an Internet portal (Chi^2 test, p = 0.828). There were also no significant differences in evaluations of the importance of specific content and elements of the portal, with the exception of discussion forums (p = 0.039). As regards acceptance of the Austrian National Tourist Office's B2B portal (including frequency of use, intention to use again, recommendation to others), there was only a significant difference in overall satisfaction (p = 0.010). This means that employees at fulfillment level were generally more satisfied with the Austrian National Tourist Office's B2B than the management and service levels.

Factors Influencing the Acceptance of the B2B Portal

In order to find out whether (or the extent to which) the three factors specified in the model–content, design and usability–influence the users' attitudes or behavioral intentions with regard to the B2B portal, multiple linear regression was carried out for each of these dimensions. The "attitude" dimension was taken into account as a multi-attribute measurement by including the variable "overall appeal of the B2B portal," while the use behavior dimension was included in the regression model using the "intention to use the portal again" variable. A stepwise regression procedure was chosen. In addition, due efforts were made to adhere to the premises of the regression model, such as linearity, completeness of the model, homoscedacity, autocorrelation, multicollinearity and the normal distribution of disturbance variables.

Factors Influencing the Overall Appeal of the B2B Portal

As shown in Figure 3, all three independent variables or factors were included in the regression equation due to their significant influence weights. Taken together, the three independent variables–usability, content and design–explain 65.1% (i.e., more than half) of the overall spread of the dependent variable "overall appeal of the B2B portal"; this can be seen in the corrected coefficient of determination. In addition, the T-test showed the influences of the three independent variables "usability," "content" and "design" to be highly significant. In order to compare the weights of the independent variables, the standardized regression coefficients (beta values) were analyzed. The results show that the usability of the B2B portal has the strongest influence on its appeal (beta = 0.590), followed by the content presented on the portal (beta = 0.470). The design of the B2B portal has the weakest influence on its overall appeal (beta = 0.330).

FIGURE 3. Factors Influencing the Appeal of the B2B Portal

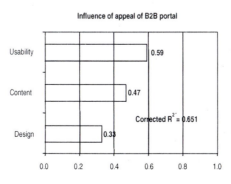

Influence of appeal of B2B portal

Factors Influencing the Respondents' Intentions to Use the B2B Portal

As shown in Figure 4 below, all three independent variables/factors were also included in the regression equation for the "intention to use the B2B portal again" dimension due to the significant weight they demonstrated in a T-test. The corrected coefficient of determination shows that 32.6% of the overall spread of the explained variable "intention to use the B2B portal again" can be attributed to the three explanatory variables of usability, content and design. In order to compare the weights of the independent variables, the standardized regression coefficients (beta values) were again analyzed in this case. As a result, the content presented in the portal turned out to have the strongest influence (beta = 0.398) on the respondents' intentions to use the portal again, followed closely by the portal's usability (i.e., user friendliness; beta = 0.373). The design of the portal had the least influence on the respondents' intentions to use the portal again (beta = 0.282) in this case as well.

The analyses performed confirm the conjecture postulated in the working model that the three factors–usability, content and design–influence the "overall appeal of the B2B portal" as well as the "intentions to use the B2B portal again." The design of the portal had the least influence in these dimensions. According to these analyses, what is far more important for the "overall appeal" and "intention to use again" dimensions are the features of "usability" and "content," where the usability of the portal exerts a stronger influence on its appeal and the content of the portal has a greater influence on the respondents' intentions to use it again.

FIGURE 4. Factors Influencing Intentions to Use the B2B Portal Again

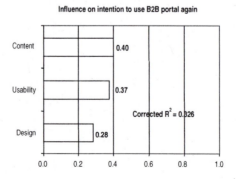

CONCLUSIONS AND IMPLICATIONS

This study deals with the evaluation of Internet portals in the tourism industry. The Internet portal of the Austrian National Tourist Office, the largest service organization in Austria's tourism industry, was chosen as an example. The results of the telephone survey of 172 B2B customers of the agency using a standardized questionnaire show that the tourism professionals surveyed assign great importance to the Internet, a fact which manifests itself in the high frequency of use indicated by respondents. The main areas in which the Internet is used are communication and information acquisition, while its importance for the purpose of purchasing goods and services is substantially lower at present. In the detailed analyses of the characteristics of a portal, it became clear that "general clarity," "clear structure," "easy orientation" as well as "highly up-to-date content" are considered very important. As regards user friendliness, "easy-to-understand operation" and "short loading times" are regarded as especially relevant.

The evaluation of the Austrian National Tourist Office's portal shows an entirely positive result among B2B users in the importance/performance matrix. Target group-specific analyses also yielded interesting results. Significant differences in evaluation appeared between the four organization categories surveyed (provincial tourism organizations, hotels, travel agencies/operators, associations) in terms of the frequency of use, the need for a portal and the expectations of a tourism portal, which can probably be attributed to the organizations' differing tasks. This means that the mere division into a B2B portal and a B2C portal is not sufficient to meet the needs of specific target groups; instead, it will be necessary to query these specific needs in greater detail and to take them into account when creating portals (Chakraborty et al., 2002).

The assumptions of the portal acceptance measurement model developed for the empirical study on the basis of the relevant literature were largely confirmed: Content and usability have the strongest influence on the appeal of a portal as well as the frequency with which users return to a portal.

Research Outline

Due to the increasing importance of the Internet, the tourist business has been investing large amounts into the development of websites. Issues involving, e.g., the evaluation of the acceptance of these websites (especially in respect of the innovative service features offered through them) and the future objectives of website development have been largely ignored by researchers and practitioners in tourism alike (Fuchs and Weiermair, 2003, 2004). The central role of the Internet in tourism is best reflected in hard-and-fast figures. In Europe 94 million travels by a total of 337 million were booked via the Internet in 2002 (IETM, 2002) and the upward trend continues.

The idea underlying the present study was to develop a standardized instrument for a B2B portal in the tourist industry so as to ensure repeated measurements for longitudinal analysis and to enable comparisons across various tourist organizations (benchmarking). The use of a standardized instrument, criteria and measures will allow sector-to-sector comparisons in the future. At present, no such standards of performance exist.

From the point of view of methodology, two points have to be highlighted for future continued research. Due to the research issues on hand, the measuring approach chosen in the present study concentrated on features that had to do with selected requirements for tourist websites, such as content, design and usability. In future studies, various other fields, mainly focusing on B2C, will open up in the context of website analyses as the application of websites and portals broadens: customer relations (e.g., customization, interactivity, safety-security etc.), value added services (e.g., networking tools, multimedia, help & service functions, file formatting etc.) and sales (e.g., segment-based customer orientation, layout and tangible forms of presentation of quality and price etc.) (Douglas and Mills, 2004; Morrison et al., 2004; Pan and Fersenmaier, 2000).

The second point concerns the attitude-oriented multi-attribute measuring process chosen in the present study and the representation of results in Importance Performance Analyses (IPA). The importance-performance relationship is i.e., discussed in the contribution by Sampson and Showalter (1999). Using partial ranking as a means to measure attribute importance, they found an inverse relationship between perceived importance and perceived performance. In their paper, Matzler and Sauerwein (2002) point to the different results obtained, depending on the method of measuring (explicitly versus implicitly derived importance) and potential stochastic dependence of importance of and satisfaction with a specific quality attribute. The use of an importance grid could be conceived as an approach for further methodological comparison (Vavra, 1997, p. 385) within which a distinction can be drawn between explicit and implicit importance; it would be equally conceivable to use Penalty-Reward-Contrast (PRC) Analysis. Both procedures lead to a three- factor structure (Basic factor, Performance factor and Excitement factor) (Matzler and Sauerwein, 2002, p. 326).

REFERENCES

Allerbeck, M., and Helmreich, R. (1984). Akzeptanz planen–aber wie? *Office Management 32*(11), pp. 1080-1082.

Bauer, H. (2001). *Unternehmensportale-Geschäftsmodell, Design, Technologie*, Bonn: Galileo Press GmbH.

BMWA (2001). *Tourismus-Jahresbericht für Österreich 2001*, Bundesministerium für Wirtschaft und Arbeit (BMWA). Retrieved December 12, 2004, from Chakraborty, G., Lala, V. & Warren, D. (2002). An Empirical Investigation of Antecedents of B2B Websites'Effectiveness. *Journal of Interactive Marketing 16*(4), pp. 51-72.

Douglas, A., and Mills, J.E. (2004). Staying Afloat in the Tropics: Applying a Structural Equation Model Approach to Evaluating National Tourism Organization Websites in the Caribbean. *Journal of Travel & Tourism Marketing, 17*(2/3), pp. 269-293.

Eidenmüller, B. (1986). *Schwerpunkte der technologischen Entwicklung bei Siemens.* In: Siemens AG (Hrsg), *Soziale Bewältigung der technologischen Entwicklung.* Berlin.

Frenko, A. (2004). Internet-Portal-Sites: Aktueller Hype oder mehr? *Online Maketer Verlag und Beratung.* Retrieved December 12, 2004, from www.autoresponder. de/onlinemarketing/hintergrund/portal-sites.htm

Frischmuth, J., Karrlein W., and Knop, J. (2001). *Strategien und Prozesse für neue Geschäftsmodelle Praxisleitfaden für E- und Mobile Business,* Berlin: Springer.

Fuchs, M., & Weiermair, K. (2003). New Perspectives of Satisfaction Research in Tourism. *Tourism Review 58*(3), 6-14.

Fuchs, M., and Weiermair, K. (2004). Destination Benchmarking–An Indicator's Potential for Exploring Guest Satisfaction. *Journal of Travel Research 42*(3), pp. 212-225.

Ganglmair, B. (2000). *Das Web-Portal–kurzlebiger Trend oder Erfolgskonzept im Internet?, Eine empirische Studie über die Akzeptanz eines Web-Portals für Studenten.* Wien: WU-Wien.

Grösswang, B. (2000). *Die Wirkung der Web-Sites der Abteilungen "Werbewissenschaft und Marktforschung," "Handel und Marketing," "Internationales Marketing und Management" und des Institutes für "Wirtschaftsinformatik" der Wirtschaftsuniversität Wien bei WU-Studentinnen und Studenten.* Wien: WU-Wien.

Hilbig, W. (1983). *Akzeptanzermittlung und Akzeptanzförderung.* Bremen: Universität Bremen.

Hilbig, W. (1984). Akzeptanzforschung neuer Bürotechnologien–Ergebnisse einer empirischen Fallstudie. *Office Management 32* (4), pp. 320-323.

Hoffmann, D., & Novak T. P. (1996). Marketing in Hypermedia Computer-Mediated Evironments–Conceptual Foundations. *Journal of Marketing 60*(3), pp. 50-68.

Inan, H. (2002). *Measuring the success of your Website*. Frenchs Forest, NSW: Pearson Education Australia.

Joseph, J. (1990). *Arbeitswissenschaftliche Aspekte der betrieblichen Einfürung neuer Technologien am Beispiel Computer Aided Design (CAD)*. Frankfurt/M.

Kollmann, T. (1998). *Akzeptanz innovativer Nutzungsgüter und –systeme*. Wiesbaden: Gabler.

Kredel, L. (1988). *Wirtschaftlichkeit von Bürokommunikationsystemen*–eine vergleichende Darstellung. Berlin.

Kurz, H. (1998). Determinanten der Akzeptanz von Firmenauftritten im Internet. *der markt*. 146/147, pp. 215-226.

Matzler, K., and Sauerwein, E. (2002). The Factor Structure of Customer Satisfaction: An Empircal Test of the Importance Grid and the Penalty-Reward-Contrast Analysis. *International Journal of Service Industry Management 13*(4), pp. 314-332.

Mills, J.E., and Morrison, A.M. (2003). Measuring Customer Satisfaction with Online Travel. *International Federation of Information and Communications Technologies in Tourism 2003* Conference Proceedings. Helsinki, Finland. January 27 - February 1, 2003.

Morrison, A.M., Taylor, J.S., and Douglas, A. (2004). Website Evaluation in Tourism and Hospitality: The Art is not yet Stated. *Journal of Travel & Tourism Marketing 17*(2/3), pp. 232-251.

net4eyes (2002). Was ist der Unterschied zwischen einem Portal und einer Homepage? *NETEYES AG*. Retrieved December 12, 2004, from Pan, B. and Fesenmaier, D. R. (2000). A Typology of Tourism Related Web Sites: Its Theoretical Background and Implications, in: Fesenmaier, D.R., Klein, S. & Buhalis, D. (Hrsg.). *Information and Communication Technologies in Tourism 2000*, Proceedings of the International Conference in Barcelona. Spain, 2000, Wien/New York: Springer.

Pöhlsen, C. (2000). Portale im Internet, *Johann Wolfgang Goethe-Universität Frankfurt am Main-Lehrstuhl für Betriebswirtschaftslehre insbesondere Electronic Commerce*. Retrieved December 12, 2004, from Preim, B. (1999). *Entwicklung interaktiver Systeme, Grundlagen, Fallbeispiele und innnovative Anwendungsfehldr*, Berlin, Heidelberg: Springer.

Pringlhuber, C. (2002). Die Organisation des Tourismus in Österreich, *BMWA*. Retrieved December 12, 2004, from

Reichwald, R. (1978). *Zur Notwendigkeit der Akzeptanzforschung bei der Entwicklung neuer Systeme der Bürotechnik, Arbeitsbericht–die Akzeptanz neuer Bürotechnologie*, Band 1, Hochschule der Bundeswehr. München.

Risak, V. (2001). Portale im Internet.*Universität Salzburg-Institut für Computerwissenschaft*. Retrieved December 12, 2004, from Sampson, S.E. & Showalter, M.J. (1999). The performance-importance response function: observations and implications. *The Service Industries Journal 19*(3), pp. 1-25.

Schönecker, H.H. (1980): *Bedienerakzeptanz und technische Innovation–Akzeptanzrelevante Einführung neuer Bürotechniksysteme*. München.

Schönecker, H.G. (1985). Kommunikationstechnik und Bedienerakzeptanz. Pircot, A/Reichwald, R, (Hrsg). *Forschungsprojekt Bürokommunikation*. Band 6, München.

Schumacher, M., Schwickert, A.C. (1999). Web-Portale-Stand und Entwicklungstendenzen. *Universität Mainz-Lehrstuhl für allg. BWL und Wirtschaftsinformatik. Arbeitspapiere WI*

Nr.4. Retrieved December 12, 2004, from Stampfli-Marzaroli, S. (2000). Zielorientierte Evaluation-Internet Portale: Die Rettung für den Zauberlehrling? *Universität Zürich-Institut für Psychologische Methodenlehre*. Retrieved December 12, 2004.

Swoboda, B. (1996). *Akzeptanzmessung bei modernen Informations-und Kommunikations-technologien-Theoretische und empirische Ergebnisse am Beispiel multimedialer Kundeninformationssysteme*. St. Gallen: Thexis-Verlag.

Vavra, T.G. (1997). *Improving Your Measurement of Customer Statisfaction: A Guide to Creating, Conducting, Analyzing and Reporting Customer Satisfaction Measurement Program*. Milwaukee. WI.

Vogel, R. (2001). *Der Weg in die NetEconommy-Märkte, Portale, Projekte*. Wiesbaden: Gabler.

Wagner, M. (2002): *Kundenakzeptanz von eCommerce-Vertriebsschiene auf dem Strommarkt-Empirische Analyse am Beispiel von* Wien: WU-Wien.

Wallau, S. (1990). *Akzeptanz betrieblicher Informationssysteme*–eine empirische Untersuchung, Arbeitsberichte des Lehrstuhl für Wirtschaftsinformatik der Universität Tübingen. Tübingen.

Wenzel, O. (2001). *Webdesign, Informationssuche und Flow*–Nutzungsverhalten auf unterschiedlich strukturierten Websites. Lohmar, Köln: Josef Eul Verlag.

Werthner, H. (2000). Bericht der AG eTourism. *Bundesministerium für Wirtschaft und Arbeit* (BMWA). Retrieved December 12, 2004.

A New Tune from an Old Instrument: The Application of SERVQUAL to a Tourism Service Business

Robert A. Home

SUMMARY. The ability to provide high quality customer service and to deliver customer value is critical to attracting customers in the competitive tourism service environment. This research seeks to explore whether the instrument developed by Zeithaml et al. (1990), referred to as SERVQUAL, can be applied to a tourism service business to provide a quantifiable method of measuring service quality. An adaptation of SERVQUAL was applied to a business operating tours through a brewery in Tasmania, Australia. The instrument proved to be adequately internally reliable and provided apparently useful and easily interpretable diagnostic data to the management of the business. It was concluded that SERVQUAL has the potential to be a useful management tool provided care is taken to adapt the instrument to the individual needs of the user while remaining within the underlying theoretical framework. Adaptation and simplification of the complicated instrument provides small tourism businesses with a new way of gaining theory-based diagnostic

Robert A. Home is a post graduate at the School of Geography and Environmental Studies, University of Tasmania, Sandy Bay, Tasmania, Australia, 7005 (E-mail: Roberthome2@lycos.com).

[Haworth co-indexing entry note]: "A New Tune from an Old Instrument: The Application of SERVQUAL to a Tourism Service Business." Home, Robert A. Co-published simultaneously in *Journal of Quality Assurance in Hospitality & Tourism* (The Haworth Hospitality Press, an imprint of The Haworth Press, Inc.) Vol. 6, No. 3/4, 2005, pp. 185-202; and: *Innovation in Hospitality and Tourism* (ed: Mike Peters, and Birgit Pikkemaat) The Haworth Hospitality Press, an imprint of The Haworth Press, Inc., 2005, pp. 185-202. Single or multiple copies of this article are available for a fee from The Haworth Document Delivery Service [1-800-HAWORTH, 9:00 a.m. - 5:00 p.m. (EST). E-mail address: docdelivery@ haworthpress.com].

Available online at http://www.haworthpress.com/web/JQAHT
doi:10.1300/J162v06n03_11

data that can be self-administered by management on an ongoing basis and is not a burden to the customers. *[Article copies available for a fee from The Haworth Document Delivery Service: 1-800-HAWORTH. E-mail address: <docdelivery@haworthpress.com> Website: <http://www.HaworthPress.com> © 2005 by The Haworth Press, Inc. All rights reserved.]*

KEYWORDS. SERVQUAL, tours, service quality, customer feedback

INTRODUCTION

The ability to provide high quality customer service and to deliver customer value is critical to attracting customers in the competitive tourism service environment. Assessment of the quality of service received by customers has proven to be difficult to measure and often relies on the intuition of the staff and management or customer feedback forms. While each method is useful in indicating whether quality is acceptable, they are both without theoretical basis and are inadequate to provide diagnostic data. This research seeks to explore whether the instrument developed by Zeithaml et al. (1990), referred to as SERVQUAL, can be applied to a tourism service business to provide a quantifiable method of measuring service quality and so allow a more objective assessment by the management of the business.

The underlying theory of SERVQUAL is that service quality can be divided into five dimensions labelled empathy, assurance, reliability, responsiveness, and tangibles. The core principle of SERVQUAL is that for each of these dimensions, the gap between customer expectations and perceptions of received service describes the quality of service. For example, if a consumer perceives to have received better service than was expected, the customer is deemed to have received high quality service in that dimension. Zeithaml et al. (1990) suggested that the gap between expectations (E) and perceptions (P) can be expressed as a single number derived from the formula $I*(P-E)$ where I is a weighting of the importance to the customer of the service dimension.

SERVQUAL was developed for application in the financial sector in the United States and some question exists whether the instrument is applicable outside the context for which it was designed and in particular whether it is applicable to the tourism industry (Babakus and Boller, 1992; Brown et al., 1993; Carman, 1990; Williams, 1998). Babakus and Boller (1992) suggest that a wide variety of services may not be able to be measured on a single measurement scale for service quality. Furthermore, application of SERVQUAL usually requires the assistance of an external consultant, which is likely to be beyond the resources of many small businesses (Williams, 1998).

However, the theory upon which the instrument is based allows some modification without affecting the theoretical integrity (Schmidt, 1995). Parasuraman et al. (1993, p. 143) stated that the SERVQUAL instrument is "the basic skeleton–that can be supplemented with context-specific items when necessary." This paper argues that the instrument must be case specific if it is to be of practical diagnostic use for the business' management and that modification is therefore necessary within, as well as across, applications. SERVQUAL is a reasonably complicated model and its application has usually required the services of external consultants (Williams, 1998). This paper takes a new approach and seeks to explore whether the core of the model, which is able to be used by naïve users, has the potential to provide useful diagnostic data, independently from the rest of the SERVQUAL model.

Ongoing internal self assessment by a tourism service provider, such as the subject of this research, allows the identification of inadequate service quality and so provides a tool for maintaining quality service across each of the dimensions. Demonstration that the SERVQUAL model could be adapted and applied to the selected tourism service would allow the conclusion that the model has the potential to provide useful diagnostic data to tourism service managers generally. However, further testing of the model in the wider context will be required before the utility of the instrument to the tourism industry can be stated with more certainty.

The primary aim of the study is to test the customer feedback section of the conceptual model of service quality proposed by Parasuraman et al. (1985) in the context of a tour service and make inferences as to its applicability and utility to such services.

The secondary aim is to assess the quality of service delivered by Subject Brewery Tours, Hobart, by comparing the quality of service that customers perceive they are receiving with the quality of service that they expect.

LITERATURE REVIEW

Quality is widely regarded as essential to attracting and retaining customers across all industries including service-based industries (Gerson, 1999). Acceptance of the importance of quality to a service industry, such as a tour provider, appears to lead to the decision to work towards enhancing the quality of service delivered. The concept of total quality management involves a "real and meaningful effort by an organisation to change its whole approach to business by making quality a guiding factor in everything the organisation does" (Davidson and Griffin, 2000, p. 744). Application of the total quality management approach to a service industry therefore means that the real and meaningful efforts are to be directed at enhancing the quality of service provided. Consequences of this approach include that there must be a commitment to continual improvement and that an understanding of what constitutes both quality and service is required (Davidson and Griffin, 2000).

The determination of service quality requires a definition of what constitutes service and of what characteristics are unique to services. Services are defined as "deeds, processes and performances (non-tangibles) that satisfy buyer or user needs' (McColl-Kennedy and Kiel, 2000, p. 335). Inherent in the service delivery of a tourism service is the notion that customers are an inseparable part of the process of production and consumption since the service cannot be provided if the customer is not present. Moreover, the quality of perceived service received by a customer is dependant upon many factors including some that are not under the control of the service provider, for example, the frame of mind of the customer at the time (McColl-Kennedy and Kiel, 2000).

Another characteristic of service is perishability because a service is consumed as it is delivered. Services are heterogenous and a perceived risk exists on the part of the buyer because of the intangibility of services and, since a service is simultaneously produced and consumed, it cannot be sampled in advance of sale (McColl-Kennedy and Kiel, 2000). Therefore the intangibility, heterogeneity, and perishability of services create difficulties for marketers in anticipating the "criteria customers use to evaluate service quality" (Zeithaml et al., 1990 p. 16).

Gerson (1999, p. 112) comments that "quality and service are the means to the ends of satisfaction and retention." Debate whether customer satisfaction is a requirement or a result of service quality (Brady, et al. 2002; Cronin and Taylor, 1992; Parasuraman et al., 1994; Teas, 1993) is of less importance than recognising that the concepts are related. While the definition of service is relatively straightforward, defining quality proves to be more difficult. "An internationally accepted definition is that quality is the totality of features and characteristics of a product or service that bear on its ability to satisfy stated or implied needs" (Davidson and Griffin, 2000, p. 741). This definition is broad but also rather vague and the quality of a service or product is open to interpretation by customers and managers causing the concept of quality to be subjective. For total quality management to become a useful approach to improving service quality, a means of quantitative measurement must be used so that an organisation can establish its goals of quality delivery and determine if they are being achieved.

MEASURING SERVICE QUALITY

One means of measuring the service quality is a culture audit, based on the premise that front-line employees have a sound knowledge of what customers expect and what they experience. A widely accepted method of carrying out a culture audit is a questionnaire covering employees' perceptions of issues such as value delivered to the customer, areas that are in need of improvement, and management's capabilities for making a quality improvement initiative succeed (Albrecht, 1992). However, Saleh and Ryan (1991) found that employee perceptions of hotel customers' expectations were incorrect in 27 of 44 attributes measured. While such an audit may be useful as a guide, a more objective and diagnostic assessment of customers' experiences of quality of service received is required for effective quality measurement.

With the recognised need for the continual improvement of service quality, it was necessary for the development of "an instrument for measuring customer's perceptions of service quality" (Zeithaml et al., 1990, p. 23). Prior to 1985, literature relating to quality was devoted to 'tangible goods quality defined in terms of conformance to manufacturers specifications' (Zeithaml et al., 1990, p. 15). The research that followed has led to the development of the SERVQUAL instrument based on the 'premise that customers can rationally rate the performance of a service compared to their expectations of that service' (Howat et al., 1999, p. 42).

The customer feedback section of the SERVQUAL instrument consists of a section containing statements to determine the general expectations of a customer regarding a service and a matching section containing statements to determine the customer's assessment of services received for each of the five attributes; empathy, reliability, responsiveness, assurance and tangibles. A refinement indicating the relative importance of the service attributes is added to provide a weighted quality score for each attribute that can be directly applied to the SERVQUAL model as a value for the gap between expectations and perceptions.

Brief descriptions of the five general attributes that influence customers' assessments of service quality are as follows (Berry and Parasuraman, 1991, p. 16):

- Reliability: The ability to perform the promised service dependably and accurately.
- Tangibles: The appearance of physical facilities, equipment, personnel, and communications materials.
- Responsiveness: The willingness to help customers and to provide prompt service.
- Assurance: The knowledge and courtesy of employees and their ability to convey trust and confidence.
- Empathy: The provision of caring, individualized attention to customers.

Several researchers, including Babakus and Boller (1992), Brown et al. (1993), Carman (1990), and Williams (1998), have questioned whether an instrument developed for application in the financial sector can reasonably be universally applied to other services and suggest that SERVQUAL may be bound by the context for which it was designed. Pitt et al. (1997) argue that a generic model allows comparisons to be made across applications while Babakus and Boller (1992) suggest that a wide variety of services may not be able to be measured on any single measurement scale for service quality. On the other hand, application of the instrument in the financial sector has consistently found reliability to be the most important and tangibles the least important drivers and that these findings have been consistent across "studies, researchers and contexts" (Parasuraman et al., 1994, p. 116), The differences that exist between the financial sector and the tourism industry suggest that at least some modification would be required for valid application of the SERVQUAL instrument.

Schmidt's (1995) assessment and refinement of the SERVQUAL scale in fitness centres concluded that a greater reliability than the original 22-item SERVQUAL scale could be achieved by revision of the SERVQUAL scale. Schmidt (1995, p. 5) noted that, although the "face validity of the SERVQUAL scale has been supported by many studies," peer assessment of his modified scale "indicated that items used– represented the concept of service quality in a fitness centre setting." Howat et al. (1999, p. 55) agree by reporting that their study, which includes perceptions of service quality in Australian leisure centre customers, "provide[s] general support for the findings of Zeithaml et al. (1990)."

Saleh and Ryan (1988), while undertaking a study of the hospitality industry, identified the need to modify the questions and length of the SERVQUAL instrument to be more relevant to the specific service being examined. Williams (1998) noted that the full SERVQUAL instrument often required the use of external consultants and the length of the instrument proved to be an excessive burden to respondents.

A further criticism of the SERVQUAL instrument is that perceptions of service received, automatically include a compensation for their expectations. Carman (1990) suggests that the dual scale could be combined into a SERVQUAL scale relating both perceptions and expectations as single items. He continues by proposing that it is reasonable to assume that perceptions of quality will be influenced by expectations and that "expectations" responses can be of little value. Cronin and Taylor in their 1992 study on measuring service quality, replicated by Brady et al. (2002) reached similar conclusions. They suggest that "service quality should be measured as an attitude" and can best be measured with a performance-based scale which they called SERVPERF (Cronin and Taylor, 1992, p. 64). Parasuraman et al. (1994) counter that, from a practical standpoint, the superior diagnostic value of SERVQUAL more than offsets the loss in predictive power. While Brady et al. (2002) demonstrated the predictive superiority of SERVPERF over SERVQUAL, they concede that SERVQUAL is widely used by service organisations and identified as an appropriate service quality measurement tool in both marketing textbooks (for example Lamb et al., 1995; McColl-Kennedy and Kiel, 2000) and academic journals (for example Akama and Kieti, 2003; Bigne et al., 2003; McAtarsney, 1999).

Teas (1994) specifies the Evaluated Performance and Normed Quality models as alternatives to the SERVQUAL (P-E) model although the model is intended to be broad enough to be useful in the development of a "goods and services" perspective of quality. Norming of expected quality relies on the assumption that customers' expectations are influenced by what they perceive to be feasible. This implies that customers give some thought to the challenges faced by service providers, which in the context of tourism services, may not be the case.

It has been shown that the delivery of quality service is essential to the survival of a service-based industry and that the quality of service delivered is enhanced with the adoption of the total quality management approach. Total quality management involves making a priority for the business to be the continual improvement of the service quality that it delivers. Some form of measurement of quality is therefore required. Despite proposals, expressed by Brady et al. (2002), that a superior instrument exists in SERVPERF, SERVQUAL has been selected as the measurement instrument because of the belief that there is useful information to be learnt from the expectations of guests, irrespective of whether they are perceived to have been met. Furthermore, the results of Schmidt's (1995), study suggests that SERVQUAL may be an appropriate instrument to measure the quality of service delivered by tourism service providers.

METHODS

Background

The research was undertaken using the case of a small brewery tour operation, named for the purposes of this paper as "Subject Brewery" in Tasmania, Australia. The service provided is a tour delivered in three stages; a safety briefing, a guided walk through the brewery, and a tasting session. The brewery employs 11 part time tour guides along with two full time administrative staff and has been operating tours for 14 years. Tour guides receive training in first aid and interpretive guiding from the Hobart College of Technical and Further Education.

Sampling

Sampling was undertaken at the Brewery Tours Visitor's Centre, in Hobart Tasmania and 157 responses, from a total number of visitors estimated at approximately 2000, were collected during January 2004. January is "high season" in Tasmania and was selected as a readily definable period in which a sufficiently large sample could be collected to apply the central limits theorem. Data collection was undertaken by placing blank survey forms in the waiting area and inviting customers to volunteer to complete the survey form. Despite the low response rate and the implicit bias, such sampling is a common method of customer feedback data collection for small businesses without the resources to assign a staff member on an ongoing basis to the task of interviewing customers. "Reliance on available subjects," or convenience sampling, is criticised by Babbie (1989, p. 205) as "almost never an adequate sampling technique" however, the method was selected in accordance with the aims of this study which include the investigation of the practical utility of SERVQUAL for ongoing quality self-assessment of a tourism service. It was decided that practicality of application should be tested within the resource constraints likely to be faced by organisations that may choose to use the instrument.

Questionnaire

With the aim of customising the instrument to the specific subject of the study, the 22 item SERVQUAL scale developed by Zeithaml et al. (1990) was adapted to form an instrument comprising three sections, with each containing 10 items.

Items one to ten consisted of a series of statements beginning with 'in your opinion tours should' followed by a case specific example of each of the five dimensions of service identified by Zeithaml et al. (1987). Two items were provided for each service dimension and the average of the two responses provided the "expectations" values.

Items eleven to twenty consisted of a series of statements beginning with either "The Subject Brewery Tour" or "The staff at Subject Brewery Tours" followed by a case specific example of each of the five dimensions. Similarly, two items were provided for each service dimension and the average of the two responses provided the "perceptions" values.

Items twenty one to thirty consisted of a series of statements beginning with "For me it is important that" followed by a case specific example of each of the five dimensions. Again two items were provided for each service dimension and the average of the two responses provided the importance values.

It was decided that asking respondents to identify whether a gap existed (for example, by simply asking "did quality received exceed quality expected?" in each service dimension) introduced that possibility of "socially desirable responding" (Axelrod, 1994) in which respondents provide the answer they believe the researcher wants to hear. The survey instrument was designed in consultation with the manager of the service under investigation and was intended to gather data for the application of the formula service quality (Q) equals importance (I) times the difference between perceptions (P) and expectations (E) ($Q = I \{P - E\}$).

The format of the questions and the use of a Likert scale allows direct application of the assigned values to the formula:

$$Q_{n1,n2,n3\ldots} = I_{n1,n2,n3\ldots} \{(P1_{n1,n2,n3\ldots} + P2_{n1,n2,n3\ldots})/$$
$$2 - (E1_{n1,n2,n3\ldots} + E2_{n1,\ n2,n3\ldots})/2\}$$

where Q is the single number score, or rating, of the quality of service received.

The possible range of the Q value is negative twenty to positive twenty. A score of negative twenty would occur with a value of five for "importance," five for "expectations" and one for "perceptions," i.e., 5 (1-5) = –20. Similarly a score of positive twenty would occur with a reversal of the values given for expectations and perceptions, i.e., 5 (5-1) = 20. A score of zero would occur when perceptions of service received were equal to expectations and a greater gap between expectations and perceptions would give a score further from zero.

RESULTS AND DISCUSSION

All calculations were performed using SPSS version 11.1. Scale items are labelled with a 5 character code. The first character indicates an importance (i), perception (p), or expectation (e) item. The next three characters indicate a reliability (rel), tangible (tan), empathy (emp), responsiveness (res), or assurance (ass) item. The final character indicates either of the two items for each dimension/measurement combination. For example "eres2" is the second item concerning expectations of responsiveness. The itemised results of the survey are presented in Table 1.

Principal Components

The primary aim of the study is to test the conceptual model of service quality proposed by Parasuraman et al. (1985) in the context of a tour service and make inferences as to its applicability and utility to such services. It is therefore necessary to determine whether the data supports the concept that service quality is indeed separated into the expected dimensions and whether expectations are separated from perceptions in the minds of respondents. An appropriate method of examination of the data with these aims in mind is principal components analysis. An added benefit of principal components analysis is that the method has the potential to identify redundant items, thereby allowing streamlining of the instrument for practical application, as suggested by Williams (1998).

The scale proved to be internally reliable (á = 0.84). A principal component analysis with varimax rotation was carried out and returned nine components with Eigenvalues greater than one. The results are presented in Table 2.

All 10 of the "perceptions" items loaded against component 1 (explaining 14.5% of the variance) however, no reliable conclusions could be drawn from the remaining eight components (collectively explaining

TABLE 1. Itemised Results

Item	code	mean	std. dev.
Should only use guides who have been trained	eass1	4.71	0.65
Should provide individual attention	eres2	3.52	1.14
Should only give information if it is known to be true	erel1	4.42	0.95
Should have staff looking neat and tidy	etan1	4.32	0.89
Should have safety as a priority	eass2	4.57	0.65
Should have enthusiastic guides	eemp1	4.81	0.53
Should always open on time	erel2	4.41	0.85
Should have all facilities in good working order all the time	etan2	4.52	0.76
Should have approachable guides who listen to what I say	eemp2	4.59	0.74
Should change according to the needs of each visitor	eres1	3.50	1.25
Were enthusiastic	pemp1	4.67	0.82
Gave individual attention	pres1	4.51	0.82
Listened when I had something to say	pemp2	4.61	0.51
Appeared neat and tidy	ptan2	4.85	0.41
Seemed to know what I wanted from the tour	pres2	4.45	1.00
Are skilled and knowledgeable	pass2	4.72	0.54
Was everything that was promised	prel1	4.43	0.89
Was well-organised and orderly	prel2	4.77	0.55
Was conducted in a well-maintained environment	ptan1	4.66	0.74
Was conducted in a safe environment	pass1	4.86	0.46

53.5 % of the variance) comprising the remaining 20 items. One interpretation of this result is that importance is included in the concept of expectations. This would allow the importance section of the scale to be omitted. Reliability analysis of the scale without the 'importance' items was still adequately internally reliable (á = 0.78) and the 20 item scale is more user friendly and less daunting than the original 30 item scale, characteristics strongly suggested by Williams (1998). Omission of the Importance items from the data set produces the more clearly interpretable principal components output presented in Table 3.

At first glance it would seem that component 1, explaining 19.9 % of the variance and against which each of the perceptions items loaded, could be included into the single question of "how was the quality of service?" This would seem to challenge the conclusions reached by Cronin and Taylor (1994) that perceptions alone can provide diagnostic

TABLE 2. Rotated Component Matrix

	1	2	3	4	5	6	7	8	9
prel2	.815								
ptan1	.763								
prell	.749								
pass2	.695							.324	
pemp2	.682				.418				
pempl	.661								
presl	.529			.309	.320	-.361			
ptan2	.432						.403		
irell		.783							
itan1		.711			.375				
irel2		.581							
etan1		.555		.398					
erel2		.436	.350	.339					
iemp2			.835						
iempl			.805						
iresl		.423	.572						
eempl				.753					
eemp2				.612		.370			
ires2					.767	.309			
pres2	.340				.597				
itan2		.360			.437		.339		
eresl						.807			
eres2					.336	.767			
iass2							.805		
pass 1	.497						.557		
eass 1				.421				.718	
iassl			.351				.661		
etan2		.380						.396	.305
erell								.767	
eass2				.414			.314		.636

Extraction Method: Principal Component Analysis.
Rotation Method: Varimax with Kaiser Normalization. Rotation converged in 10 iterations.

TABLE 3. Rotated Component Matrix (I Data Omitted)

	Component				
	1	2	3	4	5
pass2	.780				
ptan2	.764				
pemp2	.701		.368		
passl	.641				
ptan 1	.599		.450		
pres2	.590				
pempl	.554		.397		
presl	.554			−.324	.310
etanl		.706			
erel2		.700			
erel1		.608	.433		
eass2		.580	.384		
etan2		.569			−.397
eassl		.545			.356
pre12	.440		.772		
prel1	.336		.697		
eres2				.845	
eresl				.818	
eempl					.666
eemp2				.336	.650

Extraction Method: Principal Component Analysis. Rotation method: Varimax with Kaiser.
Normalization. Rotation converged in 11 iterations.

data as it would seem that perceptions were not separated into quality dimensions. However, perceptions of reliability loaded more strongly against component 3 suggesting that, in this case, reliability was perceived to be a separate and individual construct. Similarly, expectations of responsiveness and of empathy loaded against components four and five respectively and were separated from the construct made up of the remaining three expectations quality dimensions. A reasonable conclusion is that each dimension should be retained for both expectations and perceptions items.

The survey instrument contained two items for each service dimension and in every case these pairs of items loaded against the same component. While this adds confidence to the underlying theory of SERVQUAL, omission of the second redundant item should not alter the theoretical effectiveness of the test if simplification of the questionnaire were desired. However, omission of items makes the instrument more general and is likely to reduce the specific diagnostic capabilities. A balance between a shorter instrument, that is more user-friendly for the customers asked to complete it, and a tool providing thorough diagnostic data may be achieved with a 20 item scale with 10 items for perceptions and 10 items for expectations, each containing two items from the five dimensions of service quality. Further simplification could, however, be achieved by selecting one of the pair of expectations items provided the selected item was applicable to both of the corresponding perceptions items.

PRACTICAL APPLICATION

Expectations of Brewery Visitors

Parasuramans et al.'s (1994) assertion that reliability and tangibles are respectively the most and least important drivers of visitor expectations has not been supported by this study. In the case of visitors to Subject Brewery, empathy was rated as most important ($\mu = 4.7$) and responsiveness as least important ($\mu = 3.51$). The expectations of tangibles ($\mu = 4.42$), reliability ($\mu = 4.41$) and assurance ($\mu = 4.64$) all loaded against component two (explaining 12.5% of the variance). This may be explained by the tour being conducted in an industrial site where visitors are unlikely to have sufficient experience to be comfortable and therefore feel dependent upon their guide. The item worded 'tours should *only* use guides who have been trained' returned a mean of 4.71 and it would appear that tangibles and reliability are regarded as being reflective of guide training and grouped into a common construct.

Responsiveness and empathy were differentiated into components four and five (respectively explaining 8.8 % and 7.5 % of the variance). The mean response of the responsiveness expectations items ($\mu = 3.51$) allows the surprising conclusion that responsiveness is not greatly expected by a brewery tour visitor. Several respondents commented that the group size (typically 20 tour participants) does not readily encourage catering to individual responses so such responses are not expected. This finding adds support to Teas' (1993) assertion that practicalities are considered in the formation of expectations and further suggests that tour participants are generous in their allowances for the difficulties of tour guides.

The mean response of empathy expectations items ($\mu = 4.7$) suggests that, in the context of this study, empathy is of critical importance to tour providers. Interestingly, the second empathy item, worded 'tours should have approachable guides who listen to what I say' ($\mu = 4.59$) shows that listening is expected of tour guides. Less expectation that tours should change according to individual participants has been shown and it can therefore be concluded that participants do consider the practicalities of group tours when interacting with the guide, thus providing further support for Teas' (1994) conclusions. The contention that the method of reaching expectations is of less importance to a tour provider than understanding what the expectations are has not, however, been addressed by this research.

Gap According to the SERVQUAL Model

An advantage of the SERVQUAL gap model is that results are returned as a single number that is readily interpreted. The mean responses to the equation P-E (With weighting "I" data omitted) for each service dimension are presented in Table 4.

Returned Q values for the service quality dimensions reliability, responsiveness, assurance, and tangibles were greater than zero, thus providing evidence that the expectations of respondents were exceeded by their perceptions of service received. While this result is encouraging for the tour provider, more useful diagnostic data was gained by examining the means of the specific expectations items as discussed in the previous section.

Consultation with management revealed that empathy had previously been assumed to be of less importance than the principles of thematic guiding, namely entertainment, reliability, organisation and engagement. Empathy is likely to be related to the personality of the individual tour

TABLE 4. Quality Scores for Each Service Dimension

	Reliability	Tangibles	Assurance	Responsiveness	Empathy
Mean Q value	0.19	0.33	0.15	0.97	−0.06
Mean Expectation	4.41	4.42	4.64	3.51	4.70
Mean Perception	4.60	4.75	4.79	4.48	4.64

guide and cross tabulation of empathy Q values has the potential to be used as a tool for assessment of guide performance. While individual tour guides were not identified in the survey instrument used in this study, the possibility has been flagged for future research. In this study however, the empathy items returned a Q value of less than zero, identifying a problem for which a solution should be found. Reporting the results of the application of the SERVQUAL instrument to management encouraged the formulation of strategies and procedures to address the identified problem.

A culture audit of front line staff initially voiced a collective opinion that service quality was of the highest standard until they were made aware of the results of the customer survey. Inadequacies in the empathy of service delivered were then attributed by the group to task overload in the time immediately before tours commenced. A strategy was selected by which staff, in the time immediately before a tour, were free to socialise (and empathise) with the tour participants. A follow up survey conducted in February 2004 (n = 17) returned a Q value of -0.01 with two participants from 17 reporting that expectations of staff empathy were not met although only one reported that empathy expectations were exceeded.

CONCLUSION

The results of this study provide evidence that SERVQUAL has the potential to provide useful and easily interpretable diagnostic data in the tourism service context. It appears that the five dimensions identified by Zeithaml et al. (1990) adequately describe service quality in the tour setting. However, further testing of the instrument in wider contexts will be required to confirm the utility of the instrument and allow more confident generalisations to be made about whether the tourism service quality is indeed five dimensional.

Inclusion of "importance" items does not change the sign of the difference between perceptions and expectations but does change the magnitude of the gap. However, it was found that results could be adequately interpreted without a weighting value, leading to the conclusion that the value of data obtained may not be worth the extra burden placed on the respondents (or customers) asked to provide it. The results suggested that the importance of a quality dimension to a respondent is included in their expression of expectations of that dimension. Furthermore, evidence was found to support Teas' (1994) conclusions that expectations

Robert A. Home 201

include a compensation for what the consumer deems to be reasonable in given circumstances.

It should be restated that the instrument must be specific to the service provided and that 'a one size fits all' diagnostic instrument for tourism service providers is neither likely nor desirable (Saleh and Ryan, 1991). Provided that the items selected by designers of future survey instruments fall within the theoretical framework of SERVQUAL, there is no reason that such instruments should not provide useful diagnostic data. The challenge then is for managers to interpret returned data and to seek solutions to the identified problems.

In the case of Subject Brewery Tours, empathy was found to be the most important driver of perceived service quality while studies in other industries have consistently found reliability to be of paramount importance. Higher expectations are more difficult to exceed which goes some way to explaining the consistent negative gap in the empathy dimension. This result is intuitively reasonable, given that tours are primarily undertaken for pleasure and the experience will be enhanced if the participant finds the guide to be likeable. However, further study is needed to determine whether this finding will be repeated in wider tourism contexts so that generalisations can be made.

What can be confidently stated is that ongoing application of the instrument has the potential to provide easily interpretable data to allow early identification of service quality problems. SERVQUAL is able to be applied with minimal commitment of resources and is therefore likely to be an attractive diagnostic tool for management of small businesses typically found in the tourism sector. A tourism service business with a commitment to continual quality improvement has much to gain from an objective means of internal self assessment. Once the business has a clear picture of their quality performance, those searching for innovative solutions will have the advantage of direction.

REFERENCES

Akama, J., and Kieti, D. (2002). Measuring Tourist Satisfaction with Kenya's Wildlife Safari: A Case Study of Tsavo West National Park, *Tourism Management* 24(1), pp. 73-81.

Albrecht, K. (1992). *The Only Thing That Matters*, Harper Business, New York.

Axelrod, L. (1994). Balancing Personal Needs with Environmental Preservation: Identifying the Values that Guide Decisions in Ecological Dilemmas. *Journal of Social Issues* 50(3), pp. 85-104.

Babakus, E., and Boller, G. (1992). An Empirical Assessment of the SERVQUAL Scale. *Journal of Business Research 24*(3), pp. 253-268.

Babbie, E. (1989) *The Practice of Social Research*, 5th edn., Wadsworth, Belmont, USA.

Berry, L., and Parasuraman, A. (1991). *Marketing Services–Competing Through Quality*, The Free Press, New York.

Brady, M., Cronin, J., & Brand, R. (2002). Performance-Only Measurement of Service Quality: A Replication and Extension. *Journal of Business Research 55*(1), pp. 17-31.

Brown, T., Churchill Jr. G., and Peter, J. (1993). Research Note: Improving the Measurement of Service Quality. *Journal of Retailing 69*(1), pp. 127–139.

Carman, J. (1990). Customer Perceptions of Service Quality: An Assessment of the SERVQUAL Dimensions. *Journal of Retailing 66*(1), pp. 33-55.

Cronin, J., and Taylor, S. (1994). Measuring Service Quality: A Re-examination and Extension. *Journal of Marketing 56*(3), pp. 55-68.

Davidson, P., & Griffin, C. (2000). *Management–Australia in a Global Context*, John Wiley & Sons, Brisbane.

Gerson, R. (1999). *Members For Life–Proven Service and Retention Strategies for Health-Fitness and Sports Clubs.* Human Kinetics, Champaign, Il.

Howat, G., Murray, D., and Crilley, G. (1999). The Relationships between Service Problems and Perceptions of Service Quality, Satisfaction, and Behavioural Intentions of Australian Public Sports and Leisure Center Customers. *Journal of Park and Recreation Administration 17*(2), pp. 42-64.

Lamb C., Hair J., McDaniel C. (1995). *Marketing* 3rd edn., Southwestern Publishing, Cincinnati, OH.

McAtarsney D. (1999). Review, Critique, and Assessment of Customer Care. *Total Quality Management 10*(4/5), pp. 636-646.

McColl-Kennedy, J., and Kiel, G. (2000). *Marketing–A Strategic Approach*, Nelson Thomas Learning, Melbourne.

Parasuraman, A., Berry L., and Zeithaml, V. (1993). Research Notes: More on Improving Service Quality Measurement. *Journal of Retailing 69*(1), pp. 140-147.

Parasuraman, A., Zeithaml, V., Berry, L. (1994). Reassessment of Expectations as a Comparison Standard in Measuring Service Quality: Implications for Further Research. *Journal of Marketing 58*(1), pp. 111-124.

Pitt, L., Watson, R., and Kavan, C. (1997). Measuring Information Systems Service Quality: Concerns for a Complete Canvas. *MIS Quarterly 21*(2), pp. 209-221.

Saleh, F., and Ryan, C. (1991). Analysing Service Quality in the Hospitality Industry Using the SERVQUAL Model. *The Service Industries Journal 11*(3), pp. 324-346.

Schmidt, C. (1999). *An Assessment and Refinement of the SERVQUAL Scale in Fitness Centres*, Griffith University, Brisbane.

Teas, R. (1994). Expectations as a Comparison Standard in Measuring Service Quality: an Assessment of a Reassessment. *Journal of Marketing 58*(1), pp. 132-139.

Williams, C. (1998). Is The SERVQUAL Model an Appropriate Management Tool for Measuring Service Delivery Quality in The UK Leisure Industry. *Managing Leisure 3*(2), pp. 98-110.

Zeithaml, V., Parasuraman, A., & Berry, L. (1990). *Delivering Quality Service: Balancing Customer Perceptions and Expectations*, The Free Press, New York.

Index